THIRD EDITION

2 LET'S GO

TEACHER'S BOOK

Ritsuko Nakata

Karen Frazier

Barbara Hoskins

with songs and chants by Carolyn Graham

OXFORD

UNIVERSITY PRESS

OXFORD
UNIVERSITY PRESS

198 Madison Avenue
New York, NY 10016 USA

Great Clarendon Street, Oxford OX2 6DP UK

Oxford University Press is a department of the University of Oxford.
It furthers the University's objective of excellence in research, scholarship,
and education by publishing worldwide in

Oxford New York

Auckland Cape Town Dar es Salaam Hong Kong Karachi
Kuala Lumpur Madrid Melbourne Mexico City Nairobi
New Delhi Shanghai Taipei Toronto

With offices in

Argentina Austria Brazil Chile Czech Republic France Greece
Guatemala Hungary Italy Japan Poland Portugal Singapore
South Korea Switzerland Thailand Turkey Ukraine Vietnam

OXFORD and OXFORD ENGLISH are registered trademarks of
Oxford University Press

ISBN-13: 978 0 19 439481 9
ISBN-10: 0 19 439481 6

Photocopying

The Publisher grants permisson for the photocopying of those pages marked
"Permission granted to reproduce for instructional use" according to the
following conditions. Individual purchasers may make copies for their own
use or for use by classes they teach. School purchasers may make copies
for use by their staff and students, but this permission does not extend to
additional schools or branches. In no circumstances may any part of this book
be photocopied for resale.

Senior Editor: Paul B. Phillips
Editor: Joseph McGasko
Art Director: Maj-Britt Hagsted
Design Project Manager: Amelia L. Carling
Designers: Elsa Varela, Sangeeta Ramcharan
Art Editor: Judi DeSouter
Production Manager: Shanta Persaud
Production Controller: Eve Wong

Printing (last digit): 10 9 8 7 6 5 4 3 2 1

Printed in Hong Kong.

ACKNOWLEDGMENTS

To our editors at Oxford University Press, and to the design team, thank you
for your creativity and hard work. To our husbands and children, thank you
for your support, understanding, and willingness to eat fast food. We would
like to dedicate this series to the many teachers and students who have
crossed our paths over the years. You have been our inspiration.

Illustrations: Fran Newman: 174, 177, 182, 184; Ruth Flanigan: 175; Chris Reed:
176, 186, 189; Linda Howard Bittner: 179, 185; Mike Dammer: 180; Susan
Miller: 181, 188; Dan Sharp: 183, 187

Cover Illustration: Janet Skiles

Table of Contents

Introduction

DESCRIPTION OF THE COURSE: PHILOSOPHY AND PRINCIPLES

Let's Go Third Edition is a seven-level course designed for children learning English for the first time. The themes and situations throughout the books are universal to children everywhere.

Let's Go emphasizes communication within a carefully controlled grammatical syllabus. Beginning with the first lesson, students are provided with a variety of activities that focus on interactive communication. The activities gradually increase in difficulty. Students are regularly presented with new vocabulary and structures so that they have adequate language to communicate with at each new level.

Experiences that are familiar to children are featured throughout the course in dialogues, songs, and exercises. This enables students to quickly begin speaking in English about situations to which they can easily relate.

The activities and exercises in each lesson are highly student-centered. Students are encouraged to communicate with one another, first in groups and then in pairs, after they have developed sufficient confidence and familiarity with the language. This pairwork is crucial, since it is here that students are really communicating with one another in situations most closely resembling life outside the classroom.

The lessons in *Let's Go* incorporate techniques from several methods that have been repeatedly proven successful in teaching English to children. Among the numerous methods and techniques drawn upon for this course are the following:

- **The MAT (Model, Action, Talk) Method**, which emphasizes the use of actions and brief, intensive drills that enable students to learn a maximum of English skills in a minimum amount of time.

- **Total Physical Response (TPR)**, which is based in part on the idea that linking physical action with language will aid retention.

- **The Functional Approach**, which emphasizes the proper context in which to use certain language patterns and expressions.

- **The Communicative Approach**, which is based on the idea that language used in the classroom should be used to communicate thoughts and feelings that are meaningful to the students.

- **The Audio-Lingual Approach**, which focuses on the sounds and syntax of the language.

- **The Grammatical/Structural Approaches** examine grammar, focusing on patterns and structure in language to aid comprehension and retention.

This new edition of *Let's Go* has also incorporated more recent scholarship into its instruction. These include the educational theory of Multiple Intelligences, which includes the idea that students' aptitudes for learning fall into a wide range of strategies. Additionally, Process-focused Learning emphasizes the importance of establishing proper models through repetition in order to set up the best neural pathways for the language process.

DESCRIPTION OF THE LEVELS

Let's Begin

This new level for *Let's Go* Third Edition is the initial entry-point into *Let's Go*. It follows the same unit structure as the other levels but is intended for students who have had no formal instruction in English. Structured around thematic topics and corresponding simple grammar patterns, this pre-reading level introduces students to some basic classroom phrases, useful vocabulary, and the letters of the alphabet and their sounds. Further instruction and support for phonics is available in the new *Let's Go Phonics* books.

Level 1

This level is also an entry-point into *Let's Go* intended for students who already have some familiarity with the English alphabet. Level 1 focuses on the development of basic oral language through functional dialogues, question-and-answer patterns, and vocabulary work.

This new edition includes more vocabulary in each unit to give students more varied opportunities to communicate with each other. Language patterns focus on first-person use of *Be*, *Like*, *Can*, along with both *Wh-* and *Yes/No* question forms. Depending on whether or not your students learn reading skills at this level, there are ample opportunities through dialogues, songs, and short conversation to practice reading skills. A review of the alphabet letters and their initial sounds at this level can also be supplemented by the new *Let's Go Phonics* series.

Level 2

This level is for students who have completed Level 1 and are familiar with basic question-and-answer patterns, grammatical structures, and vocabulary. New patterns and concepts include further expansion of third-person plural forms and the present continuous tense.

Level 3

This level focuses on expanding the students' ability to use the grammar patterns introduced in Level 2. Students are gradually required to read these structures and sight words in short reading passages.

Level 4

This level expands on vocabulary and grammar from the previous levels and introduces more new structures. It also offers slightly longer reading passages that incorporate familiar structures and high-frequency sight words. At this stage, songs and chants are replaced by other reading focuses and performance opportunities, such as poems, short dialogues, and readings.

Level 5

This level continues to recycle language from the previous levels while introducing new structures. Dialogues now appear in script form instead of "speech bubbles" for a more mature appearance. The reading sections in Level 5 include passages that are three to four paragraphs long. These passages incorporate familiar grammar patterns from earlier levels.

Level 6

This level consolidates the language from the previous five levels and introduces new structures. Students are given many opportunities to use their language skills to talk about themselves, their opinions, and their feelings. As in Level 5, the reading passages are three to four paragraphs long.

MAIN COMPONENTS

Each level of *Let's Go* Third Edition features basic components that are designed to be closely coordinated in the classroom. These include the Student Book (available with a new CD-ROM for study and games at home), the Workbook, a new Skills Book with audio CD, the Teacher's Book, Audio Compact Disc, Teacher Cards, Student Cards, Tests and Quizzes, and Readers.

STUDENT BOOK

The Student Books feature beautiful full-color illustrations in a clear and attractive format. Creative activities, utilizing a wide range of skills, engage students in a variety of learning experiences. Each Student Book contains eight units, providing material for five to seven 50-minute lessons, as well as four review units. This Third edition includes a new Unit structure focusing on four consistent and flexible lessons per unit. Songs appear in the Let's Sing portion of each Unit's first lesson, and also appear at strategic points in other lessons, some of which are interactive listening exercises on the Student Book page.

Let's Go Third Edition CD-ROM is available with Student Books and features fun games for students to play on their computers at home. A wide variety of games help reinforce the language and vocabulary students have learned in fun, motivating ways. They also provide many hours of educational English practice for your students at home.

WORKBOOK

The Workbooks provide reading and writing practice to further reinforce the language introduced in the Student Book. The activities in them are designed for study at home or in the classroom. Extra activity pages at the back of each Workbook provide additional writing practice using personalization and consolidation of the material students have learned throughout the level. There is a new parent's sign-off box at the bottom of each page that can be useful for homework management.

SKILLS BOOK

The Skills Books provide additional practice in reading, writing, and listening to reinforce the language introduced in the Student Book. The Skills Book audio CD includes a variety of listening comprehension exercises and tasks to help students understand natural, spoken English. The activities are designed for study at home or in the classroom. These books also feature the new parent's sign-off box at the bottom of each page.

TEACHER'S BOOK

The Teacher's Books contain easy-to-follow lesson plans. Each lesson begins with a list of the vocabulary and patterns to be covered, plus an outline of the materials needed for that lesson. The lesson plans contain activities designed to present, practice, and reinforce the new language. Group dynamics are carefully considered, with activities organized into class, small-group, or pair arrangements. Extra teaching tips are highlighted throughout: pronunciation tips, grammar tips, cultural tips, and suggestions for how to adapt lessons for larger or smaller classes. An audio tapescript of the language and dialogues that appear on the audio CD is incorporated into the teacher's notes.

The end of each section contains suggestions for extra practice as well as links to other components including the following:

- *Let's Go Picture Dictionary*
- *Let's Go Readers*
- *Let's Chant Let's Sing*
- *Let's Go CD-ROMs*

The back of the Teacher's Book features instructions and answer keys for all the Workbook and Skills Book activities. There are also reproducible worksheets in the back of the Teacher's Book that can be used to supplement your lessons. Detailed instructions are included. The structure key (or syllabus), the Word List, and the list of Teacher and Student Cards are also included in the Teacher's Book for reference.

Audio Compact Discs

Compact discs contain everything from the body of the Student Book:

- dialogues
- narratives
- language patterns
- vocabulary
- question-and-answer practices
- alphabet letters and sounds
- original songs and chants by Carolyn Graham
- listening activities in each review unit

A new feature unique to the Third Edition is a rhythmic presentation of the grammar patterns on the audio CD. This feature helps students learn the natural rhythm and intonation of spoken English by first presenting students with a spoken model of the pattern, then a repeat of the spoken model combined with a drum beat rhythm, and finally the rhythm alone. Students can listen to both spoken and rhythmic models, and then practice the language along with the beat. These tracks are identified by a drum icon in the Student Book and Teacher's Book:

Teacher Cards and Student Cards

A set of large Teacher Cards and playing-card size Student Cards accompany each level of *Let's Go*. The Teacher's Books contain suggestions for many different games and drills utilizing the cards.

SUPPLEMENTAL COMPONENTS

Let's Go Phonics

Let's Go Phonics is a brand new phonics course accompanying *Let's Go* Third Edition that covers phonics material in more depth. The books feature writing, listening, reading, and pronunciation practice to help students develop a basic foundation in English letters and spelling rules, as well as the system of sounds in English. *Let's Go Phonics* can be taught in conjunction with the *Let's Go* Student Books or independently of them. The course is split into three levels, and it keeps within the language level of *Let's Go* Levels 1 and 2. The course is flexibly linked to the *Let's Go* Third Edition syllabus without a rigid correspondence to it.

Let's Go Third Edition Readers

This new series features eight *Readers* at each level. Each *Reader* focuses on the cumulative language, vocabulary, and topics of the corresponding unit in the Student Books. Colorful, interesting stories help motivate students through meaningful reading experience.

Comprehension and practice exercises are located at the back of each *Reader* along with a new words list.

Let's Go Tests and Quizzes

Available for each level of *Let's Go* Third Edition are *Let's Go Tests and Quizzes*, which provide quizzes for every lesson in each unit as well as for the Let's Learn About lessons. In addition, there is a test after each unit, a Units review test after every two units, a midterm test, which can be given after completing Unit 4, and a final exam for the end of the book.

COMPONENTS FROM *LET'S GO* SECOND EDITION

Picture Dictionary

The beautifully illustrated *Let's Go Picture Dictionary* contains 975 high-frequency words taught in the *Let's Go* series, plus many other topically related words. Many of the Student Book lessons can be extended by introducing new words from the Dictionary. Suggestions as to when and how to use a Dictionary page in conjunction with your Student Book lessons appear throughout the Teacher's Book. A cassette with all the words from the Dictionary is also available.

Let's Chant Let's Sing

Songs and chants help students remember new vocabulary and structures. They also reinforce the natural stress and pronunciation of spoken English. *Let's Chant Let's Sing 1-6* by Carolyn Graham contain all the songs and chants from *Let's Go* Second Edition, as well as other songs and chants that are also based on the vocabulary and structures taught in that edition. Each chant and song is labeled so that you can easily correlate them with the lessons in the Student Book. These books present songs in musical notation for teachers and students who can read music. Extension activities are suggested on all the chant pages. Cassettes and compact discs are also available for these books.

ORGANIZATION OF A UNIT

Organization of Level Two

Each of the eight units in Student Book 2 is organized around a basic theme and is divided into four lessons: Let's Start, Let's Learn, Let's Learn More, and Let's Build. A Listen and Review lesson appears after every two units along with a new section, Let's Learn About..., that introduces useful topical vocabulary. The same titles and page numbers are used in the Workbook and Skills Book to help teachers and students identify corresponding pages for homework and extra practice assignments.

Each lesson builds on previously learned language and introduces new vocabulary and structures. Both review and new language are clearly identified in the Teacher's Book lesson plans.

Each lesson focuses on specific purposes in language development:

Let's Start builds functional fluency through Let's Talk, Let's Sing, and Let's Move. Let's Talk introduces a short functional dialogue relating to the topic of the unit. Let's Sing practices the dialogue language and reinforces natural pronunciation, rhythm, and intonation. Let's Move combines useful action verb phrases with useful patterns in which to use them. Many of the verbs are also useful classroom commands and language.

Let's Learn builds grammatical accuracy. In this lesson, students learn vocabulary related to the unit theme, practice using the vocabulary in the context of a sentence pattern, and finally, practice using the sentence pattern to answer *Wh-* questions. This building sequence allows students to make statements as well as to respond to questions. The grammar patterns are presented rhythmically to reinforce natural intonation and pronunciation.

Let's Learn More expands on the language introduced in Let's Learn by introducing additional thematic vocabulary and a *Yes/No* question-and-answer pattern. The lesson provides opportunities for students to use vocabulary from the previous lesson with the new patterns.

Let's Build unlocks the creative power of English through reviewing, recycling, and recombining language they have already learned. Students review and consolidate structures and vocabulary learned across the units. Then, they learn how to combine these structures to expand their ability to express themselves in English.

Listen and Review provides a one-page listening assessment after every two units. As they prepare for the listening tasks, students review the material from previous units, further strengthening the base from which they can then move on to more advanced language.

Let's Learn About appears after each two units, and introduces special, topic-based vocabulary and language. In Level Two, students learn essential vocabulary for Numbers 20–100, Months, Seasons, and Time.

LESSON PLANNING GUIDELINES

A lesson plan should be developed for every lesson taught. When planning, establish specific goals and objectives. Activities and exercises to practice the language should be carefully selected to help ensure that these goals are achieved. It is always better to over-plan and have more activities than you need, as the same activity will not always work equally well with all groups of students. In addition, use various types of activities to appeal to students' different learning styles. Careful planning also helps you cope with the unexpected situations that sometimes occur in class.

Lessons in the *Let's Go* Teacher's Book use time effectively. Every lesson activity, drill, or game has a purpose in advancing language proficiency. For example, the Warm Up activity at the beginning of each lesson serves two purposes—it helps activate students' English when coming from a non-English environment (eg., after school), and it reviews previously learned language that will be built on in the lesson.

The Teacher's Book pages for each lesson contain suggested activities, explanations of potential problem areas, and tips for teaching each specific language point. All lessons build on the lesson models in the following pages. Activities can be replaced with others from appropriate sections to suit the needs of your class.

Books Open / Books Closed

Generally, students keep their books closed during the presentation of new language so they can focus on hearing and understanding the language before having to see it on a page. After the closed-book presentation, students open their books and listen to the audio and do the exercises for that lesson. Finally, students close their books to focus on real communication with their classmates for the suggested Games and Activities.

TIME GUIDELINES

The majority of class time should be spent on presenting and practicing the new language. Books should be closed more than open since *Let's Go* focuses on developing communicative competence. The timing of a typical class in which one lesson is completed might be:

Warm Up and Review	5 minutes
Presentation and Practice	30 minutes
Games and Activities	15 minutes

The length of classes will of course vary, depending on various factors.

PACING

The pacing of a language class for children must be lively. To maintain the students' interest, activities should be changed approximately every five to seven minutes, or whenever the students' interest starts to wane. It is much better to stop an activity while the children are still involved in it than to wait until they are no longer interested. Favorite activities can always be used again later. This also holds true for drills and practices, which should be done at a challenging pace to establish natural English rhythm and intonation.

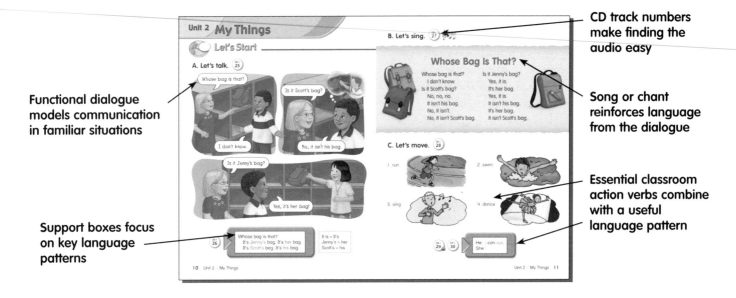

CD track numbers make finding the audio easy

Functional dialogue models communication in familiar situations

Song or chant reinforces language from the dialogue

Essential classroom action verbs combine with a useful language pattern

Support boxes focus on key language patterns

WARM UP AND REVIEW

Start the lesson with the suggested review activity or select an activity from Drills and Games (p. 21). Every class should begin with an oral review of language recently studied. This helps the students to remember previous material and starts the class on a positive note since the students are using familiar language.

PRESENT THE LANGUAGE

📖 BOOKS CLOSED

It's important to present new material to your students in a way that focuses on understanding meaning. Presenting new material with the books closed helps focus student attention on your demonstration. Lesson notes generally follow these steps.

Present the dialogue.

1. Introduce the dialogue.
Model the conversation dialogue with puppets or student volunteers. Using puppets or volunteers provides a physical reminder that conversation is communication between two or more people.

2. Practice the dialogue.
Use puppets or volunteers to cue students in practice, moving from whole class practice to two-group practice to partner conversations.

📖 BOOKS OPEN

Students open their books and look at the illustrated dialogue that reinforces the language just introduced. Steps are generally as follows:

A. Let's talk.

1. Listen to the dialogue.

a. Have students look at the scene and describe what they see.

b. Play the audio track and have students point to the items they hear in their books.

c. Play the audio again. Students repeat after the characters.

2. Practice the dialogue.

a. Write the sentence pattern on the board or direct student attention to the pattern in their books. Play the audio track. Students point to the speech bubbles as they listen. Then, have students repeat after the audio.

b. If there is a contraction in the sentence pattern, direct your students attention to it and make sure they understand. Use the contraction cards and instructions on pages 196–197 to help demonstrate the meaning and formation of contractions.

c. Students practice in pairs or groups of three, depending on the conversation.

B. Let's sing.

Books remain open throughout this portion so students can get cues from the illustration. The lesson notes generally follow these steps:

1. Play and listen.
Play the song first, and have students identify familiar words they hear and familiar items in the illustration.

2. Practice the rhythm.
Introduce the song rhythmically. Have students clap to keep the beat as you model the song line by line.

Demonstrate any actions or movements that go with the song. Have students repeat after you. For difficult and longer phrases, you can use a backward build-up technique. Begin by saying the last word in the phrase and gradually add the words before it until the phrase is complete.

3. Do the song activity.

Play the song again and divide the class, with half singing one part and half singing the other. If the song has a question-and-answer pattern, act it out with students taking turns singing questions and responses. Add gestures to go with the song lyrics. Whenever possible, include actions with the songs. Students enjoy moving, and shifting the focus from language to activity often improves fluency. Suggested actions are included in many lessons, but you can also encourage students to create their own movements for songs.

4. Read the lyrics and sing.

Have students point to and read words that they recognize. Then repeat the words of the song line by line and model them for the class. Students repeat after you until they have learned the song. Sing the song several times together.

📖 BOOKS CLOSED

Presenting new material with the books closed helps focus student attention on your demonstration. Individual lesson notes generally follow these steps.

Present the verb phrases.

1. Introduce the verb phrases.

a. Introduce the verbs with actions or gestures to reinforce meaning and retention. In addition to helping students remember the meaning of new verbs, gestures reinforce correct word order and improve fluency in speaking.

b. To check understanding, say the phrases in random order and have students do the appropriate action.

c. Show Teacher Cards and have students say the phrase and do the action.

d. Divide the class into two groups and have the groups take turns saying the commands and doing the actions.

2. Introduce the language pattern.

Notes for each lesson present strategies for integrating verb phrases with useful sentence patterns, such as *He can _____, I _____ at school,* and *I _____ in the morning.*

📖 BOOKS OPEN

Students open books for this part of the lesson, as the pictures on the page are necessary for demonstration. Lesson notes generally follow the steps below.

C. Let's move.

1. Listen and point to the verb phrases.

a. Play the audio track and have students listen and point to the verb phrases, then listen again and repeat.

2. Practice the pattern rhythmically.

a. Students listen to the pattern as it is spoken, then listen to the rhythmic beat of the pattern, and finally listen to the pattern as it is spoken along with the rhythm.

b. Play audio again. Have students tap or clap the rhythm as they listen one time. Then replay the audio and have students repeat the sentence with the spoken model, the drum beats, and the rhythmic model.

3. Practice the verb phrases with the pattern.

a. Students listen and point to the appropriate pictures.

b. Students repeat the sentences, or questions and answers, along with the audio.

GAMES AND ACTIVITIES

Games and Activities recycle the material from the lesson in innovative and engaging ways to reinforce what the students have learned. This is also a good way to end a class since the students will leave with a sense of accomplishment, wanting to learn more. You will find detailed instructions in each Teacher's Book lesson and in the Drills and Games section of this introduction (p. 21).

EXTRA PRACTICE

Extra Practice contains various ancillary materials for further practice of the language taught in the lesson. Workbook and Skills Book instructions and Answer Keys, as well as reproducible Worksheets and their instructions, are located in the back of the book.

COMPONENTS LINK

Components Link lists resources for further practice, assessment, and learning additional material. These include *Let's Go CD-ROM, Let's Go Tests and Quizzes, Let's Go Readers, Let's Chant Let's Sing,* and *Let's Go Picture Dictionary.*

Lesson Structure of Let's Learn

Hosts Sam and Ginger demonstrate lesson's language

Topic-based vocabulary

Substitution vocabulary highlighted in language patterns

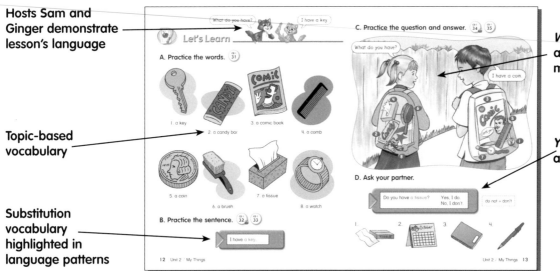

Wh- question-and-answer pattern modeled in scene

Yes/No question-and-answer practice

WARM UP AND REVIEW

Start the lesson with the suggested review activity or select an activity from Drills and Games. Every class should begin with an oral review of language recently studied. This helps the students to remember previous material and starts the class on a positive note since the students are using familiar language.

PRESENT THE LANGUAGE

📕 BOOKS CLOSED

It's important to present new material to your students in a way that focuses on understanding meaning. Presenting new material with the books closed helps focus student attention on your demonstration. Lesson notes generally follow these steps.

Introduce the words.

1. Use Teacher Cards to introduce the new words, focusing on pronunciation and rhythm. When introducing verb vocabulary, use gestures or actions to reinforce meaning. Speak with natural pronunciation and intonation as you model the vocabulary or play the audio. Make sure that students understand the meaning of the words and can say them easily.

2. Check and correct students' pronunciation so you don't have to return to teaching pronunciation once vocabulary has been introduced. The introduction and drill of new vocabulary should be done thoroughly but quickly here so that you only have to introduce new vocabulary once, and after that, students are using and practicing the words in context.

Introduce the sentence pattern.

Model the new sentence pattern with natural speed, rhythm, and intonation. Then, practice vocabulary in the context of the sentence. As soon as students are able, have them form sentences from Teacher Card cues (instead of repeating the teacher's words). This gives them a chance to recall the words for themselves. Give students a chance to practice the sentence pattern and vocabulary in pairs, with activities or drill and game alternatives (see pages 21–26).

📖 BOOKS OPEN

Students open their books and look at the illustrations that reinforce the language just introduced. Steps are generally as follows:

A. Practice the words.

1. Play the audio and have students listen and point to the vocabulary on the page.

2. Play the audio again and have students repeat the vocabulary.

B. Practice the sentences.

1. Listen to the sentences.

   a. Write the sentence pattern on the board or direct student attention to the pattern in their books. Play the audio track. Students listen to the sentence pattern as it is spoken, then listen to the sentence as it is spoken along with the rhythm, and finally listen to the rhythm alone.

   b. Play the audio again. Have students tap or clap the rhythm as they listen one time. Then replay the audio and have students repeat the sentence with the spoken model, the rhythmic model, and the rhythm alone.

c. If there is a contraction in the sentence pattern, direct your students' attention to it and make sure they understand. Use the contraction cards and instructions on pages 196–197 to help demonstrate the meaning and formation of contractions.

2. Practice the sentence pattern with vocabulary.

a. Students listen and point to the appropriate pictures.

b. Students repeat the sentences along with the audio.

c. Do short activities to solidify the vocabulary and sentence pattern. Suggestions for activities can be found in the lessons.

📖 BOOKS CLOSED

Presenting new material with the books closed helps focus student attention on your demonstration. Individual lesson notes generally follow these steps.

Introduce the question form.

The Let's Learn lesson generally introduces a *Wh-* question-and-answer pattern. Because students learn the answer first (in the sentence pattern), the teacher can introduce the question naturally.

1. Show Teacher Cards to elicit sentences. Then ask the question before showing them the card, modeling pronunciation and intonation. Students' statements become the answer to the question. Switch the student focus to the question and its natural intonation. Drill the question only until students can say it naturally.

2. Use Teacher Cards to cue answers as students practice asking questions.

3. Divide the class into two groups. One group asks the question and the other answers. As the groups grow confident with the pattern, switch roles to make sure both groups can ask and answer the question. Students should either ask the question or answer it (rather than simply repeating both after the teacher) so that even basic language practice reinforces natural communication.

📖 BOOKS OPEN

Students open books for this portion, as the pictures on the page are necessary for demonstration. Lesson notes generally follow these steps:

C. Practice the question and answer.

1. Listen to the question-and-answer pattern.

a. Have students look at the page and describe the things they see.

b. Play the audio track. Students listen to the question-and-answer pattern as it is spoken, then listen to the pattern as it is spoken along with the rhythm, and finally listen to the rhythm alone.

c. Play the audio again. Have students tap or clap the rhythm as they listen one time. Then replay the audio and have students repeat the question and

answer with the spoken model, the rhythmic model, and the rhythm.

2. Practice the question-and-answer pattern with vocabulary.

a. Present the pattern by writing it on the board or direct student attention to it in the book.

b. Play the audio track. Point to the words as students listen. Have students repeat the questions and answers after the audio.

c. If there is a contraction in the sentence pattern, direct your students' attention to it and make sure they understand. Use the contraction cards and instructions on pages 196–197 to help demonstrate the meaning and formation of contractions.

d. When students are confident enough, have them ask and answer each other in pairs, using picture cards or actual items as cues.

D. Practice.

Many Let's Learn lessons feature a practice activity to reinforce the vocabulary and the question-and-answer pattern. These vary throughout the book and include listening exercises, songs, fill-in charts, and personalized activities. Notes for instructing students on these exercises can be found in the individual lessons.

GAMES AND ACTIVITIES

Games and Activities recycle the material from the lesson in innovative and engaging ways to reinforce what the students have learned. This is also a good way to end a class since the students will leave with a sense of accomplishment, wanting to learn more. You will find detailed instructions in each Teacher's Book lesson and in the Drills and Games section of this introduction (p. 21).

EXTRA PRACTICE

Extra Practice contains various ancillary materials for further practice of the language taught in the lesson. Workbook and Skills Book instructions and Answer Keys, as well as reproducible Worksheets and their instructions, are located in the back of the book.

COMPONENTS LINK

Components Link lists resources for further practice, assessment, and learning additional material. These include *Let's Go CD-ROM, Let's Go Tests and Quizzes, Let's Go Readers, Let's Chant Let's Sing, and Let's Go Picture Dictionary.*

Lesson Structure of Let's Learn More

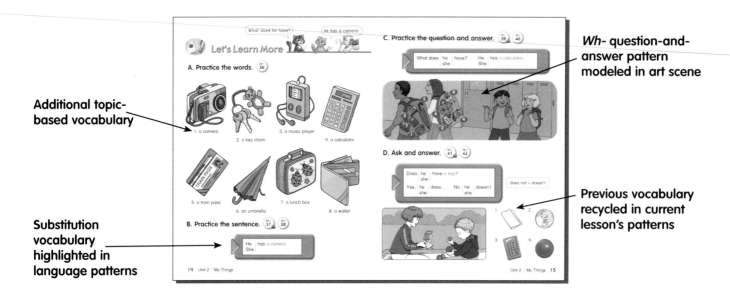

Additional topic-based vocabulary

Substitution vocabulary highlighted in language patterns

Wh- question-and-answer pattern modeled in art scene

Previous vocabulary recycled in current lesson's patterns

WARM UP AND REVIEW

Start the lesson with the suggested review activity or select an activity from Drills and Games. Every class should begin with an oral review of language recently studied. This helps the students to remember previous material and starts the class on a positive note since the students are using familiar language.

PRESENT THE LANGUAGE

BOOKS CLOSED

It's important to present new material to your students in a way that focuses on understanding meaning. Presenting new material with the books closed helps focus student attention on your demonstration. Lesson notes generally follow these steps.

Introduce the words.

1. Use Teacher Cards to introduce the new words, focusing on pronunciation and rhythm. Speak with natural pronunciation and intonation as you model the vocabulary or play the audio. Make sure that students understand the meaning of the words and can say them easily.

2. Check and correct students' pronunciation so that you don't have to return to teaching pronunciation once vocabulary has been introduced. The introduction and drill of new vocabulary should be done thoroughly but quickly so that you should only have to introduce new vocabulary once, and after that students are using and practicing the words in context.

Introduce the sentence pattern.

Model the new sentence pattern with natural speed, rhythm, and intonation. Then, practice vocabulary in

the context of the sentence. As soon as students are able, have them form sentences from Teacher Card cues (instead of repeating the teacher's words). This gives them a chance to recall the words for themselves. Give students a chance to practice the sentence pattern and vocabulary in pairs, with activities or drill and game alternatives (see pages 21–26).

BOOKS OPEN

Students open their books and look at the illustrations that reinforce the language just introduced. Steps are generally as follows:

A. Practice the words.

1. Play the audio and have students listen and point to the vocabulary on the page.

2. Play the audio again and have students repeat the vocabulary.

B. Practice the sentences.

1. Listen to the sentences.

   a. Write the sentence pattern on the board or direct student attention to the pattern in their books. Play the audio track. Students listen to the sentence pattern as it is spoken, then listen to the sentence as it is spoken along with the rhythm, and finally listen to the rhythm alone.

   b. Play the audio again. Have students tap or clap the rhythm as they listen one time. Then replay the audio and have students repeat the sentence with the spoken model, the rhythmic model, and the rhythm alone.

   c. If there is a contraction in the sentence pattern, direct your students' attention to it and make sure they understand. Use the contraction cards and instructions on pages 196–197 to help demonstrate the meaning and formation of contractions.

2. Practice the sentence pattern with vocabulary.

a. Students listen and point to the appropriate pictures.

b. Students repeat the sentences along with the audio.

c. Do short activities to solidify the vocabulary and sentence pattern. Suggestions for activities can be found in the lessons.

BOOKS CLOSED

Presenting new material with the books closed helps focus student attention on your demonstration. Individual lesson notes generally follow these steps:

Introduce the question form.

The Let's Learn More lesson generally introduces a *Yes/No* question-and-answer pattern. Because students learned the sentences first, it is very easy for them to learn to change the sentences into *Yes/No* questions.

1. Show Teacher Cards to elicit sentences. Then ask the question while pointing to the item on the card, modeling pronunciation and rising intonation essential to *Yes/No* questions. If you prefer, use word cards to physically show how the verb moves to the front when changing a sentence to a *Yes/No* question. Elicit a *Yes* answer and model the full form: *Yes, it is. Let's Go* emphasizes teaching full sentence answers to *Yes/No* questions because otherwise students don't learn the difference in meaning between *Yes, it is*; *Yes, they are*; *Yes, I am*; *Yes, I can*; or *Yes, I do*. Repeat for several Teacher Cards, with you asking the questions and students answering.

2. Use Teacher Cards to cue students to ask questions. The teacher answers.

3. Divide the class into two groups. One group asks the question and the other answers. As the groups grow confident with the pattern, switch roles to make sure both groups can ask and answer the question. Students should ask the question or answer it (rather than simply repeating both after the teacher) so that even basic language practice reinforces natural communication.

Introduce the *No* form.

Steps are repeated almost identically to those for learning the *Yes* form. If questions do not naturally elicit negative answers, turn your Teacher Cards upside down to cue students for *No*.

BOOKS OPEN

Students open their books and look at the illustrations that reinforce the language just introduced. Steps are generally as follows:

C. Practice the question and answer.

Students open books for this portion, as the pictures on the page are necessary for demonstration. Lesson notes generally follow the steps below.

1. Listen to the question-and-answer pattern.

a. Have students look at the page and describe the things they see.

b. Play the audio track. Students listen to the question-and-answer pattern as it is spoken, then listen to the pattern as it is spoken along with the rhythm, and finally listen to the rhythm alone.

c. Play audio again. Have students tap or clap the rhythm as they listen one time. Then replay the audio and have students repeat the question and answer with the spoken model, the rhythmic model, and the rhythm.

2. Practice the question-and-answer pattern with vocabulary.

a. Present the pattern by writing it on the board or direct student attention to it in the book.

b. Play the audio track. Point to the words as students listen. Have students repeat the questions and answers after the audio.

c. If there is a contraction in the sentence pattern, direct your students' attention to it and make sure they understand. Use the contraction cards and instructions on pages 196–197 to help demonstrate the meaning and formation of contractions.

d. When students are confident enough, have them ask and answer each other in pairs, using picture cards or actual items as cues.

D. Practice.

Many Let's Learn More lessons feature a practice activity that brings back the vocabulary from the Let's Learn lesson and practices it in the *Yes/No* question-and-answer pattern just studied. The activities vary throughout the book and include listening exercises, songs, fill-in charts, and personalized activities. Notes for instructing students on these exercises can be found in the individual lessons.

GAMES AND ACTIVITIES

Games and Activities recycle the material from the lesson in innovative and engaging ways to reinforce what the students have learned. This is also a good way to end a class since the students will leave with a sense of accomplishment, wanting to learn more. You will find detailed instructions in each Teacher's Book lesson and in the Drills and Games section of this introduction (p. 21).

EXTRA PRACTICE

Extra Practice contains various ancillary materials for further practice of the language taught in the lesson. Workbook and Skills Book instructions and Answer Keys, as well as reproducible Worksheets and their instructions, are located in the back of the book.

COMPONENTS LINK

Components Link lists resources for further practice, assessment, and learning additional material. These include *Let's Go CD-ROM, Let's Go Tests and Quizzes, Let's Go Readers, Let's Chant Let's Sing,* and *Let's Go Picture Dictionary.*

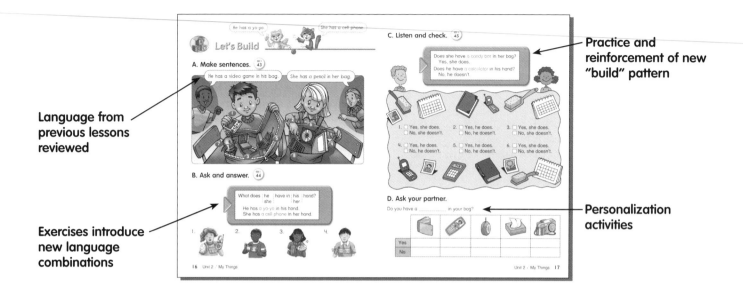

Language from previous lessons reviewed

Exercises introduce new language combinations

Practice and reinforcement of new "build" pattern

Personalization activities

Note on the Let's Build approach: Let's Build stimulates students' interest by expanding their possibilities for expression. The structure of the lesson varies more than any other lesson in *Let's Go*. Main features are:

- Recycling of material from previous units
- Recombinations of patterns the students know
- Introduction of a new pattern, built upon what students already know

WARM UP AND REVIEW

Start the lesson with the suggested review activity, or select an activity from pages 21–26. Every class should begin with an oral review of language recently studied. This helps the students to remember previous material and starts the class on a positive note since the students are using familiar language.

EXERCISES A THROUGH D

The majority of Let's Build exercises feature practice activities to demonstrate new combinations of vocabulary and language patterns. These vary throughout the book, and include listening exercises, songs, fill-in charts, and personalized activities. Notes for instructing students on these exercises can be found in the individual lessons.

Books remain open throughout the lesson, as the illustrations are necessary for demonstration. Contents and activities vary greatly according to the language in each unit, but frequently appearing activities are briefly described below:

Ask and answer. / Practice.

Presentation and practice of these exercises are similar to activities in Let's Learn and Let's Learn More. Steps and progression will vary with each unit. The following steps are common:

1. Practice the words. Show Teacher Cards, objects, or the pictures in the book to review familiar vocabulary.

2. If an audio track accompanies the exercise, play it and have students listen and point to the appropriate pictures. Replay the audio and have students repeat, then speak to each other.

3. Model the sentence or question-and-answer pattern. Use gestures or pictures while saying the target patterns. Have students repeat.

4. Divide the class into two groups. One group asks the question and the other answers. As the groups grow confident with the pattern, switch roles to make sure both groups can ask and answer the question. Students should either ask the question or answer it, so that even basic language practice reinforces natural communication.

5. Have students take turns asking and answering the questions in pairs.

Ask your partner.

The steps and progression are similar to **Ask and answer** and **Practice**, but this exercise focuses more on personalized pair practice.

Listen and circle. / Listen and number.

These exercises allow students to interact with the book and demonstrate their understanding. Steps and progression will vary with each unit. The following steps are common:

1. Have students look at the art and describe what they see. Encourage them to guess what language they might hear.

2. Play the audio track and have students listen the first time. The second time they should circle or number the correct items. The third time they should check their answers.

3. Pair and group question-and-answer activities can be done if desired.

Listen and sing.

Songs in Let's Build reinforce the new language combinations built up in the lesson. Steps and progression will vary with each song. The following principles are common:

1. Have students look at the pictures and describe what they see. Have them point to and read words they recognize.

2. Use backwards build-up to teach phrases, or model the song line by line.

3. When playing the audio track, have students listen and point to the pictures.

4. When playing the song again, have students sing along all together, or divide the class according to the number of parts in the song.

GAMES AND ACTIVITIES

Games and Activities recycle the material from the lesson in innovative and engaging ways to reinforce what the students have learned. This is also a good way to end a class since the students will leave with a sense of accomplishment, wanting to learn more. You will find detailed instructions in each Teacher's Book lesson and in the Drills and Games section of this introduction (p. 21).

EXTRA PRACTICE

Extra Practice contains various ancillary materials for further practice of the language taught in the lesson. Workbook and Skills Book instructions and Answer Keys, as well as reproducible Worksheets and their instructions, are located in the back of the book.

COMPONENTS LINK

Components Link lists resources for further practice, assessment, and learning additional material. These include *Let's Go CD-ROM, Let's Go Tests and Quizzes, Let's Go Readers, Let's Chant Let's Sing,* and *Let's Go Picture Dictionary.*

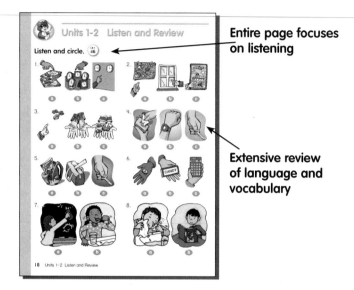

Entire page focuses on listening

Extensive review of language and vocabulary

This is a lesson in two parts. Part One, titled Listen and Review, quizzes material from the immediately preceding two Units. Part Two, titled Let's Learn About, introduces important new vocabulary in four topic areas: Numbers 20–100, Months, Seasons, and Time.

PART ONE: LISTEN AND REVIEW

Review Activities

Since Listen and Review culminates in a listening exercise covering all the material from the prior two units, the majority of time is spent reviewing vocabulary and language patterns through games and activities. This helps the students to remember previous material and starts the class on a positive note, since the students are using language with which they are comfortable and familiar. There are review activities for all language from Let's Start (Let's Talk, Let's Sing, Let's Move), as well as for Let's Learn and Let's Learn More. These activities include games, drills, and dialogues. Make sure to have your Teacher Cards ready, and have the students prepare their Student Cards, too.

Introduce Listen and Review

BOOKS CLOSED

It's important to review material in a way that focuses on recognition and recall. Reviewing material with the books closed helps focus student attention on your demonstration. Lesson notes generally follow these steps:

1. Put three Teacher Cards on the chalkrail to resemble the activity on the Listen and Review page in the

Student Book. Draw a letter *a* under the first card, a letter *b* under the second, and a letter *c* under the third. Have a student stand by the cards. Identify one of the cards and have the student point to the correct card and circle the appropriate letter. Repeat as necessary until all students understand the procedure.

BOOKS OPEN

Students open books in order to do the listening assessment. Steps are as follows:

A. Listen and circle.

1. Open your book and show the page to the class. Have students identify the items and actions shown.

2. Have students open their books to the same page.

   a. Play the audio track. Have students listen and point to the appropriate pictures.

   b. Play the audio again. Have students do the exercise as a written test.

   c. Correct the test with the students.

3. Use the page for further review. Pair off the students or have them work in groups. Have them ask each other questions about the illustrations. Focus on aspects for which language was not used in the quiz. For example:

   a. Have students ask what objects there are.

   b. Have students identify the colors of objects.

   c. If there is more than one object, have students ask what there is/what there are. You can then have them ask how many there are.

   d. For verb phrases, ask about the other pictures. When possible, use them to personalize the questions, particularly after studying *can* and *can't*.

By the time later units are being covered, the amount of language available will expand the possibilities for recycling. Make an effort to re-combine the language that students have learned to that point, and encourage the students to do likewise.

Listen and Review Test

In addition to the Listen and Review exercise in the Student Book, a Units Listen and Review test is available in Let's go Tests and Quizzes. It covers the same two units as the Student Book exercise, but includes written items.

Part 2: Lesson Structure of Let's Learn About

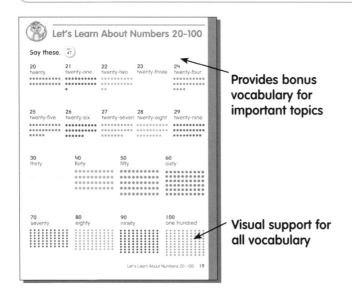

Provides bonus vocabulary for important topics

Visual support for all vocabulary

Note about the lesson: Generally, the Let's Learn About lesson follows the presentation and practice model found in the other lessons. However, steps vary according to the content. The following presentation is a generalized example.

PART TWO: LET'S LEARN ABOUT

BOOKS CLOSED

It's important to present new material to your students in a way that focuses on understanding meaning. Presenting new material with the books closed helps focus student attention on your demonstration. Lesson notes generally follow these steps:

Present the topic

Ask students questions about the topic. See how much students know. Don't feel you need to correct them at this point—the goal is to see what they already know about the topic.

1. Introduce the words.

Use Teacher Cards to introduce the new words, focusing on pronunciation and rhythm. When introducing verb vocabulary, use gestures or actions to reinforce meaning. Speak with natural pronunciation and intonation as you model the vocabulary or play the audio. Make sure that students understand the meaning of the words and can say them easily.

2. Introduce the question and answer.

Check and correct students' pronunciation so that you don't have to return to teaching pronunciation once vocabulary has been introduced. The introduction and drill of new vocabulary should be done thoroughly but quickly here so that you should only have to introduce new vocabulary once, and after that students are using and practicing the words in context.

BOOKS OPEN

Students open their books and look at the illustrations that reinforce the language just introduced. Steps in the lesson notes vary depending on the topic. The following sequence is a general example:

A. Say these. / Ask and answer.

1. Practice the words.

    a. Play the audio and have students listen and point to the vocabulary on the page.

    b. Play the audio again and have students repeat the vocabulary.

2. Practice the pattern.

Write the pattern on the board or direct students' attention to it in their books. Point to the item in the book and model the language. Have students listen to the audio. Then, have them answer and repeat as necessary.

B. Practice. / Say these.

The B exercise will also vary, but will generally offer further vocabulary practice, often demonstrated with a support box. Make sure to play the audio if instructed, and to allow for a variety of practice methods: divide the class in two, pairwork, games and drills, etc.

GAMES AND ACTIVITIES

Games and Activities recycle the material from the lesson in innovative and engaging ways to reinforce what the students have learned. This is also a good way to end a class since the students will leave with a sense of accomplishment, wanting to learn more. You will find detailed instructions in each Teacher's Book lesson and in the Drills and Games section of this introduction.

EXTRA PRACTICE

Extra Practice contains various ancillary materials for further practice of the language taught in the lesson. Workbook and Skills Book instructions and Answer Keys, as well as reproducible Worksheets and their instructions, are located in the back of the book.

COMPONENTS LINK

Components Link lists resources for further practice, assessment, and learning additional material. These include *Let's Go CD-ROM, Let's Go Tests and Quizzes, Let's Go Readers, Let's Chant Let's Sing,* and *Let's Go Picture Dictionary.*

TEACHING TECHNIQUES AND PROCEDURES

VOCABULARY

Use actual objects or Teacher Cards to present new key words. Hold up an object or picture card and say the word. Have the students repeat the word several times. Then practice the word with drills, using familiar language whenever possible.

The Teacher's Book describes a number of drills and activities designed to develop and reinforce the students' vocabulary knowledge. There are two types of vocabulary or language that all language learners develop—receptive language and productive language.

Receptive language is the language students understand but are not necessarily able to produce yet. When you speak to the students in English, it is inevitable that you will sometimes use language that they have not yet studied. This is not a problem and is even desirable since it exposes the students to additional language. They will gradually pick up the meaning from the context if the language is used often enough. For example, if you write the number *1* on the board and tell the students to open their books and look at page 1, receptive language is being developed; they have not yet learned the number or the command, but will pick up the meaning from your actions.

To practice receptive language, students must recognize and physically respond to vocabulary words. For example, place the Teacher Cards for *book* and *pencil* on the chalk or marker rail. Say *book* and have one or more students point to the *book* card, or place several Teacher Cards on the rail and select two students to come to the front of the class. Say one of the vocabulary words and have the students race to touch the correct card. Whoever touches the card first is the winner.

While receptive language is language understood but not necessarily spoken by students, productive language is the language spoken by students. Productive language practice requires students to say the vocabulary words as they identify the objects. Play the games as described above, but have the students touch the correct cards and orally identify the objects.

After being initially modeled or done as a whole class, all the games for receptive and productive language can be continued in small groups of three or four students each. Small-group practice is especially important for large classes. When the students are first learning new vocabulary, use one set of Student Cards per group. Call out the words and have the students, one at a time, touch the correct picture card. If a student is incorrect, the other students in the group can help.

PRONUNCIATION

In order to be understood, students need to clearly articulate words and sentence patterns. This is why *Let's Go* emphasizes natural speed and intonation in both introducing and practicing language. This is also why verbs are generally introduced as part of verb phrases, rather than as basic verbs. It is best, however, not to single out individual students and ask them to repeat a word or phrase over and over in front of the class. When one or more students are having difficulty articulating something, have the whole class practice the troublesome pattern several times. Walk around the class listening to all the students, but pay particular attention to those who are having difficulty. Later, when the students are in pairs, spend some time with the individual students if they are still having trouble.

It is important to remember that even native English-speaking children have difficulty in learning certain English sounds, among them *r*, *l*, *sh*, and *th*. It takes time and maturity to be able to properly articulate them. Consequently, it is important that you be patient and allow time for the language learner to produce the correct sound.

In the *Let's Go* Student Books, pronunciation drills and practice do not receive major emphasis. This stems from the belief that it is desirable, especially with younger children, to begin language instruction without placing undue stress on the exact pronunciation of each word or phrase. Too much attention to this can result in student frustration, lack of confidence, and lack of interest in the language. It is important at the first stage to develop ease in communicating in the new language, as well as a desire to speak it without worry about making errors in pronunciation at every step. This is crucial for students' motivation.

The lessons in the Teacher's Book do, however, incorporate some pronunciation practice at each stage. This is done through choral repetition and further oral practice in small groups and pairs. During this time, you should circulate around the classroom listening to the students and helping those who are having trouble. The Teacher's Book also includes occasional pronunciation tips to help teachers identify and deal with the more troublesome areas for students. A new feature of this third edition of *Let's Go* is the inclusion of drum rhythm tracks on the audio to help students practice using natural rhythm and stress for each new language pattern. Regular practice with the drum will help students achieve more natural and fluent English.

CONTRACTIONS

Let's Go teaches both contracted and non-contracted language, but it stresses the use of contractions in order to foster naturally spoken speech. Learning how to use *isn't* and *I'm* in conversation, for example, allows students to sound more fluent and to better understand natural English, and gives them an advantage when they begin to read and write. Students are given many opportunities to practice both the full and contracted forms of words.

Individual contractions are explained in Teacher's Book lessons and corresponding contraction cards are found on pages 196–197. The contraction cards provide a simple way for students to see how two words become one in speech.

In Levels 2-6, contractions are incorporated into the paradigm boxes (except for the paradigms introducing the past tense, which revert to the style used in the earlier levels).

GROUPING THE STUDENTS FOR LANGUAGE PRACTICE

Varying the way in which new structures are practiced helps to keep students interested in the language. After modeling a new structure, have the whole class repeat it. If the language is complicated, or if there are more than one or two items being introduced, it can be practiced in a drill. Keep the drill moving to maintain the students' attention. After the whole class practices the new structure, place the students into two groups to practice again, this time with each group taking a part of the dialogue or pattern. Practicing in two groups allows the students to become more familiar with the patterns within the secure setting of speaking with other students.

You can then place the students in small groups or pairs where they can further practice in a realistic one-on-one exchange. Practicing in pairs or small groups is an ideal way for students to learn from one another since they can share information and ask questions about points they are unsure of.

For example, the following progression shows how to move a question-and-response from whole-class practice to individual response:

Part A: *How are you?*	Part B: *I'm fine.*
1. Puppet A (teacher)	Puppet B (teacher)
2. Puppet A (teacher)	Whole class
3. Whole class	Puppet B (teacher)
4. Group A (half class)	Group B (half class)
5. Group B	Group A
6. Student A	Student B
7. Student B	Student A

Let's Go uses games, interviews, questions about pictures, and dialogues that can easily be done in small groups or pairs. You should closely monitor the students by walking around the classroom, listening to each group, and helping as needed. Only after adequate whole-class and group practice should you ask students to speak in front of the class. (The latter should be done more as a game or a role play than as a method of testing.)

TEAM TEACHING

Team teaching is a very useful technique in the language classroom. Two teachers can bring the dialogues and conversations to life by acting as models.

Likewise, practice exercises can be clearly demonstrated by two teachers. Team teachers can lead different halves of the class in two-group practice or team games. They can also give more individualized attention to students when circulating around the class for small-group practice and pairwork.

MODELING

Clear, careful modeling is essential to demonstrate to students the procedure for certain activities. The more complicated the activity and the language involved, the more essential it becomes to prepare the students before they begin. Good modeling saves time later and helps the students get the most out of an activity linguistically, since they will not be wasting energy in confusion about what they should be doing. Finally, and most importantly, modeling enables you to explain a structure or an activity so that the students can carry out the activity using only English.

Modeling Sentence Patterns

New question-and-answer patterns can be modeled in several ways. You can act as two people, work with a student volunteer, or use puppets. When modeling, use actual objects or visual aids whenever possible along with corresponding gestures.

Teacher: (holding up a book) *What's this?*
Student: *It's a book.*

Modeling Practice Activities

To model a practice activity, you can walk the students through the activity, move them into position, and say what they are supposed to say. For example, if the students are supposed to mingle and ask questions, you can walk several students around the room, guiding them by the shoulders. By following this physical approach, students can learn even a very complex activity.

MODEL, ACTION, TALK (MAT)

The Model, Action, Talk method (also known as MAT) was developed by Ritsuko Nakata. Many of the activities in the Teacher's Book refer to MAT techniques to help students acquire and practice new language.

The MAT method begins by providing students with an accurate and clear model of the target language using either the teacher or audio as model. The teacher then has students associate the target language with a physical movement. Associating a kinesthetic memory with rote memorization enables students to improve retention. A final key feature of MAT is that students speak from the start—there is no prolonged silent period. The model starts off slowly and clearly, but it builds up to natural speed so that students are speaking naturally from the first lessons. Using language as they acquire it encourages students to communicate rather than recite or memorize and feel more confident in their ability to use their new language skills.

READING

Let's Go offers reading material that can be approached in different ways depending on educational goals and course syllabi. Level 1 of *Let's Go* is a beginning reading level in which the Let's Build lesson includes an alphabet section that focuses on learning and practicing the alphabet via initial letters of words. For students proficient with the alphabet, vocabulary and phonics can be focused on. Students should be encouraged to read by looking for the same words or sentences on the page and by pointing to each word as they listen to the audio. In this way, they will get familiar with the words in the lesson and will be able to read what is in the Workbook and Skills Book. Finally, there is an independent three-level *Let's Go Phonics* course.

For more information on reading in *Let's Go,* see the following sections in this introduction: "Description of the Levels" (page 4), "Supplemental Components" (page 6), and "Using the Readers" (page 20).

WRITING

Written exercises for Level 2 are in the accompanying Workbook and Skills Book. In Level 2, students are not expected to write words or sentences without a spelling model on the page. These exercises can be done in class or at home; however, if Workbook exercises are to be done at home, it is advisable to spend some class time going over each exercise orally and doing one or two to show the students how to do them.

USING THE *READERS*

Each *Let's Go Reader Pack* contains eight separate Readers and an audio CD. As there is a Reader for each Unit, students will be ready to read and understand the corresponding *Let's Go Reader* upon completion of a Unit.

Below are suggested guidelines to follow when presenting a story. Although the following sequence is suggested, the pace at which it is used may vary. For example, to provide a brief break from the Student Book, an entire class lesson can be devoted to a *Reader* story. Or, the last ten minutes of several classes may be devoted to studying a story, breaking up the suggested guidelines into manageable segments. *Readers* may also be assigned as homework. There is also an audio CD with the *Readers*. There is no one preferred way to incorporate the Readers into your lessons. Rather, each teacher must consider time constraints as well as the students' age level, which may influence their tolerance for focused activities.

Step 1: Preview the story

a. Look at the cover illustration with the students and read the title aloud to them. Have students describe the picture, as their level permits.

b. Picture Walk. Have students flip through the pages of the story and look at the pictures. If desired, you can have them cover the text with a piece of paper so it won't distract them. Encourage students to talk about what they see, using language they know (or using their native language, if necessary). Ask questions to help students talk about the pictures: *Who's in it? Where is it? What's happening?*

As you progress through the book in this manner, see if the students can predict what might happen next or what the story might be about. Keep in mind that this task will get easier for your students as their level increases.

Step 2: Read aloud

Read the entire story aloud while students follow along in their books. Have students run their fingers under the words as they listen.

Step 3: Focus on vocabulary

Read the story again, page by page. For each page, do the following:

a. Look at the new vocabulary at the bottom of the page and make sure students understand the new words. Use the glossary pictures and the main scenes to help you explain them.

b. As you read the page again, have students listen for the new words. Ask them to raise their hands whenever they hear one.

Step 4: Repeated readings

Once students have learned the new vocabulary and have a basic understanding of the story, have them read the story again a number of times. This can be done over a period of several days or weeks, depending on how often you meet with your students.

Whenever students are reading aloud or a story is being read to them, it is a good idea to be sure they are actively engaged in the activity and not listening passively. Here are some ideas for keeping students actively involved in the readings:

- As you read the story aloud, pause and ask for predictions about what will happen next.

- Invite students to read parts of the story individually or in groups.

- Have students read the story in chorus. Since choral reading tends to slow down the language and make it sound unnatural, you may want to have students repeat after you, line by line, and try to copy your speed and intonation as much as possible.

- Have students read in pairs, with partners taking turns and helping each other with troublesome vocabulary and pronunciation. You should circulate during this activity and help students as necessary.

- Have students take the *Reader* home, where they can read silently, read aloud to their parents, or read aloud with their parents.

Step 5: Comprehension exercises

Comprehension exercises are included at the end

of each story. These exercises check students' understanding, and help students solidify and incorporate what they have studied. They can be done orally in class or assigned as homework (if students are able to write).

Step 6: Extension / Follow-up activities

That's Not Right

As you read the story to the students, try to trick them by changing some of the words. When students hear a mistake they shout out, *That's not right!* Then have them supply the correct sentence.

Readers Theater

For this activity, assign parts (including the narrator) to students and have them read the entire story aloud. If desired, you can have them memorize the lines and move around as if they are on-stage.

Role Play

This activity differs from Readers Theater (above) in that the focus is more on the elements of the story than on the actual language in the story. By doing this activity you will be able to see if students understood what they read in English.

Have students act out the story. If the students in your class all speak the same language, assign them roles and have them act out the story entirely in their native language. Students who speak different languages will have to do this activity in English. They can use some of the lines directly from the reading, but it doesn't have to be exact. The point of this activity is to retell the story, not to recite it verbatim.

Student-generated Story (Language Experience Approach)

This activity can be done as a whole class. Allow students to create their own story, using the *Reader* story as a model. Have them use the patterns and vocabulary from the *Reader,* and supply them with new vocabulary as needed. Write the story on the board as the class dictates it to you, and correct grammar as necessary. (Try to get the students to self-correct as much as possible.) When the story is complete, read it aloud to the class. If possible, type out the story and give copies to the students, or have them copy the story from the board (if they are able to write). Allow the students to illustrate their "Readers."

DRILLS AND GAMES

DRILLS

Drilling is a time-efficient, enjoyable way to review or present material in a tightly organized manner. Be sure to keep drills short and rhythmic—several seconds each, then repeat as many times as necessary. Short, quick drills will keep the students' attention and they will learn faster as they concentrate on the drills. While doing drills, it is a good idea to alternate between choral and individual responses. When doing the latter,

choosing students in random order and maintaining a quick pace will help keep their attention.

There are many kinds of drills to choose from. Brief descriptions of several kinds of drills and the procedures for doing them follow.

Repetition Drill

Model vocabulary words or new language patterns for the class to repeat. Teacher: *a window, a window.* Students: *a window.* Teacher: *clocks, clocks.* Students: *clocks.*

or:

> Teacher: *That's a window.*
>
> Students: *That's a window.*
>
> Teacher: *Those are clocks.*
>
> Students: *Those are clocks.*

Substitution Drill

To do a substitution drill, use picture cards or actual objects as cues.

> T: *Where are the cooks?* (show a picture of cooks in a kitchen) *They're in the kitchen.*
>
> Ss: *They're in the kitchen.*
>
> T: (show a picture of cooks in a bedroom)
>
> Ss: *They're in the bedroom.*

or:

> T: (show a picture of a peach) *This is a peach. I want a peach.*
>
> Ss: *This is a peach. I want a peach.*
>
> T: (show a picture of an omelet)
>
> Ss: *This is an omelet. I want an omelet.*

Chain Drill

In a chain drill, you should use objects or picture cards as cues. Show an object or picture card to the first student and ask a related question. The student answers and turns to the next student to ask the same question with appropriate substitutions. Continue until all the students have had a chance to ask and answer the question. Divide larger classes into three or four small groups, and have each group do a chain drill.

> T: (show a picture of a workbook to S1) What's this?
>
> S1: *It's a workbook.* (show a picture of a calendar to S2) *What's this?*
>
> S2: *It's a calendar.*

Six-second Drill

To make drills fun and exciting, after modeling several times, have students say the vocabulary or sentence in a quick series of three and raise their hands and say, *Finished!* Repeat several times for each word. Doing these drills several times in a series of three, you will be able to have the students say the target language many times even in one minute. They will be talking at natural speed (to be the first student to say *Finished!*), and drills become games.

> Ss: *Picture, picture, picture! Finished!*
>
> T: *Again! (Can you say it better this time? Say* Finished! *and clap two times.)*
>
> Ss: *Picture, picture, picture! Finished!*
>
> T: *Again!* (add a task)

Sentence pattern drill: *I like peaches.*

> Ss: *I like peaches, I like peaches, I like peaches. Finished!*
>
> T: *Again! (Can you say it faster this time? Say* Finished! *and stand up.)*
>
> Ss: *I like peaches, I like peaches, I like peaches. Finished!*
>
> T: *Again!* (add a task)

Question form: *What does he like?*

> Ss: *What does he like, what does he like, what does he like? Finished!*
>
> T: *Again! (Can you say it louder this time? Say* Finished! *and tap your head.)*
>
> Ss: *What does he like, what does he like, what does he like? Finished!*
>
> T: *Again!* (add a task)

GAMES

Games need not be considered simply entertainment, and therefore unimportant to language learning; rather, they serve as a way to reinforce the material presented in the lesson in a way that engages students in a very effective manner. In most cases, games serve the same function as the drills listed above because they offer an organized and fun way to review or present material. Drills tend to be more repetitive and teacher-centered (which can be helpful when learning new structures and vocabulary), while games tend to be more open-ended and student-centered, which leads to creative use of the language.

There are many games to choose from. Some focus on vocabulary, some focus on structures, and some exploit both vocabulary and structures. Brief descriptions of some of the games used in Level 2 and the procedures for doing them follow.

Games for Drilling Vocabulary

Bingo

This game encourages vocabulary memorization and listening comprehension. Give each student a nine-square grid, with three rows of three squares each. The students select nine of their word or picture cards (based on the lesson vocabulary) and arrange them randomly on the grid. The caller (either you or a student) picks a card from a duplicate set of cards and calls out the word or phrase indicated on the card. If the students have that card on their grids, they turn the card over or cover it with a piece of paper. The first student to cover three

squares across, down, or diagonally wins the game. Variations: Instead of using a grid, students can simply arrange their Student Cards in the shape of a grid (i.e., in columns and rows). Also, instead of using word or picture cards, students can simply write the vocabulary words in their grids.

Board Race

There are many variations to this activity, all of which involve having the students compete to demonstrate their recall of new vocabulary. One variation is to divide the class into teams. Place a row of word or picture cards along the chalk or marker rail. Say one of the words; one student from each team races to the board to touch the correct card. Or, instead of placing the cards along the chalk or marker rail, have team representatives stand at the board; say a word and have the team representatives compete to draw a picture of the word. The first team member to call out the correct word wins a point for his or her team. The team with the most points wins.

Another variation that works well with smaller classes is to have the class form a line near the board. Line up picture cards along the rail. The first two students in line come up to the chalk rail. Give each student a pointer (e.g., a ruler or a marker). Call out one of the words. Students race to touch the card and repeat the word. The winning student remains at the chalk rail to challenge the next player. The losing student passes the pointer to the next student in line. Repeat the activity until all students have had a chance to compete at least once.

Charades

There are several ways to do this activity, which involves using gestures to express meaning. In its basic form, begin by placing word or picture cards facedown in a pile. One student takes a card from the top of the pile without showing it to the rest of the class. After looking at the card, the student acts out the word using gestures. The class must guess the action. Instead of using word or picture cards, you can also simply whisper the word or phrase to the student.

Concentration

This activity helps build memory skills. Separate the students into pairs or groups of three or four. Give two sets of picture cards to each group and place them facedown in random order on the desk. One at a time, students turn over two cards and try to find two identical cards. As each student looks at the cards, he or she says the word or phrase that is shown. If the cards match, the student keeps them and gets a point.

File Grids

Make one nine-square grid (the squares should be numbered) inside a file folder for each student. Divide the class into pairs. S1 draws pictures of objects from previous units in each square of his or her grid. S2 must recreate S1's grid by asking questions. S2: *One. What is it?* S1: *It's a (bat).* After completing one grid, partners compare their pictures. Reverse roles after several exchanges.

Guess the Word

This activity reviews vocabulary while at the same time encouraging students to make guesses. Divide the class into groups of three to five students each. S1 thinks of a word and writes one letter from the word on a piece of paper. The other students try to guess the word. If no one has guessed correctly after the round, S1 adds another letter to the word. The student who guesses S1's word thinks of the next word.

Hidden Words

This game requires word or picture cards, as well as number cards. The number cards should be large enough to cover the word or picture cards. Place the word or picture cards along the chalk rail. Cover each card with a number card. Divide the class into two teams. S1 from Team A calls out a number. Reveal the word or picture card that is under that number card. Give the student a count of three to say the word. If the student says the word correctly or identifies the picture, give the team a point. If the student is incorrect, cover the word up again and allow S1 from Team B to call out a number. Play alternates back and forth between teams until all the words have been said.

Picture Game

This activity involves drawing pictures to express meaning, but more importantly it encourages guessing and recall of previously learned vocabulary. Divide the class into small groups (3–4 students). Give scratch paper and pencils to each group. One student from each group comes up to the front of the class as a representative. Gather the representatives together and whisper a word to them. When the representatives have heard the word, they return to their groups and draw a picture of the word. They cannot speak or gesture, only draw. The first team to guess the word correctly gets a point.

As a fun alternative, prepare a list of ten vocabulary items. Instead of whispering the word to the representatives, show them the word at the top of the list. The representatives then return to their groups and draw a picture of the word. When one of the team members guesses the word, he or she comes up and whispers it to you. This student then becomes the new representative. Show this new representative the next word on the list. The activity continues as before. The first team to complete the list wins the game.

Rhythm

Form a circle with the students. Establish a one-two rhythm: two slaps to the thighs, two claps twice, snap fingers of your right hand once, snap fingers of your left hand once. Repeat until all can keep the rhythm. Begin by calling out your name on the right-hand snap, then a student's name on the left-hand snap. Continue until all have participated. For example:

> All: (two slaps, two claps)
> T: *Ms. Lee* (snap), *Ken* (snap)
> All: (two slaps, two claps)
> S1 (Ken): *Ken* (snap), *Mari* (snap)
> All: (two slaps, two claps)
> S2 (Mari): *Mari* (snap), *Jenny* (snap)

This game can be played with added vocabulary as you progress through the course.

Scramble

This activity encourages vocabulary memorization and listening comprehension. It is also a good choice when the students need a chance to be active. Students sit in a circle (or several circles for large classes). There are two ways to play the game. One way is to assign a different word to each student. Call out two words at random. Those two students stand and exchange seats. To cue all students to change seats, call out *Scramble!* The first time you call *Scramble!*, remove one chair from the circle. Now one student will have to remain standing in the center of the circle. When two students exchange seats, they will have to race with the student in the center to get a seat. Another way you can play this game is to assign several students the same word. Call out only one word and take away a chair. All students assigned that word must switch places.

As an option, especially for the second variation, give each student a word or picture card with the assigned object written or drawn on it. The first time a student is left in the center of the circle, take away this student's object card. After that, any student going into the center will always give his or her object card to the student he or she is replacing.

Show Me

Hold up a Teacher Card. Ask the students to identify the item and hold up the matching Student Cards.

> T: *What are these?*
> Ss: (hold up a Student Card) *They're (peaches).*

Have student volunteers ask some of the questions.

Slap

Students enjoy the fast-paced challenge of this activity. Place students in small groups. Give each group a set of designated word or picture cards, placed faceup on the table within reach of all the students. The caller (either you or a student volunteer) should have a duplicate set of cards piled in random order. The caller calls out the word or phrase pictured on the top card. The first student in each group to slap the correct card and produce the word or phrase shown on the card takes it. The student in each group holding the most cards is the winner. This can also be played with a caller in each group. In this case, each group would need two sets of cards.

Vocabulary Race

Students place Student Cards face up in a row (or use the pictures on the Practice the Words page). S1 begins by touching the card at one end of the row and saying the word. S2 begins at the opposite end of the row. Students work their way toward their opponent's side, pointing to cards and saying the words shown. When students meet somewhere in the middle (both fingers touch the same card), they play **Rock, Paper, Scissors** (see page 26). The winner remains in place and the loser returns to the beginning of the vocabulary row. The first student to move from one end of the row to the other wins. Very young students can place Teacher Cards on the floor and hop from card to card as they say the words. This can also be done with students saying sentences as they touch each card.

Whisper Relay

This game practices listening skills and memorization. Divide the class into teams and have them stand or sit in a line looking at the back of the student in front of them. Whisper the same word to the first person in each row. Say *Go!* and have S1 whisper the word to S2, who whispers it to S3, etc., as fast as possible. The last student then runs to the front of the class and tells the teacher the word. The first student to say the word correctly wins. To make this more challenging, whisper 2–3 words or a sentence to S1.

Games for Drilling Structures

Beanbag Circle

Have the class form a circle. Toss a ball or a beanbag to S1 and ask a question. S1 responds, tosses the ball to another student (S2), and asks a question. Continue until all students have had a chance to participate. For large classes, play **Beanbag Circle** in groups so that more students can participate simultaneously.

Find Your Partner

This activity provides a setting for students to use language in a meaningful way. Use word cards in multiple sets so that all the students have cards and every card has at least one duplicate. Deal out one card to each student. Do not allow students to show their cards to one another. Have the students walk around and look for another student holding the same card. To find their partners, students must ask appropriate questions related to the items on their cards. For example, a student who holds a card showing tape can ask, *Do you want tape?* When another student answers, *Yes, I do,* it means he or she has a matching card. Students can also simply repeat the items on their cards until they each find a match.

Living Sentences or Dialogues

This activity encourages students to think about sentence structure and word order. Select sentences from present or previous units. Divide the class into groups and assign one sentence to each group. Each student in the group is assigned one word in the sentence. Students are not allowed to speak except to repeat their words. They arrange themselves in the correct order. For dialogues, students are assigned sentences rather than words.

Scrambled Sentences

This activity practices word order and sentence patterns. Have pairs of groups arrange word cards into complete sentences. Set a time limit and have students see how many correct sentences they can make using the cards. Or, have students put entire sentences in order to make a complete conversation or song.

Games for Drilling Vocabulary and Structures

1-2-3-Finished!

This game is nearly identical to **Six-second Drill**. Divide the class into pairs or small groups. Have students say the vocabulary or sentence in a quick series of three and raise their hands and say Finished! Repeat several times for each word or sentence. The winner is the first student (or pair or group) to say the target language.

Interview

This activity allows students to practice language in a natural way. Distribute Interview forms (similar to the Reproducible Worksheet on page 188) to each student. Have students circulate and interview each other, asking question and writing the information they receive on their forms. When everyone is finished, call on individual students to report on what they learned about each other, or have students write out complete sentences with the information.

Say It!

This activity practices saying vocabulary at random and spontaneously. Divide the class into several groups. Give each group a set of Student Cards. Put the cards in a zig-zig line on the table. When you say *Go!*, one students starts at one end of the cards and says a sentence for each card. S2 starts immediately after S1 and S3 follows S2 so that everyone is moving along the cards at the same time. When all the students have finished, rearrange the cards and start again.

Telegram

This activity practices listening skills and forming sentences with target language. Have students form rows. Give the first student a card in an envelope. S1 looks at the card and places it back in the envelope. Then S1 hands the envelope to S2 and whispers a sentence using the word on the card (*He has a calculator*). S2 does not look at the card, but passes it to S3 and whispers the sentence. Continue to the end of the row. The last student says the sentence out loud and then opens the envelope to see if the sentence matches the picture. The team decides whether the sentence spoken aloud is the same as spoken by S1.

Back-to-Back

This activity creates a situation where students must depend on each other to complete an assignment, thus encouraging communication. To begin, pair off students. Partners sit back-to-back, or with a screen between them, so that they cannot see each other's papers. An open file folder or notebook standing on its bottom edge works well as a screen.

In one variation, provide all students with blank grids (or partially filled-in grids, depending on the activity). S1 completes his or her grid in response to your instructions. S2 tries to reproduce S1's grid by asking S1 questions, or in some cases by listening to S1's description and asking questions for reinforcement whenever necessary. When finished, partners compare grids for accuracy, and then reverse roles.

The second variation involves drawing. Provide students with blank pieces of paper (or partial drawings, depending on the activity). S1 draws a simple picture in response to your instructions. S1 then tells S2 what to draw in order to reproduce S1's picture as closely as possible. When finished, partners compare pictures for accuracy, and then reverse roles.

Card Game / Go Fish

Divide the class into small groups of 5 or 6 students. Use a double set of Student Cards for each group. Have each group choose a dealer to shuffle and deal out all the cards to the members of the group. Have students ask for cards they hold in their hands by using the question-and-answer structure they just learned. A positive answer earns the asking student the answerer's card. If a student is not holding the correct card, he or she should answer the question in the negative form. Students must try to pair all the cards they hold. The first one to do so wins. For example:

S1 (holding card 62): *Can you do a magic trick?*

S2 (not holding card 62): *No, I can't.*

S3 (holding card 60): *Can you use chopsticks?*

S4 (holding card 60): *Yes, I can.* (S4 gives card to S3)

Model the game by playing one or two open hands (cards faceup on the table) with one group while the other students watch.

For the **Go Fish** variation of this game, leave a small pile of cards facedown in the center after distributing an even number of cards amongst each group of students. If a negative answer is given, the student asking the question will choose a card from the pile instead of receiving a card from another student.

Cube Game

Make cubes from milk cartons. Cut the bottoms of two milk cartons so that each side is the length of a square. Cover one bottom with the other to make a cube. Cover with two strips of paper the width of the cube. Write words or pictures to be practiced on each side. Example: to practice pronouns *he/she*, write *he* on three sides of the cube, and *she* on the other three sides. Students throw the cube and make sentences or questions according to what is on the cube, e.g., *Who is (he)?* Cubes can be used with picture cards, e.g., *He is my (brother).* Other cube games can be played with *this/these*, etc.

Pick Up

Use multiple sets of student cards and place them facedown on the floor or on a table. Students get into pairs and do **Rock, Paper, Scissors** (see page 26). The winner picks up a Student Card and asks his or her partner a question. The partner answers, and then the pair begins again with **Rock, Paper, Scissors**. The goal is for pairs to accumulate as many Student Cards as possible, continuing until all the cards have been picked up.

Guessing Game

Divide the class into two teams. Put small classroom objects (pencil, eraser, pen, ruler, small book) in a bag or under a cloth. Have one student from Team A reach in the bag or under the cloth, choose an object, and ask, *Is this an (eraser)?* A student from Team B must feel the object (without looking) and respond either *Yes, it is* or *No, it isn't. It's a (pen).* Each team scores one point for a correct question or answer. Continue until all students have had a chance to participate.

Relay Race

There are many variations to this game. In each variation the class is divided into teams, with each team sitting in a row. Assign a word, phrase, or sentence to the first student in each row (S1), who then repeats the word to the next student in the row (S2). The students continue in this manner until the information reaches the last student in the row. At this point, the last student either stands and says the information aloud, or races to the board to write it. The first team to finish is the winner.

Team Games

Vocabulary identification and question-and-answer practice can be done in teams. Many students enjoy the excitement of team competition, and the possibilities for activities are endless. For example: Divide the class into two or more teams. Have one student from each team come up to the front of the room. Ask a question; the first student to respond correctly wins a point for his or her team. Alternately, two students face each other. One student asks a question from the lesson and the other student answers. If the students do this correctly, both teams earn a point.

Tic-Tac-Toe

This activity uses the competition of a Tic-Tac-Toe game to encourage student participation. Divide the class into teams. Draw a nine-square grid on the board. Each square should be numbered. Ask a student from Team A a question. If the student answers correctly, the team can place an "X" or an "O" on the grid in the location of their choice, which they can indicate by stating the number. Alternate asking questions to both teams. The first team to earn three "X"s or "O"s in a row on the grid wins.

Walk and Talk

Place Student or Teacher Cards in pairs around the room (non-matching cards). Have students walk around in pairs. At the signal *Stop!*, each pair must stop at a pair of cards and exchange questions and answers, using the cards as cues.

> S1: (points to the first card) *What's this?*
>
> S2: *It's a (pencil).*
>
> Students then switch roles.
>
> S2: (points to the other card) *What's this?*
>
> S1: *It's a (pen).*

Step Away Lines may also be used for drilling structures. See description below.

Games for Drilling Conversations

Conversation Lines

Have the students stand in parallel lines facing each other so that each student has a partner in the opposite line. Partners practice the question-and-answer pattern.

> S1: *What's your name?*
>
> S2: *My name is (Kate). What's your name?*
>
> S1: *My name is (John).*

Then have the two lines move one space (left or right) in opposite directions. Have the student with no partner at the end of the line come to the front of the line so that every student has a new partner. Repeat the dialogue. Listen to the pairs at the front of the lines and help them as necessary.

Dialogue Musical Chairs

Place chairs back-to-back in two rows or at random around the room. Have one chair less than the number of students in the class. Play the recording of a song or instrumental music. As the music plays, students move around the room to greet each other and practice dialogue. When the music stops, the students sit down. The student without a chair to sit on is out of the game. Continue the game until there is one student left. For variety, remove two chairs at a time instead of one. The two students who remain standing must say a dialogue together or ask each other questions.

Step Away Lines

This activity encourages children to speak loudly. Have students stand in two rows facing each other so that each student has a partner in the opposite line. Have each pair say a dialogue. Each time a pair completes the dialogue, both partners take a giant step back and repeat the dialogue again. Every time they do so, they will naturally need to speak louder in order to hear each other.

Telephone

If possible, use toy telephones or old phones. Pair off students and give each student a phone. Have partners sit back-to-back and pretend they are talking on the phone. When facing away from each other, and since the rest of the class will be speaking, students must speak very clearly and concentrate on what their partners are saying. Have partners practice their dialogue twice so that each student can practice both parts. Circulate and help as necessary.

Games for Drilling Commands

Command Chain

Have students form circles of 8–10 each. Give and perform a command to begin the chain. T: *Touch the ruler.* One student in each circle repeats the command, does the action, and adds another command. S1: *Touch the ruler. Point to the chair.* Continue, with each student adding a new command after repeating and doing the previous commands.

Do As I Say

Give commands while modeling the actions. Try to trick the students by occasionally modeling actions that do not match the commands. Use different voices and volumes as you say the commands in order to encourage attentive listening.

Please

This is the same game as **Do As I Say,** except that it adds the word *Please.* Give the students commands at random. If you say *Please* before the command, the students should act out the command. If you do not say *Please*, students should remain still. This game becomes a stronger listening exercise if you perform the action at the same time you are giving the command. The students will tend to follow your action rather than listening for the word *Please.* Only the attentive listeners will remain standing at the end.

Rock, Paper, Scissors

This is a short, fun activity that students can do if there is no space to move around or if time is limited. In pairs, students say, *Rock, Paper, Scissors!* And show one of three gestures.

- a fist to represent a stone (stronger than scissors, but weaker than paper because paper can cover a stone)
- an outspread hand (stronger than stone, but weaker than scissors because scissors can cut paper)
- a hand with the index and third finger out like a pair of scissors (stronger than paper, but weaker than stone because a stone can break scissors)

For additional language practice, have students change the chant to practice the language from the lesson, for example, *Let's, Let's, 1, 2, 3.* The winner says a command (e.g., *Let's go fishing*) and both students do the action.

Let's Go 2 Syllabus

Unit 1   At School

Let's Start	Let's Learn	Let's Learn More	Let's Build
Hi, Scott. How are you? I'm OK, thanks. How about you? Pretty good! Good-bye, Scott. See you later! *Saying hello and good-bye* I erase the board at school. *Describing school activities*	This is a pencil sharpener. That's a clock. What's this/that? It's a workbook. Is this/that a calendar? Yes, it is./No, it isn't. *Identifying and asking about near and far school objects (singular)*	These/Those are pencil sharpeners. What are these/those? They're clocks. Are these/those doors? Yes, they are./No, they aren't. *Identifying and asking about near and far school objects (plural)*	This/that door is little/big. These/those clocks are new. Is that window small? Yes, it is./No, it isn't. Are those clocks square? Yes, they are. No, they aren't. *Identifying near and far objects with adjectives*

Unit 2   My Things

Let's Start	Let's Learn	Let's Learn More	Let's Build
Whose bag is that? I don't know. Is it Scott's bag? No, it isn't his bag. Is it Jenny's bag? Yes, it's her bag! *Talking about possessions* She can run. *Describing ability*	I have a key. *Expressing possession* What do you have? I have a coin. Do you have a tissue? Yes, I do./No, I don't. *Asking about possessions*	She has a camera. What does he have? He has a calculator. Does she have a key? Yes, she does. No, she doesn't. *Identifying the possessions of others*	He has a video game in his bag. What does she have in her hand? She has a yo-yo in her hand. Does she have a candy bar in her bag/hand? Yes, she does./No, she doesn't. Do you have a _ in your bag? *Asking about possessions and expressing their locations*

Units 1–2 Listen and Review   Let's Learn About Numbers 20–100
Counting

Unit 3   My House

Let's Start	Let's Learn	Let's Learn More	Let's Build
Where do you live, Jenny? I live in Hillsdale. What's your address? It's 16 North Street. What's your cell phone number? It's (798) 555-2043. *Asking for and giving personal information* What can he do? He can play baseball. *Asking about ability*	There's a bed in the bedroom. Where's the sofa? It's in the living room. Is there a stove in the bedroom? Yes, there is./No, there isn't. *Clarifying locations of furniture (singular)*	There's a lamp next to the sofa. There are lamps behind the sofa. Is there a stove next to the sink? Yes, there is./No, there isn't. Are there lamps behind the bed? Yes, there are./No, there aren't. *Clarifying locations of furniture (singular and plural)*	Where are the books? They're under the bed. There's a table in front of the sofa. There's a sofa behind the table. Where's the telephone? It's on the table next to the sofa. Is there a book next to the door?/Are there books on the floor? *Asking and answering singular and plural questions about the locations of objects*

Unit 4   Things to Eat

Let's Start	Let's Learn	Let's Learn More	Let's Build
What's for lunch, Mom? Spaghetti. Mmm. That's good. I like spaghetti. I do, too. Do you want spaghetti? Yes, please. No, thank you! *Asking about and expressing wants and likes* Can he/she type? Yes, he/she can. No, he/she can't. *Asking about ability*	He wants an omelet/yogurt. What does he want? He wants a peach/yogurt. Does she want cereal? Yes, she does./No, she doesn't. *Asking about the wants of others (singular)*	He likes grapes. What does she like? She likes hamburgers. Does he like stew? Yes, he does. No, he doesn't. *Asking about the likes of others (singular)*	He likes/wants hamburgers. He doesn't want a dog. He wants a cat. *Expressing likes and wants* Does she want a pear or an orange? She wants an orange. How many peaches does he want? He wants two peaches. *Asking about preferences and quantity*

Units 3–4 Listen and Review   Let's Learn About the Months
What month is it?/It's January.

Unit 5   Occupations

Let's Start	Let's Learn	Let's Learn More	Let's Build
What's the matter, Scott? I'm sick. That's too bad. Maybe Mrs. Green can help you. Who's she? She's the new nurse. Thanks for your help. You're welcome. Get better soon! *Asking about someone's health* I wake up every morning. *Describing daily activities*	She's a shopkeeper. Who's he? He's a taxi driver. Is she a farmer? Yes, she is./No, she isn't. *Making statements and asking about occupations (singular)*	They're dentists. Who are they? They're Mr. Jones and Mr. Lee. They're pilots. Are they teachers? Yes, they are. No, they aren't. *Making statements and asking about people and occupations (plural)*	I'm a nurse. Who is Mr. Jones? He's a train conductor. Is Ms. Lee a teacher or a student? She's a teacher. *Identifying self and people by occupation* Can Mrs. Hill play baseball? Yes, she can. No, she can't. *Asking about ability*

Unit 6   Locations

Let's Start	Let's Learn	Let's Learn More	Let's Build
Hi, Kate. This is Jenny. Where are you? I'm at home. Where are you? I'm at the park. Can you come to the park? Sure! *Determining location and making an invitation* What do you do every afternoon? I study English. *Describing daily activities*	She's at school. Where is she? She's at the park. Is he at home? Yes, he is. No, he isn't. He at school. *Expressing and asking about locations of people (singular)*	They're at the movies. Where are they? They're in the taxi. Are they at the park? Yes, they are. No, they aren't. *Expressing and asking about locations of people (plural)*	The shopkeeper is at the store. The students are at school. Where's the taxi driver? She's in the taxi. Where are the students? They're at the store. Is the teacher at the zoo? Yes, he is./No, he isn't. He's at the store. Are the students on the train? Yes, they are./No, they aren't. They're at the library. *Clarifying occupations and locations of people (singular and plural)*

Units 5–6 Listen and Review

Let's Learn About the Seasons

What can you do in the spring?/I can fly a kite.

Unit 7   Doing Things

Let's Start	Let's Learn	Let's Learn More	Let's Build
Let's play a game! What are you doing? I'm riding a bicycle. What are you doing? We're swimming. *Asking what someone is doing* Do you cook dinner every evening? Yes, I do./No, I don't. *Asking about frequency of daily activities*	She's dancing. What's she doing? She's swimming. Is he running? Yes, he is. / No, he isn't. *Asking about what others are doing (singular)*	They're playing soccer. What are they doing? They're singing a song. Are they doing homework? Yes, they are. No, they aren't. They're watching TV. *Asking about what others are doing (plural)*	She's walking. They're throwing a ball. What are they doing? They're sleeping. Is he doing a cartwheel? Yes, he is./No, he isn't. What is she eating? What are they playing? *Expressing and asking about what people are doing (singular and plural)*

Unit 8   After School

Let's Start	Let's Learn	Let's Learn More	Let's Build
Can you come over on Saturday? Sorry. No, I can't. I'm busy. What about Sunday? Sunday is OK. I'm free. Great! See you on Sunday! OK. See you then! *Making plans and invitations* Do you ever take a walk at night? Yes, I do./No, I don't. *Asking about frequency of daily activities*	I go to art class. What do you do on Mondays? I go to dance class. *Expressing and asking about after-school activities*	He goes to the bookstore after school. What does she do after school? She goes to the bookstore. Does he do homework after school? Yes, he does./No, he doesn't. *Expressing and asking about daily activities*	I go to my English class after school. He goes to his English class after school. What does he do on Tuesdays? He goes to his math class on Tuesdays. *Clarifying after-school activities*

Units 7–8 Listen and Review

Let's Learn About Time

What time is it?/It's 3:00.

Unit 1 At School

Let's Start

Topic: Greetings

Lesson objectives: Students greet each other and ask about each other.

New grammar: *I'm OK. Pretty good. Thanks. How about you? See you later.*

Review grammar: *Hi, (Scott). How are you? Good-bye.*

New language: *erase the board, speak English, write my name, read books, at school*

Materials: Teacher and Student Cards 1–4, CD 1 Tracks 02–07, puppets (optional), contraction card *(I'm)*

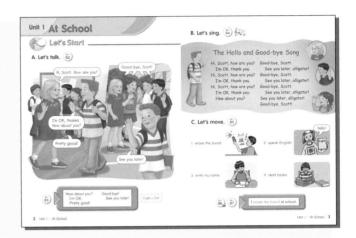

WARM UP

Choose one of the following:

1. Greet the Class practices greetings and asking about each other. As students walk into class, greet them with a cheerful *Hello!* or *Hi!* Sing "The Hello Song" from Level 1 together.

2. Greet Each Other reviews greetings and questions. Have students greet each other and add a question such as *How old are you?* or *Can you...?* Encourage students to move around the class as quickly as possible.

PRESENT THE DIALOGUE

 **BOOKS CLOSED**

Present the dialogue.

1. Introduce the dialogue.

   a. Use puppets or student volunteers to introduce the dialogue.

   Puppet A: *Hi, Scott. How are you?*
   Puppet B: *I'm OK, thanks. How about you?*
   Puppet A: *Pretty good!*
   Puppet A: *Good-bye, Scott.*
   Puppet B: *See you later!*

   b. Have students identify words they already know. Review the question *How are you?* Model the answer *I'm OK, thanks* and have students repeat after you several times.

   c. Model *Good-bye* and *See you later.* Wave and walk away as you say each phrase. Have students say *Good-bye* to you. Respond *See you later* as you wave and walk away. Practice in two groups, then in pairs.

> **Pronunciation Tip:** Make sure students are biting their tongues lightly when they say *thanks.*

> **Tip:** Explain that *How are you?* is used by the first speaker in a greeting and *How about you?* is used by the second speaker.

2. Introduce the dialogue question.

   a. Have students say *How about you?* in a series of three, several times: *How about you? How about you? How about you?* Gradually pick up speed until they are able to say it at natural speed.

   b. Divide the class into two groups. Practice the questions and answers.

   Group A: *How are you?*
   Group B: *I'm OK, thanks. How about you?*
   Group A: *Pretty good!*

   c. Keep the students in two groups. Have them combine the entire dialogue. Reverse roles.

> **Tip:** *Thanks* is a casual way of saying *Thank you.* It is usually used between friends. *Pretty good* is a casual way of saying that you are well. *I'm OK* is another simple expression students can use. Encourage students to use these alternative expressions for *I'm fine. See you later* is often used to say *Good-bye.*

BOOKS OPEN

A. Let's talk.

Students learn how to greet each other and respond to greetings.

1. Listen to the dialogue.

a. Have students look at the scene on page 2 and describe what they see.

b. Play Track 02. Have students listen to the dialogue and point to the speech bubbles. Have them identify words they hear.

 CD 1 Track 02

Kate: *Hi, Scott. How are you?*
Scott: *I'm OK, thanks. How about you?*
Kate: *Pretty good!*
Kids: *Good-bye, Scott!*
Scott: *See you later!*

c. Play the dialogue again and have students repeat each line after the characters.

d. Have students practice the full dialogue in pairs. Be sure to repeat the dialogue at least two times so that students can practice both parts.

e. Use a **Chain Drill** (p. 21) or **Step Away Lines** (p. 26) to practice the dialogue, using students' own names.

2. Practice the dialogue.

a. Present the pattern and contraction on page 2. Write the pattern on the board, or direct students' attention to their books. Play Track 03. Point to the words as students listen to the dialogue. Then have students repeat after the audio.

 CD 1 Track 03

How about you?
I'm OK.
Pretty good!
Good-bye.
See you later!

I am = I'm

b. Write the explanation of the contraction on the board: *I am = I'm*. Follow the procedure on page 196 for how to teach contractions with cards. Have students practice saying both *I am* and *I'm*. Point to the

explanation on the board as they practice.

c. Do **Conversation Lines** (p. 26) to practice the dialogue using students' own names.

B. Let's sing.

"The Hello and Good-bye Song" reinforces the language from the dialogue using rhythm and song.

1. Play and listen.

Play Track 04. Have students listen and identify words they recognize from Let's Talk.

 CD 1 Track 04

The Hello and Good-bye Song

Hi, Scott, how are you?
    I'm OK, thank you.
Hi, Scott, how are you?
    I'm OK, thank you.
Hi, Scott, how are you?
    I'm OK, thank you.
    How about you?

Good-bye, Scott.
    See you later, alligator!
Good-bye, Scott.
    See you later, alligator!
Good-bye, Scott.
    See you later, alligator!
See you later, alligator!
Good-bye, Scott!

2. Practice the rhythm.

a. Introduce the song rhythmically. Have students clap to keep the beat as you model the song line by line. Have students repeat after you.

b. Play the song again. Encourage students to sing along.

3. Do the song activity.

Play the song again, and this time have half of the class sing one part and half sing the second part. Add gestures to go with the song lyrics.

4. Read the lyrics.

Have students look at the song pictures and lyrics. Ask students to point to and read words that they recognize.

5. Work in groups.

Have students work in groups to create an original verse by inserting their names. Then, sing the song again with the new verses.

BOOKS CLOSED

Present the verb phrases

1. Introduce the verb phrases.

a. Say *erase the board* with action, and repeat the action several times. Have students repeat several times with action before going on to the next phrase. Repeat with the other phrases.

b. To check understanding, say the phrases in random order and have students do the appropriate action.

c. Show students Teacher Cards 1–4. Have them both say the phrase and do the action.

d. Divide the class into two groups. Have groups take turns saying the commands and doing the actions. Use Teacher Cards to cue the commands group.

2. Introduce *I (erase the board) at school.*

a. Add *I* and *at school* to each phrase and have students repeat the sentence and do the action.

b. Have pairs take turns saying a verb phrase with *I* and *at school*. Students do the action together as they say the sentence.

BOOKS OPEN

C. Let's move.

Students learn useful classroom language by combining rhythm and actions.

1. Listen and point to the verb phrases.

a. Play Track 05. Have students listen and point to the verb phrases.

Let's Start

 CD 1 Track 05

1. erase the board
2. speak English
3. write my name
4. read books

    b. Play the audio again. Students listen and repeat.

2. Practice the rhythm.

    a. Write the pattern on the board, or direct students' attention to their books. Play Track 06. Point to the words as students listen.

 CD 1 Track 06

I erase the board at school.

I erase the board at school.

    b. Play Track 06 again. Have students clap or tap to keep the rhythm and repeat the sentence with the audio.

    c. Have students tap or clap the rhythm and practice saying the sentence without the audio.

3. Practice the sentences.

    a. Play Track 07. Have students listen to the audio and point to the appropriate pictures.

 CD 1 Track 07

I erase the board at school.
I speak English at school.
I write my name at school.
I read books at school.

GAMES AND ACTIVITIES

1. How Are You? practices greetings. Divide the class into groups of 4–5 students. Have the students write their names on a piece of paper and fold the paper in half. Put the papers in the middle of their group. Play "The Hello and Good-bye Song." When you say *Go!*, one student in the group picks up a name and greets that student.

S1: *Hi, (Scott). How are you?*
S2: *I'm OK, thanks. How about you?*
S1: *Pretty good!*
S1: *Good-bye, (Scott).*
S2: *See you later!*

The student returns the name to the pile and another student chooses a name. Do this activity several times.

2. Rhythm (p. 23) helps develop rhythm and fluency in saying the verb phrases. Review the verb phrases in sentences with *at school*: *I write my name at school,* etc. With the one-two rhythm, slap the thighs twice, clap twice (saying *I write my name*), and snap with the right hand *(saying at)*, then the left hand (saying *school*). The student on the left continues and says another phrase. As students get used to the rhythm, gradually pick up speed. Students can also say verbs they learned in Level 1. (For example, *I eat a sandwich at school,* etc.)

3. Rock, Paper, Scissors (p. 26) practices the verb phrases. Divide the class into pairs. Have them play **Rock, Paper, Scissors**. However, tell them to change the words to *At school, at school, 1, 2, 3!* to give additional practice of the key words. The winner gives a command (*Read books!*) and the loser must say *I read books at school* while doing the action. Have them play several rounds.

EXTRA PRACTICE

WORKBOOK pages 2–3

Assign for homework or do in class. For instructions and Answer Key, see Teacher's Book page 163.

SKILLS BOOK pages 2–3

Assign for homework or do in class. For instructions and Answer Key, see Teacher's Book page 144.

COMPONENTS LINK

LET'S GO TESTS AND QUIZZES

Lesson Quiz: Explain and administer the reproducible Unit 1 Let's Start quiz from *Let's Go Tests and Quizzes,* page 8. Instructions and Answer Key are also in *Let's Go Tests and Quizzes.*

LET'S CHANT LET'S SING 2

Page 1: "The Hi Song"

This song practices greetings from the Let's Talk portion of the lesson.

Page 2: "The Good-bye Song"

This song practices farewells from the Let's Talk portion of the lesson.

Topic: Classroom objects

Lesson objectives: Students identify and ask about things they use in the classroom.

New grammar: *What's that?*

Review grammar: *What's this? It's a clock.*

New language: *a pencil sharpener, a picture, a workbook, a clock, a paper clip, a door, a window, a calendar*

Review language: *erase the board, speak English, write my name, read books, Let's*

Materials: Teacher and Student Cards 5–12, CD 1 Tracks 08–14, puppets (optional), contraction cards (*That's, What's, It's, isn't*)

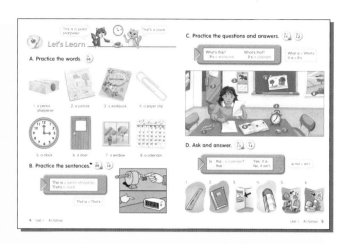

WARM UP AND REVIEW

Choose one of the following:

1. Rock, Paper, Scissors (p. 26) reviews greetings. Divide the class into two teams. The first two students from each team greet each other.

> S1: *Hello, (John). How are you?*
> S2: *I'm OK. How about you?*
> S1: *Pretty good.*

Have students play **Rock, Paper, Scissors**. However, tell them to change the words to *Hello, Goodbye, 1, 2, 3.* They exchange farewells.

> S1: *Good-bye, (John).*
> S2: *See you later.*

The loser goes back to her team and the winner plays with another member of the opposite team until she loses. Then the next person plays.

2. At School practices verb phrases with *at school*. Review the vocabulary from Let's Start, using Teacher Cards 1–4. Say the command and have students say and do the action with *at school* as quickly as possible. T: *Erase the board.* Ss: *I erase the board at school.*

Divide the class into two groups. Show one group the cards to cue the command and have the other group do the action with *Let's.* Reverse roles.

PRESENT THE LANGUAGE

💿 BOOKS CLOSED

Introduce the words.

1. Use Teacher Cards (5–12) to introduce the words. Show one Teacher Card at a time and say the name of the object. Students repeat each word several times.

2. Conduct a quick drill of the words. Do not speak as you show the cards. Have students identify the new object plus all the previously learned objects. Gradually pick up speed as students get used to saying the words.

Introduce the sentence pattern.

1. Use a pencil to introduce the sentence pattern. Hold the pencil in your hand and point to it. Say *This is a pencil. This.* Put the pencil down and move away from it. Point toward it (from a distance) and say *That is a pencil. That.* As students practice the sentence patterns, have them point to their palms for *this* and point toward something at a distance for *that* to reinforce the meaning of the two words.

2. Use Teacher Cards 5–12. Show each card and say the sentence *This is (a pencil sharpener).* Have students repeat the sentence pattern.

3. Have students practice with *This is,* substituting all the vocabulary. Students should say sentences at the same time as the teacher, not repeat after the teacher.

4. Conduct a quick drill of the sentences using Teacher Cards 5–12. Do not speak as you show the cards. Gradually pick up speed as students get used to saying the sentences.

5. Repeat steps 1, 2, and 3 with *That is (a clock).*

📖 BOOKS OPEN

A. Practice the words.

1. Play Track 08. Have students listen and point to the words.

 CD 1 Track 08

> *1. a pencil sharpener*
> *2. a picture*
> *3. a workbook*
> *4. a paper clip*
> *5. a clock*
> *6. a door*
> *7. a window*
> *8. a calendar*

2. Play the audio again and have students repeat the words.

B. Practice the sentence.

1. Listen to the sentence pattern.

a. Write the pattern on the board or direct students' attention to their books. Play Track 09. Point to the words as students listen. Then have students repeat after the audio.

 CD 1 Track 09

This is a pencil sharpener.
That's a clock.
That is = That's

This is a pencil sharpener.
That's a clock.

b. Write the explanation of the contraction on the board: *That is = That's*. See page 196 for how to use contraction cards to teach contractions. Have students practice saying both *That is a clock* and *That's a clock*.

> **Tip:** Point out to students that *This is* is never contracted.

2. Practice the rhythm.

a. Play Track 09 again. This time, have students listen to the rhythm and intonation of the sentences.

b. Play the track again. Have students tap or clap to match the rhythm of the audio. Have students listen to the spoken sentences to hear how the sentences match the rhythm, and then have them repeat the sentences along with the recorded rhythm.

c. Have students tap or clap the rhythm and practice saying the sentences without the audio.

3. Practice the sentences.

a. Play Track 10 and have students point to the vocabulary pictures as they listen.

 CD 1 Track 10

This is a pencil sharpener.
That's a pencil sharpener.
This is a picture.
That's a picture.
This is a workbook.
That's a workbook.
This is a paper clip.
That's a paper clip.
This is a clock.
That's a clock.
This is a door.
That's a door.
This is a window.
That's a window.
This is a calendar.
That's a calendar.

b. Play Track 10 again and have students repeat the sentences.

c. Divide the class into pairs and have students practice the sentences with their books open to page 4. S1 touches a picture and says *This is (a pencil sharpener)*. S2 points to a different picture and says *That's (a window)*.

BOOKS CLOSED

Introduce the question forms.

1. Introduce the *Wh-* question-and-answer pattern.

a. Use puppets or student volunteers to present the *Wh-* questions and answers.

Puppet A: *What's this?*
Puppet B: *It's a pencil sharpener.*
Puppet A: *What's that?*
Puppet B: *It's a calendar.*

b. Show Teacher Cards 5–12 and ask *What's this?* before you show each card. Have students answer *It's (a workbook)*.

c. Have students practice the question *What's this?* several times, pointing to their palms as if holding something.

> **Tip:** You can make it a game by having students stand up and sit down after saying the question three times.

d. Attach Teacher Cards (5–12) to the board and stand a short distance away. Point to the first picture and ask *What's that?* Have students answer *It's (a workbook)*. Repeat for each card.

e. Have students practice the question *What's that?* several times, pointing toward something at a distance.

f. Conduct a quick drill to make sure students understand the difference between *this* and *that*. Have students point to show they understand the importance of distance for each word. Put a classroom object or a Teacher Card in front of the class. Stand next to it and ask *What's this?* Have students answer. Next, stand a short distance away from it and ask *What's that?* and have students answer. Move the object next to a student and prompt the student to ask *What's this?* Have the rest of the class answer. Move the same object a short distance from the same student and prompt *What's that?* Continue with a few other students.

g. Divide the class into two groups. Use Teacher Cards to cue the students. Place some cards close to students to practice *this* and some cards far away from all students to practice *that*. Having the students use the proper gestures as they ask will signal to the teacher that they know how to use the words correctly. Groups take turns asking and answering both questions.

h. Repeat the question-and-answer practice in pairs.

> **Tip:** Be careful NOT to have students repeat both the question and answer at the same time as this could lead to repeating the question instead of answering it. Always have two groups or pairs do the question-and-answer sequence.

Pronunciation Tip 1: Be sure students pronounce *what's* correctly with the [ts] sound at the end.

Pronunciation Tip 2: When asking questions starting with *What*, the intonation comes down at the end of the sentence.

What's that?

2. Introduce the *Yes/No* question-and-answer pattern.

a. Show Teacher Card 12 and ask *Is this a calendar?* Encourage students to answer *Yes, it is.* Then put another card on the board and point to it saying *Is that a calendar?* Encourage students to answer *No, it isn't.*

b. Divide the class into two groups. Have one group ask and the other group answer the questions. Cue *this* and *that* by holding the cards for *Is this (a clock)?* and pointing to the cards on the board for *Is that (a calendar)?* Answer *Yes, it is* first, then turn the cards upside down to cue *No, it isn't.*

c. Divide the class into pairs and have students practice.

Pronunciation Tip: When asking *Yes/No* questions the intonation goes up at the end of the sentence.

Is that a clock?

📖 BOOKS OPEN

C. Practice the question and answer.

1. Listen to the *Wh-* question-and-answer pattern.

a. Present the pattern by writing it on the board or direct students' attention to the pattern in the book.

b. Play Track 11. Point to the words as students listen. Have students repeat after the audio.

 CD 1 Track 11

What's this?
  It's a workbook.
What's that?
  It's a calendar.
What is = What's
It is = It's

What's this?
  It's a workbook.
What's that?
  It's a calendar.

c. Write the explanation of the contractions on the board: *What is = What's* and *It is = It's.* See page 196 for how to use contraction cards to teach contractions. Have students practice saying both *What's this? It's a pencil* and *What is this? It is a pencil.* Point to the explanation on the board as they practice.

2. Practice the rhythm.

a. Play Track 11 again. This time, have students listen to the rhythm and intonation of the questions and answers.

b. Play the track again. Have students tap or clap to match the rhythm of the audio. Have students listen to the spoken questions and answers to hear how they match the rhythm, and then have them repeat the patterns along with the recorded rhythm.

c. Have students tap or clap the rhythm and practice saying the questions and answers without the audio.

3. Practice the *Wh-* questions and answers.

a. Have students look at page 5 and describe things they see.

b. Play Track 12. Have students listen and point to the appropriate pictures.

 **CD 1 Track 12**

1. *What's this? It's a paper clip.*
2. *What's that? It's a door.*
3. *What's that? It's a calendar.*
4. *What's this? It's a workbook.*
5. *What's that? It's a picture.*
6. *What's this? It's a clock.*
7. *What's this? It's a pencil sharpener.*
8. *What's that? It's a window.*

c. Play the audio again and have students repeat the questions and the answers.

d. Divide the class into question and answer groups and play the audio again. Each group repeats either the question or the answer. Repeat, with groups switching roles.

e. Have students work in pairs and take turns asking and answering questions about the pictures.

D. Ask and answer.

1. Listen to the *Yes/No* question-and-answer pattern.

a. Present the pattern by writing it on the board or direct students' attention to the pattern in the book.

b. Play Track 13. Point to the words as students listen. Have students repeat after the audio.

 CD 1 Track 13

Is this a calendar?
  Yes, it is.
Is that a calendar?
  No, it isn't.
is not = isn't

Is this a calendar?
  Yes, it is.
Is that a calendar?
  No, it isn't.

c. Write the explanation of the contraction on the board: *is not = isn't.* Follow the procedure on page 196 for how to teach contractions with cards. Have students practice saying both *is not* and *isn't.* Point to the explanation on the board as they practice.

2. Practice the rhythm.

a. Play Track 13 again and have students listen to the rhythm and intonation of the questions and answers.

b. Play the track again. Have students tap or clap to match the rhythm of the audio. Have students listen to the spoken questions and answers to hear how they match the rhythm, and then have them repeat the patterns along with the recorded rhythm.

c. Have the students tap or clap the rhythm and practice saying the questions and answers without the audio.

3. Practice the *Yes/No* questions and answers.

a. Play Track 14. Have students listen and point to the appropriate pictures.

 CD 1 Track 14

1. *Is this a ruler? Yes, it is.*
2. *Is that a poster? No, it isn't.*
3. *Is that a poster? Yes, it is.*
4. *Is this an eraser? Yes, it is.*
5. *Is that a book? No, it isn't.*
6. *Is that a picture? Yes, it is.*

b. Have students work in pairs and take turns asking and answering questions about the pictures.

GAMES AND ACTIVITIES

1. This/That challenges students to use *this* and *that* correctly. Use several sets of Student Cards 5–12. Divide the class into two teams. Have teams face each other. Divide the cards in half and display one half in front of each team. The first two students on each team play first. If you say *this*, they must make a sentence using one of their team's cards (*This is a picture*). If you say *that,* they must make a sentence using one of the other team's cards (*That's a clock*). The student who says a correct sentence first gets a point. Continue with the next two students.

2. This/That Cube Game gives students practice in asking questions with *this* and *that*. Use teacher-made cubes (see page 00) and write *this* on three sides and *that* on the remaining sides. Use several sets of Student Cards 5–12. Divide the class into two teams. The first two students from each team play **Rock, Paper, Scissors,** saying *This, That, 1, 2, 3!* The winner (S1) throws the cube and picks up a card. The loser (S2) asks *What's (this/that)?* according to what is shown on the cube and touches (*this*) or points to (*that*) S2's card. S1 answers. Different pairs continue until all the cards are taken.

3. Yes or No? encourages students to use *this/that* questions in a real situation. Divide the class into pairs and give each pair a set of Student Cards 5–12. Spread the cards on the table. Students take turns asking about the cards around them. For cards near S1, S1 points to the card and asks *Is this (a window)?* If the card is at a distance, S1 asks *Is that (a window)?* S2 picks it up and answers either *Yes, it is* or *No, it isn't.*

EXTRA PRACTICE

WORKBOOK **pages 4–5**

Assign for homework or do in class. For instructions and Answer Key, see Teacher's Book page 163.

SKILLS BOOK **pages 4–5**

Assign for homework or do in class. For instructions and Answer Key, see Teacher's Book page 144.

REPRODUCIBLE WORKSHEET, **Teacher's Book page 174**

Classroom Objects provides further fun and practice with the vocabulary of the lesson. For instructions, see page 190.

COMPONENTS LINK

CD-ROM 2

For extra fun, students can play Unit 1, Game 1 on a computer at school or at home. In this **Concentration** game, students try to find picture-word pairs. This activity reinforces reading, listening, and the Let's Learn vocabulary.

For extra fun, students can play Unit 1, Game 3 on a computer at school or at home. Students follow the prompts to sort the items into the correct categories. This activity reinforces listening and the Let's Learn vocabulary grammar structures *This is a.../ That's a....*

LET'S GO TESTS AND QUIZZES

Lesson Quiz: Explain and administer the reproducible Unit 1 Let's Learn quiz from *Let's Go Tests and Quizzes*, page 9. Instructions and Answer Key are also in *Let's Go Tests and Quizzes.*

LET'S CHANT LET'S SING 2

Page 3: "What's This? What's That?"

This chant practices the question-and-answer pattern *What's this? This is a spider. What's that? That's a cat.*

Page 4: "Look at That! What's That?"

This chant practices the question-and-answer pattern *What's that? It's a cat.* Students also practice location phrases *on your hat, on your desk,* and *in your bag.*

LET'S GO PICTURE DICTIONARY

Use pages 50–51, School Supplies, to supplement the Let's Learn portion of the lesson and increase challenge.

1. Review familiar words on page 50–51, and point out new words you wish to teach.

2. Practice the words with the question-and-answer pattern *What's this/that? It's a pencil sharpener.*

Let's Learn More

Topic: Classroom objects

Lesson objectives: Students identify and ask about classroom objects with *these* and *those*.

New grammar: *Those are (paper clips). What are those? They're (clocks).*

Review grammar: *These are (clocks). What are these?*

New language: *pencil sharpeners, clocks, paper clips, workbooks, pictures, calendars, windows, doors*

Materials: Teacher and Student Cards 5–20, CD 1 Tracks 15–21, contraction cards *(aren't, They're)*

WARM UP AND REVIEW

Choose one of the following:

1. Using verb phrases from Unit 1 and from Level 1, have students try to make as many sentences with *at school* as possible. Tell students that some phrases may not make sense, for example, *I take a bath at school.*

2. What's This/That? reviews classroom objects and how to ask *What's this?* and *What's that?* Have students get into pairs and take out classroom objects they may have (pen, pencil sharpener, book, eraser, ruler, etc.) and put them on the table. Cover them with a handkerchief or paper. Have pairs ask each other *What's this?* for their own things, and *What's that?* for their partner's things, pointing from the appropriate distance. For a variation, practice with *Yes/No* questions: *Is this/that (a pencil sharpener)?*

PRESENT THE LANGUAGE

📖 BOOKS CLOSED

Introduce the words.

1. Use Teacher Cards 13–20 or actual items. Say the word (*pencil sharpeners*) and emphasize the final /s/ sound. Have the students repeat each word three times before going on to the next word. Repeat with the rest of the words.

2. Conduct a quick drill of the objects after you introduce each object. Use Teacher Cards 13–20. Don't speak as you show the cards. Have students identify the new objects plus all the previously learned objects.

3. Show the cards again and have students say the singular form and then the plural form of each object.

Introduce the sentence patterns.

1. Show Teacher Card 5 (*pencil sharpener*) and elicit the sentence *This is a pencil sharpener.* Show Teacher Card 13 (pencil sharpeners) and say *These are pencil sharpeners. These.* Place Teacher Card 5 on the board and point to it from a distance. Elicit the sentence *That's a pencil sharpener.* Replace with Teacher Card 13 and say *Those are pencil sharpeners. Those.* Use the same pointing gestures from Let's Learn to reinforce the distance between *these* and *those.*

2. Use Teacher Cards 13–20. Show a card and say the sentence *These are (pencil sharpeners).* Then put the card on the board and point to it saying *Those are (pencil sharpeners).* Have students repeat the sentence patterns several times, using the correct gesture for *these* or *those* before moving on to the next word.

3. Practice the patterns substituting all the words. Students should say

the sentences at the same time as the teacher, not repeat after the teacher.

4. Conduct a quick drill. Show Teacher Cards 13–20 in random order and have students make sentences. Cue *these* and *those* by pointing to your palm for *these* and pointing to something at a distance for *those.* Increase the speed of the drill until students are speaking at natural speed.

📖 BOOKS OPEN

A. Practice the words.

1. Play Track 15. Have students listen and point to the words.

 CD 1 Track 15

1. pencil sharpeners
2. paper clips
3. clocks
4. workbooks
5. calendars
6. pictures
7. windows
8. doors

2. Play the audio again and have students repeat the words.

Let's Learn More

B. Practice the sentences.

1. Listen to the sentence pattern.
Write the patterns on the board or direct students' attention to their books. Play Track 16. Point to the words as students listen to the audio. Then have students repeat.

 CD 1 Track 16

These are pencil sharpeners.
Those are pictures.

These are pencil sharpeners.
Those are pictures.

2. Practice the rhythm.
a. Play Track 16 again. This time, have students listen to the rhythm and intonation of the sentences.

b. Play the track again. Have students tap or clap to match the rhythm of the audio. Have students listen to the spoken sentences to hear how the sentences match the rhythm, and then have them repeat the sentences along with the recorded rhythm.

c. Have students tap or clap the rhythm and practice saying the sentences without the audio.

3. Practice the sentences.
a. Play Track 17 and have students point to the vocabulary pictures as they listen.

 CD 1 Track 17

These are pencil sharpeners.
Those are pencil sharpeners.
These are paper clips.
Those are paper clips.
These are clocks.
Those are clocks.
These are workbooks.
Those are workbooks.
These are calendars.
Those are calendars.
These are pictures.
Those are pictures.
These are windows.
Those are windows.
These are doors.
Those are doors.

b. Play Track 17 again and have students repeat the sentences.

c. Divide the class into pairs and have students practice the sentences with their books open to page 6. S1 touches a picture and says *These are (pictures).* S2 points to a different picture and says *Those are (doors).*

📖 BOOKS CLOSED

Introduce the question forms.

1. Introduce the *Wh-* question-and-answer pattern.
a. Hold up Teacher Cards 13–20 and ask *What are these?* Model the answer for students to repeat *They are (pencil sharpeners).* Then have them repeat it in a series of three, several times.

b. Model the question *What are these?* Have students repeat the question several times, pointing to their palms to reinforce the meaning of *these* (nearness to speaker).

c. Divide the class into two groups. Use Teacher Cards to cue the asking group. Groups take turns asking *What are these?* and answering.

d. Display the Teacher Cards on the board and step away. Point at a card and ask *What are those?* Prompt students to answer *They're (pictures).* Have them repeat it in a series of three, several times.

e. Model the question *What are those?* Have students repeat the question several times. Have students point to something at a distance to reinforce the meaning of *those* (distance from speaker).

f. Divide the class into two groups. Use Teacher Cards to cue the asking group. Place some cards close to students to practice *these* and some cards far away from all students to practice *those.* Having the students use the proper gestures as they ask will signal to the teacher that they know how to use the words correctly. Groups take turns asking and answering questions.

2. Introduce the *Yes/No* question-and-answer pattern.
a. Hold up Teacher Card 20 and ask *Are these doors?* Students answer *Yes, they are.* Then put the card on the board and point to it asking *Are those doors?* Students answer. Point to the same card and ask *Are those windows?* Encourage students to answer *No, they aren't.*

b. Practice asking questions with *these* and *those* by placing Teacher Cards 13–20 around the classroom (some near and some far from students). Point to each card and ask the appropriate question. Students answer.

c. Practice the questions. Have students repeat both questions several times. Then, point to the cards again and have students ask the questions. The teacher answers.

d. Divide the students into two groups with one group asking and the other answering the questions. Point to Teacher Cards to cue students.

📖 BOOKS OPEN

C. Practice the questions and answers.

1. Listen to the *Wh-* question-and-answer pattern.
a. Present the pattern by writing it on the board or direct students' attention to the pattern in the book.

b. Play Track 18. Point to the words as students listen. Have students repeat after the audio.

CD 1 Track 18

What are these?
    They're clocks.
What are those?
    They're pictures.

What are these?
    They're clocks.
What are those?
    They're pictures.

2. Practice the rhythm.

a. Play Track 18 again. This time, have students listen to the rhythm and intonation of the questions and answers.

b. Have students tap or clap to match the rhythm of the audio. Play the track again. Have students listen to the spoken questions and answers to hear how they match the rhythm, and then have them repeat the patterns along with the recorded rhythm.

c. Have students tap or clap the rhythm and practice saying the questions and answers without the audio.

3. Practice the *Wh-* questions and answers.

a. Have students look at page 7 and describe things they see.

b. Play Track 19. Have students listen to the questions and answers and point to the appropriate pictures.

 CD 1 Track 19

1. *What are these? They're crayons.*
2. *What are these? They're pencils.*
3. *What are these? They're pencil sharpeners.*
4. *What are these? They're erasers.*
5. *What are those? They're pictures.*
6. *What are those? They're kites.*
7. *What are those? They're bicycles.*
8. *What are those? They're balls.*

c. Play the audio again and have students repeat the questions and answers.

d. Divide into question and answer groups and play the audio again. Each group repeats either the question or answer. Repeat, with groups switching roles.

e. Have students work in pairs and take turns asking and answering questions about the pictures.

D. Ask and answer.

1. Listen to the *Yes/No* question-and-answer pattern.

a. Present the *Yes/No* question-and-answer pattern by writing it on the board or direct students' attention to the pattern in the book.

b. Play Track 20. Point to the words as students listen. Have students repeat after the audio.

 CD 1 Track 20

Are these doors?
    Yes, they are.
Are those doors?
    No, they aren't.
are not = aren't

Are these doors?
    Yes, they are.
Are those doors?
    No, they aren't.

c. Write the explanation of the contraction on the board: *are not = aren't.* See page 196 for how to use contraction cards to teach contractions. Have students practice saying both *aren't* and *are not.*

2. Practice the rhythm.

a. Play Track 20 again. This time, have students listen to the rhythm and intonation of the questions and answers.

b. Have students tap or clap to match the rhythm of the audio. Play the track again. Have students listen to the spoken questions and answers to hear how they match the rhythm, and then have them repeat the patterns along with the recorded rhythm.

c. Have students tap or clap the rhythm and practice saying the questions and answers without the audio.

3. Practice the *Yes/No* questions and answers.

a. Play Track 21. Have students listen and point to the appropriate pictures.

 CD 1 Track 21

1. *Are those doors? Yes, they are.*
2. *Are these clocks? No, they aren't.*
3. *Are those tables? Yes, they are.*
4. *Are these pictures? No, they aren't.*

b. Have students work in pairs and take turns asking and answering questions about the pictures.

GAMES AND ACTIVITIES

1. These/Those Cubes gives students practice in using *these* and *those* spontaneously. Use teacher-made cubes (see page 25) and write *these* on three sides and *those* on the remaining sides. Use several sets of Student Cards 13–20. Divide the class into two teams. The first two students from each team play **Rock, Paper, Scissors** saying *These, Those, 1, 2, 3!* The winner (S1) throws the cube and picks up a card. The loser (S2) asks *What are (these/those)?* according to what is shown on the cube and touches (*these*) or points to (*those*) S1's card. S1 answers. Different pairs continue until all the cards are taken.

2. What Are These/Those? gives students practice in asking these questions fluently. Divide the class into several groups. Give each group Student Cards 13–20 or review plural cards. Spread them on a desk with half of the cards facing up, and the other half facing down. In pairs, students ask each other *What are these?* for cards facing up, and *What are those?* for cards facing down.

When all the cards have been used, reverse the position of the cards and play again.

3. Are These, Those...? uses the pictures in the book to practice *Yes/No* questions. Use page 6 of the Student Book. Have students get into pairs and work with one book. They play **Rock, Paper, Scissors** with *Are these, are those, 1, 2, 3!* The winner asks a *Yes/No* question and the loser has to answer it correctly. Make sure students sometimes ask questions that will elicit a *no* response.

EXTRA PRACTICE

WORKBOOK **pages 6–7**

Assign for homework or do in class. For instructions and Answer Key, see Teacher's Book page 163.

SKILLS BOOK **pages 6–7**

Assign for homework or do in class. For instructions and Answer Key, see Teacher's Book page 144.

REPRODUCIBLE WORKSHEET, **Teacher's Book page 175**

Singular/Plural Game provides further fun and practice with the vocabulary of the lesson. For instructions, see page 190.

COMPONENTS LINK

CD-ROM 2

For extra fun, students can play Unit 1, Game 2 on a computer at school or at home. Students spell the words to match the pictures. This activity reinforces listening, spelling, and the Let's Learn and Let's Learn More vocabulary.

For extra fun, students can play Unit 1, Game 4 on a computer at school or at home. Students put the words in order to build a sentence and beat the clock. This activity reinforces reading and the Let's Learn More vocabulary and grammar patterns.

LET'S GO TESTS AND QUIZZES

Lesson Quiz: Explain and administer the reproducible Unit 1 Let's Learn More quiz from *Let's Go Tests and Quizzes*, page 10. Instructions and Answer Key are also in *Let's Go Tests and Quizzes*.

LET'S CHANT LET'S SING 2

Page 5: "This, That, These, Those"

This chant practices the question-and-answer pattern *What are these? What are those? These are frogs. Those are dogs.* It also practices *this, that, these,* and *those.*

Page 6: "Yes, It Is. / No, It Isn't."

This chant practices the question-and-answer pattern *Is that a frog? Yes, it is. Is this a pencil case? No, it isn't.* It also practices the question-and-answer pattern *Are these cassettes? Yes, they are. No, they aren't.*

Let's Build

Topic: Using adjectives to describe classroom objects

Lesson objectives: Students describe classroom objects.

Review grammar: *this, that, these, those*

Review language: *round, little, big, new, square, small, long,* classroom objects

Materials: Teacher and Student Cards 5–20, actual items, CD 1 Tracks 22–24, contraction card (*aren't*)

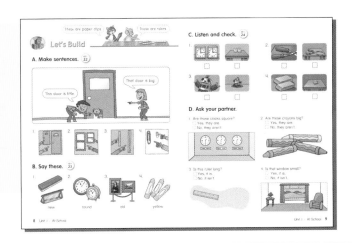

WARM UP AND REVIEW

Choose one of the following:

1. Pick Up (p. 25) reviews verb phrases. Put verb phrase cards 1–4 on the table or floor. Have several sets ready for a more exciting game. Students get into pairs and play **Rock, Paper, Scissors**, saying *At school, at school, 1, 2, 3!* The winner picks up a card and tells his or her partner what gesture to perform (*I erase the board at school*). Have students play several rounds.

2. Make a Long Sentence uses adjectives and colors to make long sentences. Review adjectives and colors from Level 1. Divide the class into teams and use several sets of singular and plural noun student cards. Mix the singular and plural cards and put them facedown in a pile on the table. Students of each team take turns picking up a card. S1 picks up a card and Team B asks *What's that?* or *What are those?* S1 must try to make a long sentence (*They are big, long, green and yellow pencils*). Team A gets one point for each adjective S1 uses (up to 4). Teams count the total number of adjectives at the end of the game.

PRESENT THE LANGUAGE

BOOKS CLOSED

Introduce the sentence pattern.

1. Review adjectives from Level 1 with Teacher Cards 5–20. Then show the cards, one at a time.

> T: *What's this?*
> Ss: *It's a clock.*
> T: *Is it big?*
> Ss: *No, it isn't. It's little.*
> T: *That's right! This clock is little.*

Have students repeat the last sentence several times. Continue with other words in the same way.

2. Have students practice the pattern *This (clock) is (little)* in pairs.

3. Display the cards on the board and step away. Point at each card and say *That clock is little, That calendar is big, That pencil sharpener is square,* etc.

4. Have students repeat each sentence several times.

5. Have students practice the pattern *That (calendar) is (big)* in pairs.

BOOKS OPEN

A. Make sentences.

1. Have students look at the pictures on page 8 and describe what they see. Encourage them to guess what language they will hear.

2. Play Track 22. Have students listen to the audio and point to the pictures.

CD 1 Track 22

This door is little. That door is big.

1. *This door is little. That door is big.*
2. *That window is big. This window is little.*
3. *This ruler is little. That ruler is big.*
4. *That paper clip is big. This paper clip is little.*

3. Play the audio again. Students listen and repeat.

4. Divide the class into pairs. Have students describe the pictures to each other, making one long sentence for each picture. Ask several students for their answers.

B. Say these.

1. Have students look at the pictures on page 8 and describe what they see. Encourage them to guess what language they will hear.

2. Play Track 23. Have students point to the pictures as they listen to the audio.

Let's Build

 CD 1 Track 23

These pencil cases are new.
Those clocks are round.
1. These pencil cases are new.
2. Those clocks are round.
3. Those pictures are old.
4. These crayons are yellow.

3. Play the audio again and have students repeat after each sentence.

4. Have students work in pairs and take turns making sentences about the pictures.

C. Listen and check.

1. Have students look at the first picture and describe it. Then play the first question and answer of Track 24.

2. Play the rest of the audio. Play the audio at least twice so that students can check their answers.

 CD 1 Track 24

1. Are these clocks square?
    Yes, they are.
2. Is that jump rope long?
    Yes, it is.
3. Is this robot thin?
    No, it isn't.
4. Are these erasers square?
    No, they aren't.

D. Ask and answer.

1. Hold up Teacher Cards 13–20 or actual items. Ask a student *Are these (pencils) (long)?* If the description is correct, the student should answer *Yes, they are.* If not, he or she should answer *No, they aren't.* With the *no* answer, encourage the student to describe the items correctly.

2. Continue with the entire class, asking about the rest of the items.

3. Divide the class into pairs. Have them ask and answer questions about each of the pictures.

4. Ask several students for the answers.

1. Show and Tell practices language students have learned with actual items. Have students walk around the classroom while you play background music. When the music stops, students pick up an item near them. Have students do a "show and tell" with the items they find, describing them to the class.

2. Pick Up (p. 25) practices *this, that, these,* and *those* with cards. Have ready several sets of singular and plural cards. Spread them facedown on the table. Have student pairs alternate picking up a card and describing it to their partner. If S1 picks up a card, he or she has to describe it with *this* or *these.* S2 has to describe the same card with *that* or *those.* S1: *This apple is red.* S2: *That apple is red.*

EXTRA PRACTICE

WORKBOOK pages 8–9

Assign for homework or do in class. For instructions and Answer Key, see Teacher's Book page 164.

SKILLS BOOK pages 8–9

Assign for homework or do in class. For instructions and Answer Key, see Teacher's Book page 145.

COMPONENTS LINK

LET'S GO TESTS AND QUIZZES

Lesson Quiz: Explain and administer the reproducible Unit 1 Let's Build quiz from *Let's Go Tests and Quizzes,* page 11. Instructions and Answer Key are also in *Let's Go Tests and Quizzes.*

Unit Test: Explain and administer the reproducible Unit 1 Test from *Let's Go Tests and Quizzes,* page 44. Instructions and Answer Key are also in *Let's Go Tests and Quizzes.*

LET'S GO READER

Now that students have completed Unit 1, they are ready to read "Let's Go Magic School." See Teacher's Book page 20 for suggestions on how to present *Readers* and incorporate them into your lesson plans.

Unit 2 My Things

Let's Start

Topic: Personal possessions

Lesson objectives: Students talk about personal possessions.

New grammar: *Whose (bag) is that? his, her, (Jenny)'s*

Review grammar: *can*

New language: *run, swim, sing, dance*

Materials: Teacher and Student Cards 21–24 and 5–20 (Level 1), CD 1 Tracks 25–30, puppets (optional), contraction card (*It's*)

WARM UP AND REVIEW

Choose one of the following:

1. This/That Is My Pencil reviews vocabulary from Unit 1 and Level 1. Use Student Cards 5–12 from Unit 1 and Level 1. Divide the class into pairs and distribute a set of cards to each pair. Tell students to divide their cards in half and put one half facedown in front of each student. S1 turns over a card and says a sentence using the object on the card. If the card is close to S1, he/she should say *This is (a pencil case)*. If the card is closer to his or her partner, S1 should say *That is (a pencil case)*. Then S2 takes a turn.

2. Charades (p. 22) reviews verb phrases from Unit 1 and Level 1. Use Teacher Cards. Divide the class into three or four teams. Show one student a card and have him or her perform the action. The team that guesses the verb phrase first wins a point. Play to a time or point limit.

PRESENT THE DIALOGUE

📖 BOOKS CLOSED

Present the dialogue.

1. Introduce the dialogue.

a. Use puppets or student volunteers to introduce the dialogue. Put Teacher Card 7 from Level 1 (*bag*) on the board. Say and act out the beginning of the dialogue by pointing to the card for the question and then shrugging your shoulders for the answer.

> Puppet A: *Whose bag is that?*
> Puppet B: *I don't know.*

b. Divide the class into groups and practice the first part of the dialogue using gestures.

> **Pronunciation Tip:** In questions with *whose*, make sure students put stress on the object they are asking about: *Whose pencil is that?*

c. Introduce the rest of the dialogue with puppets or student volunteers.

> Puppet B: *Is it Scott's bag?*
> Puppet A: *No, it isn't his bag.*
> Puppet B: *Is it Jenny's bag?*
> Puppet A: *Yes, it's her bag!*

d. Do a quick drill with *his* and *her*. Use Teacher Cards 5–20 from Level 1 or actual items. Walk around the class and hold a card over a female student's head. Ask *Whose (bag) is that?* Students answer *It's her (bag).* Hold the card over a male student's head. Ask *Whose (bag) is this?* Students answer *It's his (bag).* Move quickly around the classroom.

e. Divide the class into two groups and combine the entire dialogue. Reverse roles.

📖 BOOKS OPEN

A. Let's talk.

Students learn how to ask about another person's possessions.

1. Listen to the dialogue.

a. Have students look at the scene on page 10 and describe what they see.

b. Play Track 25. Have students listen to the dialogue and point to the speech bubbles. Have students identify words they hear.

> **CD 1 Track 25**
>
> Kate: *Whose bag is that?*
> Andy: *I don't know.*
> Kate: *Is it Scott's bag?*
> Andy: *No, it isn't his bag.*
> Kate: *Is it Jenny's bag?*
> Andy: *Yes, it's her bag!*

c. Play the dialogue again and have students repeat each line after the characters.

2. Practice the pattern.

a. Write the pattern on the board, or direct students' attention to their books. Play Track 26. Point to the words as students listen to the dialogue. Then have students repeat after the audio.

 CD 1 Track 26

Whose bag is that?
It's Jenny's bag. It's her bag.
It's Scott's bag. It's his bag.
It is = It's
Jenny's = her
Scott's = his

b. Write the explanation of the contractions on the board: *It is = It's*. Follow the procedure on page 196 for how to teach contractions with cards. Have the students practice saying both *It is her bag* and *It's her bag*. Point to the explanation on the board as they practice.

3. Practice the dialogue.

a. Ask one of the questions from the dialogue and have a volunteer answer. Repeat for the other question. Then ask the questions out of order and have volunteers answer. To make this more challenging, give one of the answers from the dialogue and have students ask the matching question.

b. Do **Conversation Lines** (p. 26) to practice the dialogue.

c. Have students practice the full dialogue in pairs, using names of other students in the class. Be sure to repeat the dialogue at least twice so that students can practice both parts.

B. Let's sing.

"Whose Bag Is That?" reinforces the language from the dialogue using rhythm and song.

1. Play and listen.

Play Track 27. Have students listen and identify the words they recognize from Let's Talk.

 CD 1 Track 27

Whose Bag Is That?

Whose bag is that?
  I don't know.
Is it Scott's bag?
  No, no, no.
  It isn't his bag.
  No, it isn't.
  No, it's not Scott's bag.
Is it Jenny's bag?
  Yes, it is.
  It's her bag.
  Yes, it is.
  It isn't his bag.
  It's her bag.
  It's not Scott's bag.

2. Practice the rhythm.

a. Introduce the song rhythmically. Have students clap to keep the beat as you model the song line by line. Have students repeat after you.

b. Play the song. Encourage students to sing along.

3. Do the song activity.

Play the song again. This time have half of the class sing one part and half sing the second part. Add gestures to go with the song lyrics.

4. Read the lyrics.

Have students look at the song pictures and lyrics. Ask students to point to and read words that they recognize.

5. Work in groups.

Have students work in groups to create an original verse by inserting each others' names. Then, sing the song again with the new verses.

 BOOKS CLOSED

Present the verbs

1. Introduce the verbs.

a. Say *run* with action, and repeat the action several times. Have students repeat several times with action before going on to the next word. Repeat with the other words.

b. To check understanding, say the words in random order and have students do the appropriate action.

c. Show students Teacher Cards 21–24. Have them both say the word and do the action.

d. Divide the class into two groups. Have the groups take turns saying the commands and doing the actions. Use Teacher Cards to cue the command group.

2. Introduce *He/She can (run)*.

a. Add *he can* or *she can* to each verb and have students repeat the verb and do the action.

b. Have pairs take turns saying a verb with *he can* or *she can* as they point to a male or female student in the class. Have both students point and do the action together when they say the sentence.

 BOOKS OPEN

C. Let's move.

Students learn useful classroom language by combining rhythm and actions.

1. Listen and point to the verbs.

a. Play Track 28. Have students listen and point to the appropriate pictures.

 CD 1 Track 28

1. run
2. swim
3. sing
4. dance

b. Play the audio again. Students listen and repeat.

2. Practice the rhythm.

a. Write the pattern on the board, or direct students' attention to their books. Play Track 29. Point to the words as students listen.

CD 1 Track 29

He can run.
She can run.

He can run.
She can run.

b. Play Track 29 again. Have students clap or tap to keep the rhythm and repeat the sentence after the audio.

3. Practice the sentences.

a. Play Track 30. Have students listen to the audio and point to the appropriate pictures.

 CD 1 Track 30

She can run.
He can swim.
He can sing.
She can dance.

b. Play the audio again and have students repeat the sentences.

c. Have students work in pairs and take turns pointing to the pictures on page 11 and making sentences.

GAMES AND ACTIVITIES

1. Whose Is It? practices questions and answers. Put students into small groups and give each student an object. S1 describes the object *This is my (pencil)*. S1 then puts the object into a bag and passes the bag to the next student. S2 identifies his or her object, puts it into the bag, and passes the bag to S3. Continue until all students in the group have identified their object and put it into the bag. Then S1 pulls out an object and asks *Whose (pencil) is this?* Another student answers *It's (Tina's) (pencil).* Continue until all students in the group have asked a question and all the objects have been identified.

To practice *Whose (pencil) is that?* place objects around the room that belong to students in the class. Have a volunteer point to an object and ask *Whose (pencil) is that?* The class answers.

2. Try To Guess gives students the chance to practice using the dialogue language spontaneously. Put students into pairs or small groups. Have them place their personal items on a desk and practice "guessing" which objects belong to which students. Have the students look at the objects and ask *Is that (Lori's) (eraser)?* Other students answer *Yes, it is. It's (Lori's) (eraser). / I don't know. / No, it isn't.* When all of the objects have been discussed, have the students move to the next desk and repeat the activity.

3. Concentration (p. 22) practices recognizing and using the verbs. Divide the class into groups of three, preferably with a mix of girls and boys. Use a double set of Student Cards 21–24. Have S1 identify the first card and then flip over the second card. S1 identifies that card and if the two cards match, S1 says *He/She can (run)*, performs the action, and keeps the pair of cards. S2 then chooses cards. Continue until all cards are gone.

EXTRA PRACTICE

WORKBOOK pages 10–11

Assign for homework or do in class. For instructions and Answer Key, see Teacher's Book page 164.

SKILLS BOOK pages 10–11

Assign for homework or do in class. For instructions and Answer Key, see Teacher's Book page 145.

COMPONENTS LINK

CD-ROM 2

For extra fun, students can play Unit 2, Game 1 on a computer at school or at home. Students listen and choose the correct pictures in time to beat the clock. This activity reinforces verbs.

LET'S GO TESTS AND QUIZZES

Lesson Quiz: Explain and administer the reproducible Unit 2 Let's Start quiz from *Let's Go Tests and Quizzes*, page 12. Instructions and Answer Key are also in *Let's Go Tests and Quizzes*.

LET'S CHANT LET'S SING 2

Page 27: "Whose Watch Is That?"

This song practices the question-and-answer pattern *Whose watch is that? It's Jenny's watch.* Teach the question-and-answer pattern *Whose books are those? They're Jenny's books.*

Let's Learn

Topic: Personal possessions

Lesson objectives: Students talk about personal possessions.

New grammar: *What do you have? I have (a key).*

Review grammar: *Do you have (a key)? Yes, I do. No, I don't.*

New language: *a key, a candy bar, a comic book, a comb, a coin, a brush, a tissue, a watch*

Review language: classroom objects

Materials: Teacher and Student Cards 25–32, CD 1 Tracks 31–35

WARM UP AND REVIEW

Choose one of the following:

1. Walk and Talk reviews asking about personal possessions. Have students draw one personal item or classroom object on a piece of paper and write their name. Students place the drawings on their desks. In pairs, students walk to other desks and ask each other questions about the drawings. S1: *Whose (watch) is that?* S2: *That's (Christie's) watch.*

2. He/She Can practices verb phrases with *can*. Review the vocabulary from Let's Move, using Teacher Cards 21–24. Say the verb as you point to a student. That student acts out the verb. The rest of the class then says *He/She can (run).*

PRESENT THE LANGUAGE

BOOKS CLOSED

Introduce the words.

1. Use Teacher Cards 25–32 to introduce the words. Show one Teacher Card at a time and say the word. Students repeat each word several times.

2. Practice the words by saying the word and have students suggest gestures for the word. Choose one of their gestures. Say all the words again with gestures and have

students repeat. Next, just do the gesture and have students say the word.

3. Conduct a quick drill of the words. Do not speak as you show the cards. Have students identify the new object plus all the previously learned objects. Gradually pick up speed as students get used to saying the words.

Introduce the sentence pattern.

1. Use a key to introduce *have.* Cup your hands (as if holding something) and hold the key. Say *I have a key. Have.*

2. Use Teacher Cards 25–32. Show each card and say *I have (a key).* Have students repeat the sentence and perform the gesture. Repeat with all the vocabulary. Students should say sentences at the same time as the teacher, not repeat after the teacher.

BOOKS OPEN

A. Practice the words.

1. Play Track 31. Have students listen and point to the words.

 CD 1 Track 31

1. *a key*
2. *a candy bar*
3. *a comic book*
4. *a comb*
5. *a coin*
6. *a brush*
7. *a tissue*
8. *a watch*

2. Play the audio again and have students repeat the words.

B. Practice the sentence.

1. Listen to the sentence pattern. Write the pattern on the board or direct students' attention to their books. Play Track 32. Point to the words as students listen to the audio. Then have students repeat after the audio.

 CD 1 Track 32

I have a key.

I have a key.

2. Practice the rhythm.

a. Play Track 32 again. This time, have students listen to the rhythm and intonation of the sentences.

b. Play the track again. Have students tap or clap to match the rhythm of the audio. Have students listen to the spoken sentence to hear how it matches the rhythm, and then have them repeat the sentence along with the recorded rhythm.

c. Have students tap or clap the rhythm and practice saying the sentence without the audio.

3. Practice the sentences.

a. Play Track 33 and have students point to the vocabulary pictures as they listen.

 CD 1 Track 33

I have a key.
I have a candy bar.
I have a comic book.
I have a comb.
I have a coin.
I have a brush.
I have a tissue.
I have a watch.

b. Play Track 33 again and have students repeat the sentences.

c. Have students practice the sentences with a **Pass The Card** activity. Give a stack of Student Cards 25–32 (personal possessions) to S1 in each row. Have the student say *I have (a key)* and then pass the card to S2. S2 says the sentence and passes the card to S3. Each row continues to pass all its cards until every student in the row has practiced the sentence pattern with each card.

📖 BOOKS CLOSED

Introduce the question forms.

1. Introduce the *Wh-* question-and-answer pattern.

a. Use student volunteers to present the question and answer *What do you have? I have a coin.* Give a student Teacher Card 29 (*coin*) and ask *What do you have?*

Model the answer *I have a coin* and have students repeat. Have students use the gesture for *have* (cupping hands) to reinforce the meaning of the verb. Give other Teacher Cards to students and ask the question. Students answer each time.

b. Have students repeat the question. Practice the question several times.

c. Have students practice asking the question. Ss: *What do you have?* Hold up a Teacher Card and answer. T: *I have a coin.* Repeat for the remaining vocabulary.

d. Divide the class into two groups. Use Teacher Cards to cue the students. Groups take turns asking and answering questions.

e. Divide the class into pairs. Have students put several of their own personal items in a bag or in their hands behind them. Pairs ask each other *What do you have?*

2. Introduce the *Yes/No* question-and-answer pattern.

a. Give Teacher Card 25 to a student volunteer and ask *Do you have (a key)?* Encourage students to answer *Yes, I do.* Give Teacher Cards to other students and practice the question and *yes* answer several times. Then, point to the first student volunteer and ask *Do you have (a tissue)?* Encourage students to answer *No, I don't.* Repeat with the remaining Teacher Cards.

b. Divide the class into two groups. Give each group four Teacher Cards to cue questions and answers. Have one group ask and the other group answer the questions. Repeat so that both groups have a chance to ask and answer.

c. Divide the class into pairs. Have students practice with Student Cards or items from their desks or book bags.

📖 BOOKS OPEN

C. Practice the question and answer.

1. Listen to the *Wh-* question-and-answer pattern.

a. Present the pattern by writing it on the board or direct students' attention to the pattern in the book.

b. Play Track 34. Point to the words or speech bubbles as students listen. Have students repeat after the audio.

 CD 1 Track 34

What do you have?
    I have a coin.

What do you have?
    I have a coin.

2. Practice the rhythm.

a. Play Track 34 again. This time, have students listen to the rhythm and the intonation of the question and answer.

b. Play the track again. Have students clap or tap to match the rhythm of the audio. Have students listen to the spoken question and answer to hear how it matches the rhythm, and then have them repeat the pattern along with the recorded rhythm.

c. Have students tap or clap the rhythm and practice saying the question and answer without the audio.

3. Practice the *Wh-* questions and answers.

a. Have students look at page 13 and describe things they see.

b. Play Track 35. Have students listen and point to the appropriate pictures.

Let's Learn _____

CD 1 Track 35

1. *What do you have?*
   I have a comic book.
2. *What do you have?*
   I have a candy bar.
3. *What do you have?*
   I have a coin.
4. *What do you have?*
   I have a tissue.
5. *What do you have?*
   I have a comb.
6. *What do you have?*
   I have a brush.
7. *What do you have?*
   I have a watch.
8. *What do you have?*
   I have a key.

c. Play the audio again. Have students repeat the questions and answers.

d. Divide the class into question and answer groups and play the audio again. Each group repeats either the question or the answer. Repeat, with groups switching roles.

e. Have students work in pairs and take turns asking and answering questions about the pictures.

D. Ask and answer.

1. Practice the *Yes/No* question-and-answer pattern.

a. Have students look at the pictures on page 13 and identify objects they recognize. Review the *Yes/No* question-and-answer pattern by writing it on the board or direct students' attention to the pattern in the book. Practice the question and answer before beginning the activity.

b. Put students in pairs and have them ask and answer questions about the pictures.

GAMES AND ACTIVITIES

1. Guessing Game (p. 25) practices the question-and-answer pattern. Use Teacher Cards of personal possessions and classroom objects. Have each student hide one in his or her desk. Divide the class into

groups and have students in each group try to guess what each person has hidden in his or her desk. Ss: *Do you have (a watch)?* S1: *Yes, I do. / No, I don't.*

2. Say It! (p. 24) practices saying vocabulary at random and spontaneously. Have several sets of Student Cards 25–32. Put the cards in a line on the table. Say *Go!* One student starts at one end of the cards and says them in order: *I have a key, I have a candy bar, I have...* S2 starts immediately after S1 and S3 starts immediately after S2 so that everyone is moving along the cards at the same time. When all the students have finished, rearrange the cards and start again. To make this more challenging, add Student Cards from Level 1 and Unit 1.

3. Relay Race (p. 25) practices fluency. Divide the class into teams. Give the first player of each team a personal possession card. When you say *Go!* each player asks *What do you have?* to the next player who answers the question. Then that player takes the card and asks the next student. The last student must run to the first student and ask the question. When the first student finishes answering, the team sits down. The first team to sit down is the winner.

4. Whisper Relay (p. 24) practices listening skills and memorization. Divide the class into teams and have them stand or sit in a line looking at the back of the student in front of them. Whisper the same word to the first person in each row. Say *Go!* and have S1 whisper the word to S2, who whispers it to S3, etc., as fast as possible. The last student then runs to the front of the class and tells the teacher the word. The first student to say the word correctly wins. To make this more challenging, whisper a few words or a sentence to S1.

EXTRA PRACTICE

WORKBOOK **pages 12–13**

Assign for homework or do in class. For instructions and Answer Key, see Teacher's Book page 164.

SKILLS BOOK **pages 12–13**

Assign for homework or do in class. For instructions and Answer Key, see Teacher's Book page 146.

REPRODUCIBLE WORKSHEET, **Teacher's Book page 176**

Do You Have…? Interview provides further fun and practice with the vocabulary of the lesson. For instructions, see page 190.

COMPONENTS LINK

LET'S GO TESTS AND QUIZZES

Lesson Quiz: Explain and administer the reproducible Unit 2 Let's Learn quiz from *Let's Go Tests and Quizzes*, page 13. Instructions and Answer Key are also in *Let's Go Tests and Quizzes*.

Let's Learn More

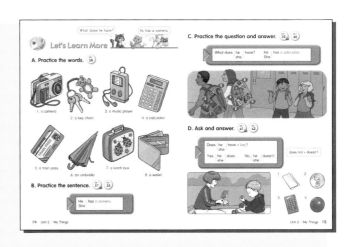

Topic: Personal possessions

Lesson objectives: Students talk about someone else's personal possessions.

New grammar: *He/She has (a key chain). What does he/she have? Does he/she have (a key chain)? Yes, he/she does. No, he/she doesn't.*

Review grammar: *What do you have? I have (a key).*

New language: *a camera, a key chain, a music player, a calculator, a train pass, an umbrella, a lunch box, a wallet*

Review language: *a key, a candy bar, a comic book, a comb, a coin, a brush, a tissue, a watch*

Materials: Teacher and Student Cards 25–40, actual items, CD 1 Tracks 36–42, contraction card (*doesn't*)

WARM UP AND REVIEW

Choose one of the following:

1. Guessing Game (p. 25). Divide the class into teams. Give a Student Card (25–32) to each student. Teams ask questions to guess what a student from the opposing team has. The object is to guess the item by asking the fewest number of questions. The team that asks the fewest questions wins the game.

2. Partners. Students in pairs ask each other about the items they brought with them to class, using *What do you have?*

PRESENT THE LANGUAGE

📖 BOOKS CLOSED

Introduce the words.

1. Use Teacher Cards 33–40 or actual items. Hold up one Teacher Card at a time and say the word. Students repeat each word several times.

2. When introducing *an umbrella* compare it with the other vocabulary (*a camera, a key chain, a music player*, etc.) and have students listen for the change *a/an*. It is not necessary here to give them the rules of how *an* is formed, but have

students drill, saying *an umbrella* many times so they can say it automatically.

3. Bring a volunteer to the front of the class. Give him or her an object and ask the class *What does he/she have?* The class responds *He/She has (a camera).* Continue with several more objects and volunteers.

4. Conduct a quick drill of the objects after you introduce each object. Use Teacher Cards 33–40. Don't speak as you show the cards. Have students identify the new objects plus all the previously learned objects. Gradually pick up speed as students get used to saying the words.

Introduce the sentence pattern.

1. Bring a volunteer to the front of the class. Give him or her a Teacher Card (or actual object) and model the sentence *He/She has (a camera).* Continue with several more objects and volunteers. Encourage students to use the gesture for *have* (cupped hands) as they speak to reinforce the meaning of the verb.

2. Use Teacher Cards 33–40. Practice the sentence pattern, substituting all the words. Students should say the

sentences at the same time as the teacher, not repeat after the teacher.

3. Conduct a quick drill. Show Teacher Cards 33–40 in random order and have students make sentences. Increase the speed of the drill until students are speaking at natural speed.

📖 BOOKS OPEN

A. Practice the words.

1. Play Track 36. Have students listen and point to the words.

> 💿 **CD 1 Track 36**
>
> 1. *a camera*
> 2. *a key chain*
> 3. *a music player*
> 4. *a calculator*
> 5. *a train pass*
> 6. *an umbrella*
> 7. *a lunch box*
> 8. *a wallet*

2. Play the audio again and have students repeat the words.

B. Practice the sentences.

1. Listen to the sentence pattern.
Write the pattern on the board or direct students' attention to their books. Play Track 37. Point to the

Let's Learn More

words as students listen to the audio. Then have students repeat after the audio.

 CD 1 Track 37

She has a camera.
He has a key chain.

She has a camera.
He has a key chain.

2. Practice the rhythm.

a. Play Track 37 again. This time, have students listen to the rhythm and intonation of the sentences.

b. Play the track again. Have students tap or clap to match the rhythm of the audio. Have students listen to the spoken sentences to hear how the sentences match the rhythm, and then have them repeat the sentences along with the recorded rhythm.

c. Have students tap or clap the rhythm and practice saying the sentences without the audio.

3. Practice the sentences.

a. Play Track 38 and have students point to the vocabulary pictures as they listen.

 CD 1 Track 38

She has a camera.
He has a key chain.
She has a music player.
He has a calculator.
She has a train pass.
He has an umbrella.
She has a lunch box.
He has a wallet.

b. Play Track 38 again and have students repeat the sentences.

c. Divide the class into pairs and have students practice the sentences with their books open to page 14. S1 touches a picture and says *She has (a music player).* S2 points to a different picture and says *He has (an umbrella).*

BOOKS CLOSED

Introduce the question forms.

1. Introduce the *Wh-* question-and-answer pattern.

a. Hold up Teacher Card 33 and give it to a male student to hold. Point to him and ask *What does he have?* Model the answer for students to repeat *He has (a camera).* Then have them repeat it in a series of three, several times. Repeat the procedure with a female student holding the card. Have students answer *She has a camera.*

b. Ask the question *What does (he) have?* while having male or female students hold Teacher Cards. Students answer with *(He) has (a key chain).*

c. Have students repeat the question several times. Point to students holding Teacher Cards and have students ask the question *What does (he) have?* Students answer each time.

d. Divide the class into two groups. Give Teacher Cards to students, and point to the students in turn to cue the questions and answers. Groups take turns asking and answering questions.

e. Further divide the two groups into smaller groups of 3–4 students. Have each student show a personal item to his or her group saying *I have (a key chain).* Students then ask each other questions like *What does Megan have?* or *What does she have?* and someone else in the group responds *He/She has (a key chain).* Continue until all students have a turn. Then have the two large groups come back together and alternate asking each other questions about their members.

Group A: *What does (Mari) have?*
Group B: *She has (a pencil).*

To make the activity more challenging, have students use color words and adjectives from Level 1 to describe the personal possessions: *She has a green pencil. He has a big bag.*

> **Pronunciation Tip:** When asking *What does he/she have?* the stress on the words can change. Model the question first with the stress on *what* and *have*, and then with the stress on *he* or *she*. Have students guess why the question would be said different ways. (The emphasis in the first instance is on what is possessed, and the emphasis in the second instance is on the person doing the possessing.)

2. Introduce the *Yes/No* question-and-answer pattern.

a. Give Teacher Card 25 to a male student and ask the class *Does he have a key?* Prompt them to answer *Yes, he does.* Give Teacher Cards to other students and practice the question (with *he* and *she*) and answer *yes* several times. Then, point to the first student volunteer and ask *Does he have (an umbrella)?* Encourage students to answer *No, he doesn't.* Repeat with the remaining seven Teacher Cards.

b. Divide the class into two groups. Give four students in each group Teacher Cards to cue questions and answers. Have one group ask and the other group answer the questions. Repeat so that both groups have a chance to ask and answer. Be sure to ask questions that elicit both *Yes* and *No* answers.

c. Divide the class into pairs, and have students practice with Student Cards or Teacher Cards attached to the board. Divide the cards into "he" and "she" piles to elicit both pronouns.

BOOKS OPEN

C. Practice the question and answer.

1. Listen to the *Wh-* question-and-answer pattern.

a. Present the pattern by writing it on the board or direct students' attention to the pattern in the book.

b. Play Track 39. Point to the words as students listen. Have students repeat after the audio.

 CD 1 Track 39

What does he have?
He has a calculator.

What does he have?
He has a calculator.

2. Practice the rhythm.

a. Play Track 39 again. This time, have students listen to the rhythm and intonation of the questions and answers.

b. Play the track again. Have students tap or clap to match the rhythm of the audio. Have students listen to the spoken questions and answers to hear how they match the rhythm, and then have them repeat the patterns along with the recorded rhythm.

c. Have students tap or clap the rhythm and practice saying the questions and answers without the audio.

3. Practice the *Wh-* questions and answers.

a. Have students look at page 15 and describe things they see.

b. Play Track 40. Have students listen to the questions and answers and point to the appropriate pictures.

 CD 1 Track 40

1. What does he have?
*   He has a wallet.*
2. What does she have?
*   She has a music player.*
3. What does he have?
*   He has a train pass.*
4. What does she have?
*   She has a camera.*
5. What does he have?
*   He has an umbrella.*
6. What does she have?
*   She has a lunch box.*
7. What does he have?
*   He has a calculator.*
8. What does she have?
*   She has a keychain.*

c. Play the audio again and have students repeat the questions and answers.

d. Divide the class into question and answer groups and play the audio again. Each group repeats either the question or answer. Repeat, with groups switching roles.

e. Have students work in pairs and take turns asking and answering questions about the pictures.

D. Ask and answer.

1. Listen to the *Yes/No* question-and-answer pattern.

a. Play Track 41. Have students listen and repeat.

 CD 1 Track 41

Does he have a key?
*   Yes, he does.*
Does she have a key?
*   No, she doesn't.*
does not = doesn't

Does he have a key?
*   Yes, he does.*
Does she have a key?
*   No, she doesn't.*

b. Write the explanation of the contraction on the board: *does not = doesn't*. See page 196 for how to use contraction cards to teach

contractions. Have students practice saying both *No, he does not* and *No, he doesn't*.

2. Practice the rhythm.

a. Play Track 41 again. This time, have students listen to the rhythm and intonation of the questions and answers.

b. Play the track again. Have students listen to the spoken questions and answers to hear how they match the rhythm, and then have them repeat the patterns along with the recorded rhythm.

c. Have students tap or clap the rhythm and practice saying the questions and answers without the audio.

3. Practice the *Yes/No* questions and answers.

a. Play Track 42. Have students listen and point to the appropriate pictures.

 CD 1 Track 42

1. Does she have a tissue?
*   Yes, she does.*
2. Does she have a coin?
*   No, she doesn't.*
3. Does he have a calculator?
*   No, he doesn't.*
4. Does he have a ball?
*   Yes, he does.*

b. Have students work in pairs and take turns asking and answering questions about the pictures.

GAMES AND ACTIVITIES

1. Telegram Drill (p. 24) practices listening skills and forming sentences with *have*. Have students form rows. Give the first student a card in an envelope. S1 looks at the card and places it back in the envelope. Then S1 hands the envelope to S2 and whispers *He/She has a calculator.* S2 does not look at the card. He or she passes the envelope to S3 and whispers *He/She has a calculator.* Continue to the end of the row. The last student says the sentence aloud and then opens

Let's Learn More

the envelope to see if the sentence matches the picture and if he or she said the same sentence as S1.

2. Yes/No practices memory and the question-and-answer patterns. First, have one male and one female student come to the front of the class. Give each of them two or three cards. Have each student show each card to the class and then hide them. Then ask a question about one of the students: *Does he have (a key chain)?* Students answer *Yes, he does* or *No, he doesn't.* When they answer *Yes* correctly, the student puts the card on the board. When all the cards are on the board, ask *What does he/she have?* and have students answer *He/She has (a key chain).* Continue with other students and other cards.

3. Walk and Talk (p. 26) practices using the question *What does he/she have?* Have four or five students sit in various places around the classroom. Give each of them two or three personal possession cards. The other students walk around in pairs. Each pair must stop by one of the seated students and take turns asking each other *What does he/she have?* Continue until pairs have talked about at least two students. Then have other students sit.

EXTRA PRACTICE

WORKBOOK **pages 14–15**

Assign for homework or do in class. For instructions and Answer Key, see Teacher's Book page 164.

SKILLS BOOK **pages 14–15**

Assign for homework or do in class. For instructions and Answer Key, see Teacher's Book page 146.

REPRODUCIBLE WORKSHEET,
Teacher's Book page 177

Do You Have...? Cards provides further fun and practice with the vocabulary of the lesson. For instructions, see page 191.

COMPONENTS LINK

CD-ROM 2

For extra fun, students can play Unit 2, Game 2 on a computer at school or at home. In this **Concentration** game, students try to find picture-word pairs. This activity reinforces listening, reading, and the Let's Learn and Let's Learn More vocabulary.

LET'S GO TESTS AND QUIZZES

Lesson Quiz: Explain and administer the reproducible Unit 2 Let's Learn More quiz from *Let's Go Tests and Quizzes*, page 14. Instructions and Answer Key are also in *Let's Go Tests and Quizzes*.

LET'S CHANT LET'S SING 2

Page 30: "Do You Have a Pencil Case?"

This song practices the question-and-answer patterns *Do you have a pencil case? Yes, I do. No, I don't. Does she have a comic book? Yes, she does. No, she doesn't.*

Let's Build

Topic: Asking about the location of personal possessions

Lesson objectives: Students talk about other people's personal possessions, about the location of personal possessions, and use possessive adjectives.

Review grammar: *in, his, her, your, He/She has, Does he/she have...? Yes, he/she does. No, he/she doesn't. What does he/she have?*

Review language: *hand, bag,* personal possessions

Materials: Teacher and Student Cards 5–12, 26–40, and personal possessions from Level 1, CD 1 Tracks 43–45

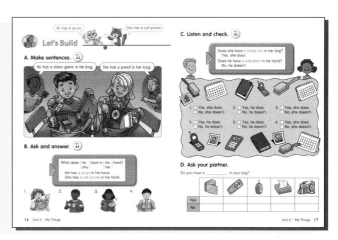

WARM UP AND REVIEW

1. Command Chain (p. 26) reviews verb phrases. Quickly show Teacher Cards 21–24 and have students say and do the actions. Then have students get into groups of 8–10 and do the command chain.

2. Concentration (p. 22) reviews personal possessions. Use a double set of Student Cards 25–40. Students turn over cards looking for a match. When students find a match, they say *I have (a key chain).* Continue until all the cards are gone. To make this more challenging, include Student Cards 5–12, or any card from Level 1 that can be a personal possession.

PRESENT THE LANGUAGE

BOOKS CLOSED

1. Show Teacher Cards 7 and 90 from Level 1 or actual items. Have a male student come to the front of the class. Have him put a video game in a bag. Point to the student and say *He has a video game in his bag.* Have students repeat. Repeat the procedure with a female student and a pencil and a bag.

2. Write the words *he, she, his, her* on the board. Model the words and have students repeat. Ask a student to come to the board. Say *He has a video game in his bag* and

have the student point to *he* and *his* when they hear it. Repeat the procedure with *She has a pencil in her bag.* Continue with several other students.

3. Prepare a goody bag with 2–3 items (personal possessions, toys, classroom objects, electronic items, actual items or pictures) for each student or group in the class. Give a bag to each student or group. Have a volunteer show an item from his or her bag. The class identifies it with the sentence *He/She has (a pen) in his or her bag.* Repeat several times and then put students into small groups to continue practice.

BOOKS OPEN

A. Make sentences.

1. Have students look at the picture on page 16 and describe what they see. Encourage them to guess what language they will hear.

2. Play Track 43. Have students listen to the audio and point to the words and pictures.

CD 1 Track 43

He has a video game in his bag.
She has a pencil in her bag.

1. He has a video game in his bag.
2. She has a pencil in her bag.
3. He has a wallet in his bag.
4. She has a notebook in her bag.
5. He has a cell phone in his bag.
6. She has a CD in her bag.
7. He has a toy in his bag.
8. She has a calculator in her bag.

3. Play the audio again. Have students repeat after each sentence.

4. Divide the class into pairs. Have them take turns pointing to one of the objects and making a sentence for each one. Ask several students for their answers.

B. Ask and answer.

1. Have students look at the pictures on page 16 and describe what they see. Encourage them to guess what language they will hear.

2. Take an object in your hand and say *I have (a pen) in my hand.* Specifically point to your hand and repeat *in my hand.* Do this with several more objects. Then have a male volunteer come to the front. Hand him an object. Point to the student and ask *What does he have in his hand?* The class responds *He has (a pencil) in his hand.*

Let's Build

3. Put students in small groups and give them some Student Cards. Have students place the Student Cards faceup on the desk. Each student takes a turn picking up and holding a card in his or her hand so that the others can see it. The other students in the group make a sentence: *He has (a pen) in his hand.*

4. Play Track 44. Have students point to the pictures as they listen to the audio.

 CD 1 Track 44

What does he have in his hand?
He has a yo-yo in his hand.
What does she have in her hand?
She has a cell phone in her hand.

1. *What does she have in her hand?*
   She has a cell phone in her hand.
2. *What does he have in his hand?*
   He has a wallet in his hand.
3. *What does she have in her hand?*
   She has a music player in her hand.
4. *What does he have in his hand?*
   He has a key chain in his hand.

5. Play the audio again and have students repeat after each sentence.

6. Divide the class into pairs. Have them take turns pointing to one of the objects and asking and answering a question for each one. Ask several students for their answers.

C. Listen and check.

1. Give a bag with Teacher Card 26 (*candy bar*) to a female student. Ask the class *Does she have a candy bar in her bag?* Prompt the class to answer *Yes, she does.* Take the Teacher Card and give it to a male student to hold. Ask the class *Does he have a calculator in his hand?* Prompt students to answer *No, he doesn't.*

2. Play the first part of Track 45. Have students listen and point to the words. Then, have students repeat the two questions and answers.

 CD 1 Track 45

Does she have a candy bar in her bag?
   Yes, she does.
Does he have a calculator in his hand?
   No, he doesn't.

3. Have students look at the picture and describe what they see. Play the rest of the audio and have students mark the answers. Play the audio at least twice so that students can check their answers.

 CD 1 Track 45

1. *Does she have a book in her bag?*
   Yes, she does.
2. *Does he have a calculator in his hand?*
   No, he doesn't.
3. *Does she have a picture in her hand?*
   Yes, she does.
4. *Does he have a calendar in his bag?*
   No, he doesn't.
5. *Does he have a cell phone in his hand?*
   Yes, he does.
6. *Does she have a brush in her bag?*
   No, she doesn't.

D. Ask your partner.

1. Write *you* and *your* on the board. Model the question *What do you have in your bag?* as you point to the words. Then have a volunteer come to the board. Say the sentence again and have the student point to the words as you say the question. Repeat with several other students.

2. Have a student come to the front of the class. Give S1 a Student Card or an actual item. Have S1 put it in a bag and ask S1 *What do you have in your bag?*

3. Point to the pictures on page 17 and ask students what they are. Have them draw additional pictures to fill their own "bag" with personal possessions.

4. Divide the class into pairs. Students exchange "bags" and take turns asking and answering questions about what is inside them. Start with the items pictured on the page and then move on to other items.

GAMES AND ACTIVITIES

1. **What Do You Have?** reviews personal possessions and classroom objects. Divide the class into small groups. One student in each group selects a Teacher Card and hides it in his or her hand or bag so the group can't see it. The students in the group must guess what the student has in his or her hand by asking *What do you have in your (hand)? Do you have (a camera)?* Students continue to ask questions until they guess the item. Each group reports to the class by answering questions such as *What does (Ryan) have in (his) (hand)?* Students answer *(He) has (a camera) in (his) (hand).*

2. **Pantomime** combines action with speaking practice. Have one student pantomime using a personal possession. The others must guess what it is by asking *Do you have (a pencil)?* The student must answer *Yes, I do* when the item is guessed or *No, I don't* when the guess is incorrect.

3. **Change the Sentence** reviews the pronouns and personal possessions. Give a male student a Student Card. Point to the student and say *He has (a camera) in his hand.* Have students repeat. Have the student give the card to a female student. Point to her and elicit from the class *She has (a camera) in her hand.* Continue quickly around the class with different cards and students. After the first example, let students do all the speaking.

EXTRA PRACTICE

WORKBOOK pages 16–17

Assign for homework or do in class. For instructions and Answer Key, see Teacher's Book page 165.

SKILLS BOOK pages 16–17

Assign for homework or do in class. For instructions and Answer Key, see Teacher's Book page 147.

COMPONENTS LINK

CD-ROM 2

For extra fun, students can play Unit 2, Game 3 on a computer at school or at home. Students listen and sort the objects in *his* or *her* backpack. This activity reinforces listening, the Let's Learn and Let's Learn More vocabulary, and the Let's Build grammar pattern *She/He has a … in her/his bag.*

For extra fun, students can play Unit 2, Game 4 on a computer at school or at home. Students try to memorize the objects in the bag and then answer the questions. This activity reinforces listening, the Let's Learn and Let's Learn More vocabulary, and the Let's Build grammar pattern *Does she/he have a … in her/his bag? Yes, she/he does. No she/he doesn't.*

LET'S GO TESTS AND QUIZZES

Lesson Quiz: Explain and administer the reproducible Unit 2 Let's Build quiz from *Let's Go Tests and Quizzes*, page 15. Instructions and Answer Key are also in *Let's Go Tests and Quizzes*.

Unit Test: Explain and administer the reproducible Unit 2 Test from *Let's Go Tests and Quizzes*, page 46. Instructions and Answer Key are also in *Let's Go Tests and Quizzes*.

LET'S GO READER

Now that students have completed Unit 2, they are ready to read "Grandma's House." See Teacher's Book page 20 for suggestions on how to present *Readers* and incorporate them into your lesson plans.

LET'S SING LET'S CHANT

Page 29: "What Do You Have in Your Bag?"

This chant reinforces the question *What do you have (in your bag / in your hand / on your desk)? I have a coin (in my bag / in my hand / on my desk).*

Page 31: "What Does She Have in Her Book Bag?"

This chant reinforces the question-and-answer pattern *What does she/he have in her/his book bag? She/He has a candy bar.*

Units 1–2 Listen and Review
Let's Learn About Numbers 20–100

Topic: Units 1–2 Review; Numbers 20–29 and 10–100 (by tens)

Lesson objectives: Students demonstrate comprehension of language and vocabulary taught in Units 1 and 2. Students also learn to count to 100.

Review grammar: *How are you? I'm okay, thanks. How about you? Pretty good. Good-bye. See you later. Whose (bag) is that? I don't know. Is it (Scott's) (bag)? It's (his) (bag). This is (a picture). That's (a paper clip). What's this/that? It's (a workbook). Is this/that (a workbook)? Yes, it is. No, it isn't. These/Those are (windows). What are these/those? They are (windows). Are these/those (windows)? Yes, they are. No, they aren't. What do you have? I have (a key). Do you have (a key)? Yes, I do. No, I don't. What does he/she have? He/She has (a comic book). Does he/she have (a coin)? Yes, he/she does. No, he/she doesn't.*

New language: Numbers 20–29 and 10–100 (by tens)

Review language: classroom and personal objects

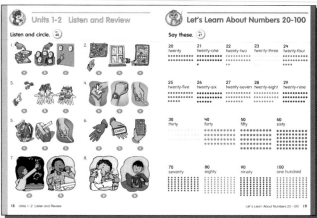

Materials: Teacher and Student Cards 1–58; CD 1 Tracks 46–4; bag and small classroom objects (for guessing game); teacher-made number and word cards for 20–29, 10, 30, 40, 50, 60, 70, 80, 90, 100; contraction cards (*can't, don't, What's*)

PART TWO: UNITS 1-2 LISTEN AND REVIEW

Review Activities

1. Let's talk / Let's sing.

a. Timed Conversations reviews the dialogue from Unit 1. With student help, create a conversation and write it on the board.

Example:
A: *Hi, _____. How are you?*
B: *I'm okay, thanks. How about you?*
A: *Pretty good!*

A: *Good-bye, _____.*
B: *See you later!*

Students circulate around the class for one minute and practice the dialogue. At first, signal students to switch every 10–15 seconds. Then, extend the time allowed and challenge students to continue talking after the greetings until the teacher signals the ending time (no longer than 30 seconds).

b. Practice the language from the Unit 2 conversation in small groups. Students empty their book bags and put the objects (and bags) in the center of their group. Then, they take turns picking up (*this*) object or pointing to (*that*) object and asking the group about ownership. S: *Whose pen is this?*

2. Let's move.

a. Six-second Drill (p. 21). Help students to think of more activities that they do at school, and write the verb phrases on the board (for example, *eat lunch, say the alphabet, count to ten, draw a picture*, etc.). In pairs, students stand and take turns saying three things they each do at school. The winners are the first pair to finish all six sentences, sit down, and say *Finished!* Repeat several times so that several pairs can win. For a greater challenge, have students talk about activities they *don't* do at school.

b. Student Interviews. Review the verb phrases from Units 1 and 2, and place the Teacher Cards on the chalk rail for reference. In pairs, students interview each other about their abilities. S1: *Can you swim?* S2: *Yes, I can.* Then, students report back to the class (or a small group, for large classes) about their partners. S1: *He can swim.*

c. Make new verb phrases. Write the base verbs from the Unit 1 and 2 Let's Move lessons on the board: *erase, speak, write, read, run, swim, sing, dance.* Have students work in groups to think of additional verb phrases using these base verbs (for example, *erase a word, speak Japanese*, etc.). Write the new phrases on the board under each base verb. Then, have pairs or groups of students place teacher-made cards of base verbs facedown on a desk. Students turn over one card at a time and make a sentence using a new verb phrase.

3. Let's Learn / Let's Learn More

a. Slap (p. 23). Use Student Cards 5–12, 26–40 (classroom and personal objects). For the simplest game, call out the vocabulary word. For more of a challenge, use each word in a sentence.

b. Hidden Words (p. 23). Hold up a Teacher Card for one of the Unit 1 or 2 vocabulary items, covered by a large piece of cardboard. Show students a portion of the card (for example, the bottom, the word only, the side) for one second or less. Students guess the vocabulary item. If students have difficulty guessing, gradually increase the amount of the card visible, or the amount of time it is visible.

c. Tic-Tac-Toe (p. 25). Divide the class into two teams. Teams earn an "X" or an "O" on the tic-tac-toe grid by providing either the correct answer to the teacher's question or the correct question to the teacher's answer.

d. Guessing Game (p. 25). Divide the class into two teams. Put small classroom objects (pencils, erasers, pens, rulers, small books) in a bag. Have one student from Team A look in the bag and ask *Are these (erasers)?* A student from Team B must feel the objects (without looking) and respond either *Yes, they are* or *No, they aren't.* Each team scores one point for a correct question and answer. Continue until all students have had a chance to participate. For smaller classes, this can also be played with students in a group taking turns asking the questions and answering.

e. Go Fish (p. 25). Use a double set of Student Cards for each group playing. S1: *Do you have a key?* S2: *Yes, I do. Here you are. / No, I don't. Go fish.*

Introduce Listen and Review

 BOOKS CLOSED

On the board, set up a sample to resemble the activity on page 18 of the Student Book. Put three Teacher Cards on the chalk rail. Draw a letter *a* above the first card, a letter *b* above the second, and a letter *c* above the third. Have one student stand by the cards. Identify one of the cards. T: *It's (a pencil sharpener).* The student points to the correct card and circles the appropriate letter. Repeat as necessary until all the students understand the procedure. If you want to conduct this as a formal test, do the sample

questions and then go directly to the written exercise in step 2b.

 BOOKS OPEN

A. Listen and circle.

1. Open your book to page 18. Show the page to the class. Have students identify the items in numbers 1–6. T: *What's this? Is this a (pencil sharpener)?* Have students identify the actions shown in numbers 7–8.

2. Have students open their books to page 18.

   a. Play Track 46. Have students listen and point to the appropriate picture.

 CD 1 Track 46

1. *What are those?*
   They're clocks.
2. *Is that a poster?*
   Yes, it is.
3. *Those are pencil sharpeners.*
4. *What does he have in his hand?*
   He has a key in his hand.
5. *What does she have in her bag?*
   She has a comic book in her bag.
6. *She has a calculator in her hand.*
7. *I erase the board at school.*
8. *What does he have?*
   He has a book.

   b. Play the audio again. Have students do the exercise as a written test. Correct the test with students.

3. Use the page for further review. Pair off the students. Have partners ask each other questions about numbers 1–6 and say the commands in numbers 7–8.

PART TWO: LET'S LEARN ABOUT NUMBERS 20–100

 BOOKS CLOSED

Present the topic: Numbers one to one hundred

If students are able, ask them to count as high as they can in English. (They have already learned the numbers 0–20 in Level 1.) Don't

feel that you need to correct them at this point—the goal is to see what they already know about this topic.

A. Count from 20 to 29.

1. Hold up Teacher Card 41 or write *20* on the board. Say the number and have students repeat. Continue for the numbers 21–29.

2. Substitution Drill (p. 21). Hold up teacher-made number cards 20–29 (or point to the numbers on the board) in random order. Have students call out the numbers.

B. Count by tens from ten to one hundred.

1. Write the numbers 1–30 on the board. Circle the numbers 10, 20, and 30. Point to the circled numbers and say the words. T: *ten, twenty, thirty.* Have students repeat.

2. Hold up teacher-made number cards for the numbers 10, 20, 30, 40, 50, 60, 70, 80, 90, and 100. Say the numbers and have students repeat.

3. Repeat the Substitution Drill procedures from step A2 above for numbers 10–100.

4. Count from twenty to twenty-nine.

 BOOKS OPEN

Play the first half of Track 47. Have students listen and point to the numbers.

 CD 1 Track 47

20, 21, 22, 23, 24, 25, 26, 27, 28, 29

5. Count by tens to one hundred.

   a. Play the second half of Track 47. Have students listen and point to the numbers.

CD 1 Track 47

10, 20, 30, 40, 50, 60, 70, 80, 90, 100

   b. Play the audio again. Have students count aloud in chorus.

6. Present the pattern: *How many (pencils) are there?*

a. Have students practice saying numbers between 10 and 100 (e.g., *34, 65, 72*, etc.).

b. Practice counting objects around the classroom. If desired, have students group objects into groups of tens and ones before saying the final number.

GAMES AND ACTIVITIES

1. Give students more practice with numbers.

a. In pairs, have students take turns dictating numbers to each other. S1 says a sequence of five numbers (not in order), and S2 writes the numbers on a piece of paper. Have S1 check S2's dictation. Reverse roles.

b. Divide the class into pairs. Students take turns saying a number and then the number that follows.

S1: *25.*
S2: *26. 72.*
S1: *73.*

2. Give students practice reading and forming numbers.

Introduce students to the number words by holding up a number card and having them identify the number shown. Then, hold up the matching word card and read the word while running your fingers under the letters. Have students repeat the word with you. Once students are comfortable with the word cards, play games to reinforce the vocabulary.

a. Concentration (p. 22). Begin by placing teacher-made word cards for *twenty* through *thirty* facedown on one side of a table. Place number cards *20–30* facedown on the other side of the table (so that there are two groupings of cards). Students turn over one card from each group, looking for matching number and word cards. When students have matched *twenty/20* through *thirty/30*, add *thirty-one/31* through *forty/40* (or add *10–100*) and play again.

b. Number formation. Write the words *twenty-one* through *twenty-nine* on the board, emphasizing that only the second part of each number changes (and is the same as counting from *one* to *nine*). Then, write *thirty* on the board and ask students to tell you what comes next. Write *thirty-one* on the board, and elicit *thirty-two*. Continue to *forty*. Once students see the pattern, write numerals on the board and have students tell you how to write the number in words. If students are able, encourage them to write the number words.

3. Give students more practice counting large numbers of objects.

a. Assign each pair of students a counting task that will require them to use large numbers (e.g., counting paper clips in a box, pencils in the class, etc.). When they have finished, ask each team to report. T: *How many paper clips?* Ss: *There are 93 paper clips.* (Note: If students will have to count beyond 100, be sure students understand how—most will either guess the pattern without explanation, or understand after a few numbers are explained to them.)

b. Teach students math language. Write *50 + 2 = ___* on the board. T: *How much is 50 + 2?* Ss: *52.* Write *52* in the blank. Then run your finger under the numbers and say *Fifty plus two equals/is fifty-two.* Have students repeat. If you are teaching older children and wish to teach additional math language, continue for *50 x 2 (fifty times two), 50 - 2 (fifty minus two),* and *50 ÷ 2 (fifty divided by 2).*

4. Combine number vocabulary with Unit One and Two patterns.

a. Have students count objects around the classroom and make sentences using *this/that* and *these/those* (e.g., *There are two big tables* and *There are 40 desks*).

b. Ask one student to hold multiple objects of the same type, and ask the class *What does he have?* Ss: *He has five books.* If the student is holding so many items that it is difficult to see clearly, students may need to break this into two steps—one to count the objects together, and another to answer the question.

EXTRA PRACTICE

WORKBOOK **page 18**

Assign for homework or do in class. For instructions and Answer Key, see Teacher's Book page 165.

SKILLS BOOK **page 18**

Assign for homework or do in class. For instructions and Answer Key, see Teacher's Book page 147.

COMPONENTS LINK

CD-ROM

For extra fun, students can play the Review Units 1-2 game on a computer at school or at home. In this memory chain game, students listen and watch to repeat the pattern. This activity reinforces reading, listening, and the numbers 20–29 and 10–100 (by 10s).

LET'S GO TESTS AND QUIZZES

Units 1–2 Listen and Review Test: Explain and administer the reproducible Units 1–2 Listen and Review Test from *Let's Go Tests and Quizzes*, page 68. Instructions and Answer Key are also in *Let's Go Tests and Quizzes*.

Lesson Quiz: Explain and administer the reproducible Let's Learn About Numbers 20–100 quiz from *Let's Go Tests and Quizzes*, page 62. Instructions and Answer Key are also in *Let's Go Tests and Quizzes*.

LET'S GO PICTURE DICTIONARY

Use page 3, Numbers, to supplement Let's Review.

Unit 3 My House

Let's Start

Topic: Addresses and cell phone numbers

Lesson objectives: Students talk about where they live, their telephone number.

New grammar: *Where do you live? I live in (Hillsdale).*

Review grammar: *What's your (cell phone number)? It's (123-4567).*

New language: *address, live, cell phone, play baseball, use chopsticks, do a magic trick, ice-skate*

Materials: Teacher and Student Cards 59–62, CD 1 Tracks 48–52, puppets (optional), beanbag, contraction cards (*What's, it's*)

Unit 3 My House
Let's Start
A. Let's talk.
Where do you live, Jenny?
What's your address?
I live in Hillsdale
It's 16 North Street
What's your cell phone number?
It's (798) 555-2043.
Where do you live? What's your address?
I live in Hillsdale It's 16 North Street
What is · What's
It is · It's
20 Unit 3 · My House

B. Let's sing.
~ Hillsdale ~
Where do you live?
In Hillsdale.
Where do you live?
In Hillsdale.
I live in Hillsdale.
How about you?
I live in Hillsdale, too.
What's your address
in Hillsdale?
What's your address
in Hillsdale?
It's North Street,
Number forty-two.
I live next to you!

C. Let's move.
1. play baseball
2. use chopsticks
3. ice-skate
4. do a magic trick
What can he do? He can play baseball.
she She
Unit 3 · My House 21

WARM UP AND REVIEW

Choose one of the following:

1. Beanbag Circle (p. 24) reviews personal information. Have students stand in a circle. Toss a beanbag to a student and ask *What's your name?* S1 answers and throws the beanbag to S2 and asks *How old are you?* S2 answers and throws the beanbag to S3 and asks *How are you?* Continue with the same questions until all the students have answered at least two of the questions.

2. Ping-Pong reviews numbers. Have students stand in a circle. Say three numbers in a row and have the student to your right repeat. Then have the student to his or her right repeat, and so on around the circle. Work up to five and then seven numbers.

PRESENT THE DIALOGUE

 **BOOKS CLOSED**

Present the dialogue.

1. Introduce the dialogue.

a. Use puppets or student volunteers to introduce the dialogue. Say both parts. Repeat three times and have students identify words they hear.

> Puppet A: *Where do you live, Jenny?*
> Puppet B: *I live in Hillsdale.*
> Puppet A: *What's your address?*
> Puppet B: *It's 16 North Street.*
> Puppet A: *What's your cell phone number?*
> Puppet B: *It's (798) 555-2043.*

b. Have students practice saying the town they live in with *I live in.* Then ask *What's your address?* and have them practice saying their addresses with *It's.*

c. Explain to students the difference between a telephone number and a cell phone number. Then ask *What's your cell phone number?* and have them practice saying a cell phone number (it doesn't have to be a real number).

> **Cultural Tip:** English address order is: building or house number, street name, apartment number (if needed), city, state, zip code, country. This may be different from the order students are familiar with. If it is, spend a little time showing students how to make their addresses work with this pattern.

> **Cultural Tip:** In saying telephone numbers, there is usually a pause between area code and prefix, and between the prefix and the final four numbers. If students' telephone numbers have a different pattern, you may need to show them where to pause.

2. Introduce the dialogue question.

a. Have students say *Where do you live?* in a series of three, several times: *Where do you live? Where do you live? Where do you live?* Gradually pick up speed until they are able to say it at natural speed.

b. Divide the class into two groups. Practice the questions and answers.

> Group A: *Where do you live, Jenny?*
> Group B: *I live in Hillsdale.*
> Group A: *What's your address?*
> Group B: *It's 16 North Street.*

c. Keep the students in two groups. Have them combine the entire dialogue. Reverse roles.

d. Divide the class into pairs and have them practice the questions with their own names and addresses.

Let's Start

 BOOKS OPEN

A. Let's talk.

Students learn how to ask and answer questions about their addresses and cell phone numbers.

1. Listen to the dialogue.

a. Have students look at the scene on page 20 and describe things they see.

b. Play Track 48. Have students listen to the dialogue and point to the characters or words in the speech bubbles. Have students identify words they hear.

 CD 1 Track 48

Kate: *Where do you live, Jenny?*
Jenny: *I live in Hillsdale.*
Kate: *What's your address?*
Jenny: *It's 16 North Street.*
Kate: *What's your cell phone number?*
Jenny: *It's (798) 555-2043.*

c. Play the dialogue again and have students repeat each line after the characters.

2. Practice the pattern.

a. Write the patterns on the board, or direct students' attention to their books. Play Track 49. Point to the words as students listen. Then have students repeat after the audio.

 CD 1 Track 49

Where do you live?
I live in Hillside.
What's your address?
It's 16 North Street.
What is = What's
It is = It's

b. Write the explanation of the contractions on the board: *What is = What's* and *It is = It's*. Follow the procedure on page 196 for how to teach contractions with cards. Have

the students practice saying both *What is / What's* and *It is / It's*. Point to the explanation on the board as they practice.

3. Practice the dialogue.

a. Ask one of the questions from the dialogue and have a volunteer answer. Repeat with the other dialogue questions. Then ask the questions out of order and have volunteers answer. To make this more challenging, give one of the answers from the dialogue and have students ask the matching question.

b. Use **Step Away Lines** (p. 26) to practice the dialogue

d. Have students practice the full dialogue in pairs, using students' own names, addresses, and cell phone (or telephone) numbers. Be sure to repeat the dialogue at least twice so that students can practice both parts.

B. Let's sing.

"Hillsdale," Track 50, reinforces the language from the dialogue using rhythm and song.

1. Play and listen.

Play Track 50. Have students listen and identify the words they recognize from Let's Talk.

 CD 1 Track 50

Hillsdale

Where do you live?
In Hillsdale.
Where do you live?
In Hillsdale.
I live in Hillsdale.
How about you?
I live in Hillsdale, too!

What's your address in Hillsdale?
What's your address in Hillsdale?
It's North Street, Number
forty-two.
I live next to you!

2. Practice the rhythm.

a. Introduce the song rhythmically. Have students clap to keep the beat as you model the song line by line. Have students repeat after you.

b. Play the song again. Encourage students to sing along.

3. Do the song activity.

Play the song again. This time have half of the class sing one part, and half sing the second part. Add gestures to go with the song lyrics.

4. Read the lyrics.

Have students look at the song pictures and lyrics. Ask students to point to and read words that they recognize.

5. Work in groups.

Have students work in groups to create an original verse by inserting each other's names. (Example: *Where does Mary live? In Hillsdale.*) Then, sing the song again with the new verses.

 BOOKS CLOSED

Present the verb phrases

1. Introduce the verb phrases.

a. Say *play baseball* with action, and repeat the action several times. Have students repeat several times with the action before going on to the next phrase. Repeat with the other phrases.

b. To check understanding, say the phrases in random order and have students do the appropriate action.

c. Show students Teacher Cards 59–62. Have them both say the phrase and do the action.

d. Divide the class into two groups. Have the groups take turns saying and doing the actions. Use Teacher Cards to cue the action-saying group.

2. Introduce *What can (she) do?* and *(She) can (ice-skate).*

a. Add *(She) can* to each verb phrase and have students repeat the phrase and do the action.

b. Have students say *What can she do?* in a series of three, several times: *What can she do? What can she do? What can she do?* Repeat with *he.*

c. Have pairs ask and answer questions together. S1: *What can (she) do?* S2: *(She) can (ice-skate).*

 BOOKS OPEN

C. Let's move.

Students practice discussing abilities by combining rhythm and actions.

1. Listen and point to the verb phrases.

a. Play Track 51. Have students listen and point to the appropriate pictures.

> **CD 1 Track 51**
>
> 1. *play baseball*
> 2. *use chopsticks*
> 3. *ice-skate*
> 4. *do a magic trick*

b. Play the audio again. Students listen and repeat.

2. Practice the rhythm.

a. Write the pattern on the board, or direct students' attention to their books. Play Track 52. Point to the words as students listen to the audio.

> **CD 1 Track 52**
>
> *What can he do?*
> *He can play baseball.*
>
> *What can she do?*
> *She can play baseball.*

b. Play Track 52 again. Have students clap or tap to keep the rhythm and repeat the question and answer with the audio.

c. Have students tap or clap the rhythm and practice saying the question and answer without the audio.

3. Practice the questions and answers.

a. Play Track 53. Have students listen to the questions and answers and point to the appropriate pictures.

> **CD 1 Track 53**
>
> *What can he do?*
> *He can play baseball.*
> *What can she do?*
> *She can use chopsticks.*
> *What can she do?*
> *She can ice-skate.*
> *What can he do?*
> *He can do a magic trick.*

b. Play the audio again and have students repeat.

c. Divide the class into question and answer groups and play the audio again. Each group repeats either the question or answer. Repeat with groups switching roles.

d. Have students work in pairs and take turns asking and answering questions about the pictures.

GAMES AND ACTIVITIES

1. Scrambled Sentences (p. 24) practices word order. Copy the lyrics from "Hillsdale" onto a sheet of paper and cut it into individual sentences. In pairs or groups, have students put the sentences in order. Play the song for students to check their arrangement, and then let students sing along with the audio.

2. Walk and Talk (p. 26) builds conversation fluency. Have students form pairs. Partners must introduce each other to other pairs and ask what their address and cell phone number is. For a greater challenge, have students use greetings they have learned previously, for example:

> S1: *Hi, I'm (Jenny).*
> S2: *Hello, I'm (Ben). This is my friend, (May).*
> S1: *Where do you live?*
> S3: *I live in (Plainville). Where do you live, Jenny?*
> S1: *I live in (Jefferson).*

3. Back-to-Back (p. 26) practices listening and numbers. Have pairs of students sit back-to-back. Have S1 write down a telephone number and dictate it to S2. S2 writes it down and then checks with S1 to see if it is correct. To make the activity more

challenging, have students dictate two telephone numbers in a row, or dictate the numbers as fast as possible.

EXTRA PRACTICE

WORKBOOK pages 20–21

Assign for homework or do in class. For instructions and Answer Key, see Teacher's Book page 165.

SKILLS BOOK pages 20–21

Assign for homework or do in class. For instructions and Answer Key, see Teacher's Book page 148.

REPRODUCIBLE WORKSHEET
Teacher's Book page 178

Address Book provides further fun and practice obtaining information such as address and phone number. For instructions, see page 191.

COMPONENTS LINK

CD-ROM 2

For extra fun, students can play Unit 3, Game 1 on a computer at school or at home. Students listen and put the words in the correct order to build a sentence about the picture. This activity reinforces listening and the verb pattern *She/He can…*

LET'S GO TESTS AND QUIZZES

Lesson Quiz: Explain and administer the reproducible Unit 3 Let's Start quiz from *Let's Go Tests and Quizzes*, page 16. Instructions and Answer Key are also in *Let's Go Tests and Quizzes*.

LET'S CHANT LET'S SING 2

Page 16: "Where Do You Live?"

This chant drills the question *Where do you live?* Teach the phrases *on Green Street, next to the school, in front of the trees, behind the school.*

Page 18: "Look at Me!"

This chant drills the sentence patterns *I can climb a tree, He can swim,* and *She can run.*

Let's Learn

Topic: Rooms and objects in a house

Lesson objectives: Students identify and ask about things found in a house.

New grammar: *There's a (bed) in the (bedroom). Is there a (refrigerator) in the (bedroom)? Yes, there is. No, there isn't.*

Review grammar: *Where's the (bed)? It's in the (bedroom).*

New language: *bed, bathtub, sofa, stove, lamp, sink, toilet, TV, refrigerator, telephone, bedroom, bathroom, living room, kitchen*

Materials: Teacher and Student Cards 63–72, CD 1 Tracks 54–60, contraction cards (*Where's, it's, There's, isn't*)

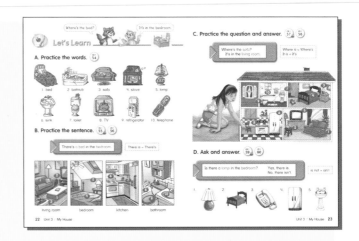

WARM UP AND REVIEW

Choose one of the following:

1. **Scrambled Sentences** (p. 24) reviews the dialogue from Let's Start. Copy the dialogue onto several pieces of paper and cut the sentences into strips. Divide the class into groups of 3–4 and have them order the strips. Then have them act out the dialogue. To make the activity more challenging, cut the sentences into phrases as well.

2. **She Can** practices verb phrases with *She can.* Review the verb phrases from Let's Move, using Teacher Cards 59–62. Say the verb phrase and have students say and do the action together with *She can* as quickly as possible. T: *play baseball.* Ss: *She can play baseball.* Divide the class into two groups. Cue one group with a card to make a sentence with *She can,* and have the other group do the action. Reverse roles.

PRESENT THE LANGUAGE

📖 BOOKS CLOSED

Introduce the words.

1. Use Teacher Cards 63–72 to introduce the words. Show one Teacher Card at a time and say the name of the object. Students repeat each word several times.

2. Conduct a quick drill of the words. Do not speak as you show the cards. Have students identify the new object plus all the previously learned objects. Gradually pick up speed as students get used to saying the words.

Introduce the sentence pattern.

1. Draw and label four large squares on the board to represent bedroom, living room, kitchen, and bathroom. Place Teacher Card 63 (*bed*) in the bedroom square. Point to it and say *There's a bed in the bedroom.* Students repeat the sentence. Place a card in each room. Point to each card and have students make a sentence: *There's a (stove) in the (kitchen).*

2. Continue until all of the furniture and room vocabulary has been practiced in sentences. Students should say sentences at the same time as the teacher, not repeat after the teacher.

3. Conduct a quick drill of the sentences using Teacher Cards 63–72. Do not speak as you show the cards. Gradually pick up speed as students get used to saying the sentences.

📖 BOOKS OPEN

A. Practice the words.

1. Play Track 54. Have students listen and point to the words.

 **CD 1 Track 54**

1. bed
2. bathtub
3. sofa
4. stove
5. lamp
6. sink
7. toilet
8. TV
9. refrigerator
10. telephone

2. Play the audio again and have students repeat the words.

B. Practice the sentence.

1. **Listen to the sentence pattern.**

a. Write the pattern on the board or direct students' attention to it in the book. Play Track 55. Point to the words as students listen to the audio. Then have students repeat after the audio.

CD 1 Track 55

There's a bed in the bedroom.
There is = There's

There's a bed in the bedroom.

b. Write the explanation of the contraction on the board: *There is=There's*. See page 196 for how to use contraction cards to teach contractions. Have students practice saying both *There is a bed in the bedroom* and *There's a bed in the bedroom*. Point to the explanation on the board as they practice.

2. Practice the rhythm.

a. Play Track 55 again. This time, have students listen to the rhythm and intonation of the sentences.

b. Play the audio again. Have students tap or clap to match the rhythm of the audio. Have students listen to the spoken sentence to hear how it matches the rhythm, and then have them repeat the sentences along with the recorded rhythm.

c. Have students tap or clap the rhythm and practice saying the sentence without the audio.

3. Practice the sentences.

a. Play Track 56 and have students point to the vocabulary pictures as they listen.

 CD 1 Track 56

1. *There's a sofa in the living room.*
2. *There's a TV in the living room.*
3. *There's a telephone in the living room.*
4. *There's a bed in the bedroom.*
5. *There's a lamp in the bedroom.*
6. *There's a stove in the kitchen.*
7. *There's a refrigerator in the kitchen.*
8. *There's a bathtub in the bathroom.*
9. *There's a toilet in the bathroom.*
10. *There's a sink in the bathroom.*

b. Play Track 56 again and have students repeat the sentences.

c. Divide the class into groups of three and have students play **Slap** (p. 23) with their books open to page 22. S1 says *There's a (bed) in the (bedroom)* and S2 and S3 rush to touch the correct part of the picture. Students switch roles and repeat.

 BOOKS CLOSED

Introduce the question forms.

1. Introduce the *Wh-* question-and-answer pattern.

✓ **a.** Use the drawing (squares) on the board and label the rooms. Place the furniture Teacher Cards in appropriate rooms and ask *Where's the (sofa)?* Prompt students to answer *It's in the (living room)*. Repeat the question for additional furniture in different rooms.

b. Have students repeat the question. Model the question and help students with pronunciation.

✓ **c.** Move the cards to different rooms. Point to one furniture card and prompt students to ask *Where's the (bed)?* T: *It's in the (living room)*. Repeat for each vocabulary item.

d. Divide the class into two groups. Use Teacher Cards placed in room squares to cue the students. Groups take turns asking and answering questions.

> **Pronunciation Tip:** Be sure students pronounce *Where's* correctly with the /s/ sound at the end.

2. Introduce the *Yes/No* question-and-answer pattern.

a. Put Teacher Card 71 (*refrigerator*) in the "kitchen" square on the board. Ask *Is there a refrigerator in the kitchen?* Prompt students to answer *Yes, there is.* Repeat with additional Teacher Cards and rooms. Then, point to the kitchen square once more and ask *Is there a sofa in the kitchen?* Prompt students to answer *No, there*

isn't. Repeat with additional Teacher Cards and rooms.

b. Divide the class into two groups. Have one group ask and the other group answer the questions. Place furniture Teacher Cards in various rooms. Point to a furniture card and a room card to cue the question. *Yes* and *No* answers depend on whether or not the furniture card is actually in the room pointed to.

c. Divide the class into pairs and have students practice with Student Cards and room squares, or by referring to Teacher Cards in the squares on the board.

 BOOKS OPEN

C. Practice the question and answer.

1. Listen to the *Wh-* question-and-answer pattern.

a. Present the pattern by writing it on the board or direct students' attention to it in the book.

b. Play Track 57. Point to the words as students listen. Have students repeat after the audio.

 CD 1 Track 57

Where's the sofa?
    It's in the living room.
Where is = Where's
It is = It's

Where's the sofa?
    It's in the living room.

✓ **c.** Write the explanation of the contractions on the board: *Where is = Where's* and *It is = It's*. See page 196 for how to use contraction cards to teach contractions. Have students practice saying both *Where's the sofa? It's in the living room* and *Where is the sofa? It is in the living room*. Point to the explanation on the board as they practice.

2. Practice the rhythm.

a. Play Track 57 again. This time, have students listen to the rhythm

Let's Learn

and the intonation of the question and answer.

b. Play the track again. Have students clap or tap to match the rhythm of the audio. Have students listen to the spoken question and answer to hear how it matches the rhythm, and then have them repeat the pattern along with the recorded rhythm.

c. Have students tap or clap the rhythm and practice saying the question and answer without the audio.

3. Practice the *Wh-* questions and answers.

a. Have students look at page 23 and describe the things they see.

b. Play Track 58. Have students listen and point to the appropriate pictures.

CD 1 Track 58

1. *Where's the sofa?*
   It's in the living room.
2. *Where's the telephone?*
   It's in the living room.
3. *Where's the lamp?*
   It's in the bedroom.
4. *Where's the bed?*
   It's in the bedroom.
5. *Where's the TV?*
   It's in the living room.
6. *Where's the refrigerator?*
   It's in the kitchen.
7. *Where's the sink?*
   It's in the bathroom.
8. *Where's the stove?*
   It's in the kitchen.
9. *Where's the toilet?*
   It's in the bathroom.
10. *Where's the bathtub?*
    It's in the bathroom.

c. Play the audio again. Have students repeat the questions and answers.

d. Divide the class into question and answer groups and play the audio again. Each group repeats either the question or answer. Repeat, with groups switching roles.

e. Have students work in pairs and take turns asking and answering questions about the pictures.

D. Ask and answer.

1. Listen to the *Yes/No* question-and-answer pattern.

a. Present the pattern by writing it on the board or direct students' attention to the pattern in the book.

b. Play Track 59. Point to the words as students listen. Have students repeat after the audio.

CD 1 Track 59

Is there a lamp in the bedroom?
   Yes, there is.
Is there a lamp in the bedroom?
   No, there isn't.

Is there a lamp in the bedroom?
   Yes, there is.
Is there a lamp in the bedroom?
   No, there isn't.

2. Practice the rhythm.

a. Play Track 59 again and have students listen to the rhythm and intonation of the question and answers.

b. Play the track again. Have students tap or clap to match the rhythm of the audio. Have students listen to the spoken question and answers to hear how they match the rhythm, and then have them repeat the patterns along with the recorded rhythm.

c. Have the students tap or clap the rhythm and practice saying the questions and answers without the audio.

3. Practice the *Yes/No* questions and answers.

a. Play Track 60. Have students listen and point to the appropriate pictures.

CD 1 Track 60

1. *Is there a lamp in the bedroom?*
   Yes, there is.
2. *Is there a bed in the living room?*
   No, there isn't.
3. *Is there a telephone in the kitchen?*
   No, there isn't.
4. *Is there a refrigerator in the kitchen?*
   Yes, there is.
5. *Is there a sink in the bedroom?*
   No, there isn't.

b. Have students work in pairs and take turns asking and answering questions about the pictures.

GAMES AND ACTIVITIES

1. What's In Your House? practices the question-and-answer pattern. Divide the class into pairs. Have each student draw four large squares on a piece of paper to represent four rooms of a house. Tell them to label the rooms *bedroom, living room, kitchen,* and *bathroom.* S1 places furniture Student Cards in each of the squares on his/her paper. S2 asks S1 about the cards in S1's rooms. S2: *Is there a refrigerator in the living room?* S1: *No, there isn't/Yes, there is.*

2. The Memory Game challenges students to see how many cards they can remember in order. Use Teacher Cards 63–72. Line the cards on the chalk rail. S1 asks *What's this?* as other students answer. Then S1 turns the card over. S1 repeats the question and turns over all the cards as they are answered. When all the cards are turned over, S1 asks *What's this?* pointing to each card in order. The other students must remember what the cards are. This can also be played in small groups.

3. Draw and Tell practices the sentence pattern and the vocabulary. Divide the class into pairs. Have students draw four large squares on a piece of paper to represent a house. Then have them draw one or two items in each room. Set a time limit to keep pictures simple. Students describe their pictures to their partners, who draw new pictures according to the descriptions: S1: *There's a bed in the bedroom*. Then partners reverse roles. When they finish, partners compare pictures.

EXTRA PRACTICE

WORKBOOK **pages 22–23**

Assign for homework or do in class. For instructions and Answer Key, see Teacher's Book page 166.

SKILLS BOOK **pages 22–23**

Assign for homework or do in class. For instructions and Answer Key, see Teacher's Book page 148.

COMPONENTS LINK

CD-ROM 2

For extra fun, students can play Unit 3, Game 2 on a computer at school or at home. Students listen and choose the correct picture to move across the maze. This activity reinforces listening and the Let's Learn vocabulary.

Explain and administer the reproducible Unit 3 Let's Learn quiz in *Let's Go Tests and Quizzes*, page 17. Instructions and Answer Key are also in *Let's Go Tests and Quizzes*.

LET'S GO TESTS AND QUIZZES

Lesson Quiz: Explain and administer the reproducible Unit 3 Let's Learn quiz from *Let's Go Tests and Quizzes*, page 17. Instructions and Answer Key are also in *Let's Go Tests and Quizzes*.

LET'S CHANT LET'S SING 2

Page 13: "Where's the Bed?"

This chant drills the question-and-answer pattern *Where's the bed? It's in the bedroom.*

LET'S GO PICTURE DICTIONARY

Use pages 30–37, Kitchen, Living Room, Bedroom, and Bathroom, to supplement the lesson and increase challenge.

1. Review familiar words on pages 30–37, and point out new words you wish to teach.

2. Practice the words with the question-and-answer pattern *Where's the bed? It's in the bedroom.*

Let's Learn More

Topic: Items in a house

Lesson objectives: Students identify and ask about the location of additional items in a house.

New grammar: *There's a (lamp) (next to) the (sofa). There are (lamps) (behind) the (sofa). Are there (lamps) (in front of) the (sofa)? Yes, there are. No, there aren't.*

Review grammar: *Is there a (lamp) (next to) the (bed)? Yes, there is. No, there isn't.*

New language: *next to, behind, in front of*

Review language: *bed, bathtub, sofa, stove, lamp, sink, toilet, TV, refrigerator, telephone, table, chair, clock, book, desk, in, under, by, on*

Materials: Teacher and Student Cards 63–79, actual items, CD 1 Tracks 61–67, contraction cards (*There's, isn't, aren't*)

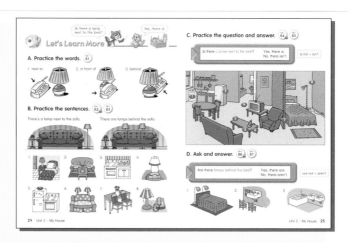

WARM UP AND REVIEW

Choose one of the following:

1. In, On, Under practices prepositions and vocabulary. Use Students Cards 63–72 (items in a house). Arrange two Student Cards on the board and have students describe their position. T: *Where is the lamp?* Ss: *It's on the bed.* Continue with other pairs of cards.

2. Slap (p. 23) practices singular and plural nouns. Use Student Cards from Let's Learn plus additional vocabulary. Have students display the cards on their desks. Call out a singular word. Students race to slap the card and say the plural form. Then call out a plural word and have students say the singular form. Let students take turns being caller.

PRESENT THE LANGUAGE

📖 BOOKS CLOSED

Introduce the words.

1. Use Teacher Cards 77–79 to practice the vocabulary. Say each word and have students repeat each word several times before going on to the next word.

2. Conduct a quick drill of the objects from Let's Learn. Use Teacher Cards 63–72. Don't speak as you show the cards. Have students identify the new words plus all the previous words.

3. Use classroom objects to present the prepositions. Arrange the two objects (to show *next to, behind, in front of*) and make a sentence describing their position. Touch each object as you say it in the sentence to help students understand the word order relative to the preposition.

Introduce the sentence patterns.

1. Use Teacher Cards 63–72. Show each card and say the sentence *There's a (lamp) (next to) the (sofa).* Have students repeat the sentence pattern several times before moving on to the next preposition. Show two Teacher Cards 67 (*lamp*) or draw two lamps on the board. Say the sentence *There are lamps (next to) the sofa.* Have students repeat the sentence pattern several times before moving onto the next preposition.

2. Practice the patterns with all the prepositions. Students should say the sentences at the same time as the teacher, not repeat after the teacher.

3. Arrange classroom objects or draw pictures on the board and have students make a sentence: *There are books on the desk* or *There's a book on the desk*. Then have volunteers come to the front of the classroom and arrange objects or draw pictures on the board. Have the other students make sentences.

> **Grammar Tip 1:** Review the importance of the plural *–s* by giving students two bags and two books (or other classroom objects) and having them arrange the items depending on your sentence. Students will quickly figure out the difference between *There are books on top of the bag* and *There is a book on top of the bag*.
>
> **Grammar Tip 2:** Explain that *There are* is never contracted.

BOOKS OPEN

A. Practice the words.

1. Play Track 61. Have students listen and point to the words.

 CD 1 Track 61

1. next to
2. in front of
3. behind

2. Play the audio again and have students repeat the words.

B. Practice the sentences.

1. Listen to the sentence pattern.
Write the pattern on the board or direct students' attention to their books. Play Track 62. Point to the words as students listen to the audio. Then have students repeat after the audio.

 CD 1 Track 62

There's a lamp next to the sofa.
There are lamps behind the sofa.

🥁

There's a lamp next to the sofa.
There are lamps behind the sofa.

2. Practice the rhythm.

a. Play Track 62 again. This time, have students listen to the rhythm and intonation of the sentences.

b. Play the track again. Have students tap or clap to match the rhythm of the audio. Have students listen to the spoken sentence to hear how it matches the rhythm, and then have them repeat the sentence along with the recorded rhythm.

c. Have students tap or clap the rhythm and practice saying the sentences without the audio.

3. Practice the sentences.

a. Play Track 63 and have students point to the vocabulary pictures as they listen.

 CD 1 Track 63

1. *There's a lamp next to the bed.*
2. *There's a TV in front of the sofa.*
3. *There's a sink next to the stove.*
4. *There's a telephone in front of the lamp.*
5. *There's a refrigerator next to the stove.*
6. *There are two lamps behind the sofa.*
7. *There are chairs in front of the table.*
8. *There's a telephone next to the lamp.*

b. Play Track 63 again and have students repeat the sentences.

c. Divide the class into pairs and have students practice the sentences with their books open to page 24. S1 says *There's a TV in front of the sofa.* S2 touches the appropriate picture and then says a different sentence.

 BOOKS CLOSED

Introduce the question forms.

1. Introduce the singular *Yes/No* question-and-answer pattern.

a. Hold up Teacher Cards 66 and 68 (*stove* and *sink*) next to each other and ask *Is there a stove next to the sink?* Model the answer for students to repeat *Yes, there is.* Have them repeat it in a series of three, several times.

b. Hold up Teacher Cards 66 and 71 (*stove* and *refrigerator*) next to each other and ask *Is there a stove next to the sink?* Model the answer for students to repeat *No, there isn't.* Then have them repeat it in a series of three, several times.

c. Ask questions showing the cards as the students answer with *Yes, there is* or *No, there isn't.* Then model the question *Is there a stove next to the sink?* Have students repeat the question several times.

d. Divide the class into two groups. Use Teacher Cards to cue the asking group. Groups take turns asking and answering questions.

e. Divide the class into pairs. Have students ask and answer questions with both *Yes, there is* and *No, there isn't.*

> **Pronunciation Tip:** Review the pronunciation of /th/. Tell students to make sure their tongues are touching the back of their front teeth. Model the difference between *thanks* and *there* and have students repeat several times.

2. Introduce the plural *Yes/No* question-and-answer pattern.

a. Hold up one Teacher Card 63 (*bed*) and two Teacher Cards 67 (*lamp*) behind it and ask *Are there lamps behind the bed?* Students answer *Yes, there are.* Then hold the lamp cards next to the *bed* card and ask *Are there lamps behind the bed?* Encourage students to answer *No, there aren't.*

b. Practice asking questions with *Are there.* Show students two object cards next to, in front of, or behind another card as they point to them and ask *Are there (lamps) (in front of) the bed?*

c. Divide the students into two groups with one group asking and the other answering the questions.

d. Divide the class into pairs and have them ask and answer questions about objects they arrange on their desks.

 BOOKS OPEN

C. Practice the question and answer.

1. Listen to the singular *Yes/No* question-and-answer pattern.

a. Present the pattern by writing it on the board or direct students' attention to the pattern in the book.

b. Play Track 64. Point to the words as students listen. Have students repeat after the audio.

Let's Learn More

 CD 1 Track 64

Is there a stove next to the sink?
   Yes, there is.
Is there a stove next to the sink?
   No, there isn't.
is not = isn't

Is there a stove next to the sink?
   Yes, there is.
Is there a stove next to the sink?
   No, there isn't.

c. Write the explanation of the contraction on the board: *is not = isn't*. See page 196 for how to use contraction cards to teach contractions. Have students practice saying both *No, there is not* and *No, there isn't*.

2. Practice the rhythm.

a. Play Track 64 again and have students listen to the rhythm and intonation of the questions and answers.

b. Play the track again. Have students tap or clap to match the rhythm of the audio. Have students listen to the spoken questions and answers to hear how they match the rhythm, and then have them repeat the patterns along with the recorded rhythm.

c. Have students tap or clap the rhythm and practice saying the questions and answers without the audio.

3. Practice the singular *Yes/No* questions and answers.

a. Have students look at page 25 and describe the things they see.

b. Play Track 65. Have students listen and point to the appropriate pictures.

 CD 1 Track 65

1. *Is there a stove next to the sink?*
   Yes, there is.
2. *Is there a refrigerator next to the stove?*
   No, there isn't.
3. *Is there a table in front of the sofa?*
   Yes, there is.
4. *Is there a TV on top of the table?*
   Yes, there is.
5. *Is there a telephone on top of the table?*
   Yes, there is.
6. *Is there a telephone in front of the sofa?*
   Yes, there is.
7. *Is there a lamp next to the bed?*
   Yes, there is.

c. Play the audio again and have students repeat the questions and the answers.

d. Divide the class into question and answer groups and play the audio again. Each group repeats either the question or the answer. Repeat with groups switching roles.

e. Have students work in pairs and take turns asking and answering questions about the pictures.

D. Ask and answer.

1. Listen to the plural *Yes/No* question-and-answer pattern.

a. Present the pattern by writing it on the board or direct students' attention to the pattern in the book.

b. Play Track 66. Point to the words as students listen. Have students repeat after the audio.

 CD 1 Track 66

Are there lamps behind the bed?
   Yes, there are.
Are there lamps behind the bed?
   No, there aren't.
are not = aren't

Are there lamps behind the bed?
   Yes, there are.
Are there lamps behind the bed?
   No, there aren't.

c. Write the explanation of the contraction on the board: *are not = aren't*. See page 196 for how to use contraction cards to teach contractions. Have students practice saying both *No, there aren't* and *No, there are not*.

2. Practice the rhythm.

a. Play Track 66 again and have students listen to the rhythm and intonation of the question and answer.

b. Have students tap or clap to match the rhythm of the audio. Play the track again. Have students listen to the spoken question and answers to hear how they match the rhythm, and then have them repeat the patterns along with the recorded rhythm.

c. Have students tap or clap the rhythm and practice saying the question and answers.

2. Practice the plural *Yes/No* questions and answers.

a. Play Track 67. Have students listen and point to the appropriate pictures.

 CD 1 Track 67

1. *Are there lamps behind the bed?*
   Yes, there are.
2. *Are there chairs in front of the sink?*
   Yes, there are.
3. *Are there sinks in front of the bathtub?*
   No, there aren't.

b. Have students work in pairs and take turns asking and answering questions about the pictures.

> **Grammar Tip:** Remind students that *There are* is never contracted.

GAMES AND ACTIVITIES

1. What's Different? gives students practice in using *there is, there are* and prepositions. Have students close their eyes. Change the arrangement of classroom furniture and objects. Tell students to open their eyes and identify what has changed. For example: *There's a chair in front of the* desk. To make this more challenging, have students make sentences with *there are* and *there aren't* as well.

2. My Bedroom gives students practice in using the vocabulary. Students draw a simple picture of their bedroom (or dream bedroom). Divide the class into pairs. Have students describe their bedroom to their partner: *There's a chair in front of the desk. There are tables next to the bed.* To make this more challenging, have students include colors and other adjectives in their sentences.

3. Step Away Lines (p. 26) gives students confidence in speaking in a loud voice. Give students Student Cards 63–72. Have them get into two lines and show a card as they ask *Yes/No* questions from Let's Learn More.

4. Are There? uses the pictures in the book as reinforcement. Use page 25 of the Student Book. Have students gets into pairs and work with one book. They play **Rock, Paper, Scissors** with *Are there, are there, 1, 2, 3!* The winner asks a *Yes/No* question and the loser has to answer it correctly.

EXTRA PRACTICE

WORKBOOK pages 24–25

Assign for homework or do in class. For instructions and Answer Key, see Teacher's Book page 166.

SKILLS BOOK pages 24–25

Assign for homework or do in class. For instructions and Answer Key, see Teacher's Book page 149.

REPRODUCIBLE WORKSHEET
Teacher's Book page 179

Look, Listen, and Circle provides further fun and practice with the vocabulary of the lesson. For instructions, see page 191.

COMPONENTS LINK

CD-ROM 2

For extra fun, students can play Unit 3, Game 3 on a computer at school or at home. Students follow the prompts to place the objects correctly in the picture. This activity reinforces listening, the Let's Learn vocabulary, and prepositions.

Explain and administer the reproducible Unit 3 Let's Learn More quiz in *Let's Go Tests and Quizzes,* page 18. Instructions and Answer Key are also in *Let's Go Tests and Quizzes.*

LET'S GO TESTS AND QUIZZES

Lesson Quiz: Explain and administer the reproducible Unit 3 Let's Learn More quiz from *Let's Go Tests and Quizzes,* page 18. Instructions and Answer Key are also in *Let's Go Tests and Quizzes.*

LET'S CHANT LET'S SING 2

Page 15: "Are There Books in the Bathtub?"

This chant drills the question-and-answer pattern *Are there books in the bathtub? Yes, there are. No, there aren't.*

LET'S GO PICTURE DICTIONARY

Use pages 14–15, Prepositions, to supplement the lesson and increase challenge.

1. Review familiar words on pages 14–15, and point out new words you wish to teach.

2. Practice the words with the question-and-answer pattern *Is there a stove next to the sink? Yes, there is. No, there isn't.*

Let's Build

Topic: Using prepositions to describe the location of things in a house

Lesson objectives: Students learn how to combine two prepositions to describe an object's location.

Review grammar: *Where are the (books)? They're (under the bed). There's a (lamp) (next to) (the bed). There are (lamps) (in front of) (the table). There's a (telephone) (on the table) (next to the sofa). There are (books) (in the bags) (on the bed).*

Review vocabulary: prepositions, furniture, toys, classroom objects

Materials: Teacher and Student Cards 5–13, 25–39, 63–72, and 16 from Level 1, CD 1 Tracks 68–71, contraction cards (*They're, There's, It's*)

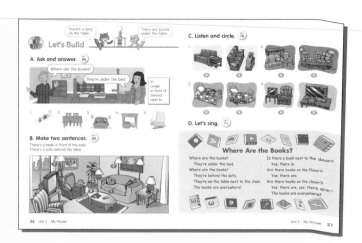

WARM UP AND REVIEW

Choose one of the following:

1. Picture Game practices prepositions. Make a list of six prepositions. Divide the class into teams. Whisper the first preposition to S1 from each team. S1s race back to their team and try to get their teammates to say the same preposition by drawing pictures or arranging objects—no speaking. S2 races up to the teacher and whispers his or her team's guess to the teacher. If correct, the team moves on to the next preposition. The first team to guess all six correctly in order wins.

2. Where Is It? practices using *there is, there are,* prepositions, and vocabulary. Say a sentence that uses two prepositions to describe the location of classroom objects (from Level 1 or Level 2). T: *There's a pencil in the book on the bag.* Students manipulate objects to match the sentence. To make this more challenging, divide the class into small groups. Have one student say a sentence and the other students manipulate the objects.

PRESENT THE LANGUAGE

BOOKS CLOSED

Introduce the question-and-answer pattern.

1. Show two books and Teacher Card 63 (*bed*). Put the books under the bed card. Model the question *Where are the books?* Have students repeat several times.

2. Still showing the books and card, ask *Where are the books?* Model the answer *They're under the bed.* Have students repeat several times.

3. Use other cards or actual items. Put them in different positions and have volunteers take turns asking the question and answering. S1: *Where are the pencils?* S2: *They're in the bag.*

4. Divide the class into pairs. Have students take turns putting classroom objects in different positions and then asking and answering questions.

BOOKS OPEN

A. Ask and answer.

1. Have students look at the pictures on page 26 and describe what they see. Encourage them to guess what language they will hear.

2. Play Track 68. Have students listen and point to the words.

 CD 1 Track 68

Where are the books?
They're under the bed.

1. Where are the balls?
   They're in the bathtub.
2. Where are the chairs?
   They're behind the table.
3. Where are the lamps?
   They're next to the sofa.
4. Where are the book bags?
   They're under the table.
5. Where are the pencils?
   They're in front of the telephone.

3. Play the audio again. Have students repeat after each sentence.

4. Divide the class into pairs. Have students take turns asking and answering questions about the pictures. Ask several students for their answers.

> **Grammar Tip:** Explain that *they* is a substitute for a plural noun. On the board, write *The pencils are on the desk.* Cross out *The pencils* and write *They* above it. Model the two sentences and have students repeat. Continue with several more sentences.

B. Make two sentences.

1. Have students look at the picture on page 26 and describe what they see. Encourage them to guess what language they will hear.

2. Show Teacher Card 65 and 16 from Level 1 (*sofa* and *table*). Have a volunteer come to the front of the class, and give him or her the cards. Say the first sentence again and have him or her position the cards to match the sentence.

3. Say the second sentence and ask the volunteer if the cards should be in a different position.

4. Divide the class into pairs. Have students use classroom objects to make two sentences that have the same meaning: *There's an eraser next to the pen. There's a pen next to the eraser.*

5. Play Track 69. Have students listen and point to the pictures.

 CD 1 Track 69

There's a table in front of the sofa.
There's a sofa behind the table.

1. *There's a table in front of the sofa. There's a sofa behind the table.*
2. *There are lamps behind the sofa. There's a sofa in front of the lamps.*
3. *There are tables next to the sofa. There's a sofa next to the tables.*
4. *There's a telephone in front of the lamp. There's a lamp behind the telephone.*
5. *There's a TV on the table. There's a table under the TV.*
6. *There's a chair next to the TV. There's a TV next to the chair.*
7. *There's a lamp behind the chair. There's a chair in front of the lamp.*
8. *There's a book on the table. There's a table under the book.*

6. Play the audio again. Have students repeat after each sentence.

7. Divide the class into pairs. Have students describe the pictures to each other. Have them take turns making two sentences about the objects in the picture. Ask several students for their answers.

C. Listen and circle.

1. Have students look at the first picture and describe it. Then play the first sentence of Track 70 and trace the circle.

2. Play the rest of the audio and have students circle the correct pictures. Play the audio at least twice so that students can check their answers.

 CD 1 Track 70

1. *Where's the telephone? It's on the table next to the sofa.*
2. *Where are the chairs? They're behind the table next to the lamps.*
3. *Where are the books? They're in the book bag on the bed.*
4. *Where's the TV? It's on the table behind the telephone.*

D. Let's sing.

1. Have students look at the pictures and describe what they see.

2. Play Track 71 and have students listen.

 CD 1 Track 71

Where Are the Books?

Where are the books?
    They're under the bed.
Where are the books?
They're behind the sofa.
    They're on the table next to the chair.
    The books are everywhere!

Is there a book next to the door?
    Yes, there is.
Are there books on the floor?
    Yes, there are.
Are there books on the chair?
    Yes, there are, yes, there are—
    The books are everywhere!

3. Play the audio again and have students sing along.

GAMES AND ACTIVITIES

1. **Where Are They?** practices prepositions. Arrange three objects and have students make a sentence using two prepositions to describe the arrangement. Write the sentences on the board. When students suggest sentences using different prepositions, or order of prepositions, help them to decide if the meaning is different or the same. For example: *The ball is on the bag next to the book* and *The book is next to the bag under the ball* describe the same arrangement even though they use different prepositions.

2. **Screens Activity** practices using prepositions spontaneously. Divide the class into two groups and select one student to act as go-between (for large classes, you might have several groups and go-betweens). On opposite sides of the classroom, provide identical sets of objects (classroom objects, toy furniture, etc.). The object sets should be behind a screen of some sort (behind books, or boxes—not visible to the other group). Group A decides on an arrangement. Then, Group A tells the go-between how to arrange the objects. The go-between tells Group B. Group B tries to put their objects in the same position as Group A. Group B can ask the go-between clarifying questions, and the go-between can move between groups. But the go-between never sees either arrangement until the end. After students have finished (set a time limit if desired), allow them to compare arrangements and see where communication broke down (if it did).

Let's Build

3. Make Sentences gives students practice in writing and saying longer sentences. Write pairs of preposition sentences (similar to the lesson model) on the board and have students combine them. Alternately, give students a handout with the sentences and have them write the combined sentence.

EXTRA PRACTICE

WORKBOOK pages 26–27

Assign for homework or do in class. For instructions and Answer Key, see Teacher's Book page 166.

SKILLS BOOK pages 26–27

Assign for homework or do in class. For instructions and Answer Key, see Teacher's Book page 149.

COMPONENTS LINK

CD-ROM 2

For extra fun, students can play Unit 3, Game 4 on a computer at school or at home. Students answer *Yes/No* questions to build a personalized picture of their own bedroom. This activity reinforces listening, prepositions, and the Let's Learn vocabulary and grammar patterns.

LET'S GO TESTS AND QUIZZES

Lesson Quiz: Explain and administer the reproducible Unit 3 Let's Build quiz from *Let's Go Tests and Quizzes*, page 19. Instructions and Answer Key are also in *Let's Go Tests and Quizzes*.

Unit Test: Explain and administer the reproducible Unit 3 Test from *Let's Go Tests and Quizzes*, page 48. Instructions and Answer Key are also in *Let's Go Tests and Quizzes*.

LET'S GO READER

Now that students have completed Unit 3, they are ready to read "I Don't Know." See Teacher's Book page 20 for suggestions on how to present *Readers* and incorporate them into your lesson plans.

LET'S CHANT LET'S SING 2

Page 14: "There's a Lamp on the Big Blue Table"

This chant practices adjectives and the sentence pattern *There's a lamp on the table*.

Unit 4 Things To Eat

Let's Start

Topic: Food

Lesson objectives: Students learn how to accept and refuse food politely.

New grammar: *Yes, please. No, thank you. I do, too. Can he/she (type)?*

Review grammar: *Do you want (spaghetti)? I like (spaghetti).*

New language: *type, wink, do a cartwheel, play Ping-Pong*

Materials: Teacher and Student Cards 81–92, cards from Level 1 Unit 7, CD 1 Tracks 72–77, puppets (optional), contraction cards (*That's, What's, can't*)

WARM UP AND REVIEW

Choose one of the following:

1. Interview (p. 24) gives students the opportunity to use extended greeting language spontaneously. Divide the class into pairs. Have students pretend to be someone famous. Have them take turns interviewing each other by saying a greeting and then asking name, age, address, and telephone number:

S1: *Hello, I'm (Bill Smith).*
S2: *Hi, I'm (Tom Johnson).*
S1: *How are you today?*
S2: *I'm pretty good. How about you?*
etc.

2. Team Race reviews verb phrases. Review verb phrases with Teacher Cards 59–62. Place Teacher Cards 59–62 on the chalk rail. Divide the class into teams. Students ask in unison *What can you do?* The teacher answers *I can (do a magic trick).* The first student in each line races to the rail to touch the card. The student who touches the card first and correctly says it wins a team point.

PRESENT THE DIALOGUE

📕 BOOKS CLOSED

Present the dialogue.

1. Introduce the dialogue.

a. Use puppets or student volunteers to introduce the dialogue. Have students identify words they hear.

Puppet A: *What's for lunch, Mom?*
Puppet B: *Spaghetti.*
Puppet A: *Mmm. That's good. I like spaghetti.*
Puppet C: *I do, too.*

b. Divide the class into three groups and practice the first part of the dialogue using gestures.

c. Play **What's for Dinner?** Use food cards from the unit and also from Level 1 Unit 7. Put the cards facedown on the table. Divide the class into pairs. S1 asks *What's for dinner?* S2 picks up a card and answers *(Spaghetti).* Then S2 says *I like (spaghetti)* and S1 responds *That's good. I like (spaghetti), too.*

> **Cultural Tip:** In the United States, *mom* is an informal word for *mother.*

> **Pronunciation Tip:** Make sure students are biting their tongue lightly when they say *that's.*

d. Introduce the rest of the dialogue with puppets or student volunteers.

Puppet B: *Do you want spaghetti?*
Puppet A: *Yes, please.*
Puppet C: *No, thank you.*

e. Do a quick drill with *Yes, please* and *No, thank you.* Model the responses with gestures. Use pictures of food items that children know. Show a picture and ask *Do you want (an apple)?* Have a volunteer answer using gestures. Move quickly around the class using different food items.

f. Divide the class into two groups and combine the entire dialogue. Reverse roles.

📖 BOOKS OPEN

A. Let's talk.

Students learn how to ask for and refuse food.

1. Listen to the dialogue.

a. Have students look at the scene on page 28 and describe what they see.

b. Play Track 72. Have students listen to the dialogue and point to the speech bubbles. Have them identify words they hear. Show Teacher Card 80 to make the meaning of *spaghetti* clear.

 CD 1 Track 72

Kate: *What's for lunch, Mom?*
Kate's mom: *Spaghetti.*
Kate: *Mmm. That's good. I like spaghetti.*
Andy: *I do, too.*
Kate's mom: *Do you want spaghetti?*
Andy: *Yes, please.*
Kate's sister: *No, thank you!*

c. Play the dialogue again and have students repeat each line after the characters.

2. Practice the pattern.

Write the pattern on the board, or direct students' attention to their books. Play Track 73. Point to the words as students listen to the dialogue. Then have students repeat after the audio.

 CD 1 Track 73

Do you want spaghetti?
    Yes, please.
    No, thank you.

3. Practice the dialogue.

a. Ask the question from the dialogue and have students answer. Repeat for the other question. For greater challenge, say one of the answers and have students ask the question.

b. Use a **Chain Drill** (p. 21) or **Step Away Lines** (p. 26) to practice the dialogue.

c. Have students practice the full dialogue in groups of four. Be sure to repeat the dialogue at least four times so that students can practice all the parts.

B. Let's sing.

"The Spaghetti Song" reinforces the language from the dialogue using rhythm and song.

1. Play and listen.

Play Track 74. Have students listen and identify the words they recognize from Let's Talk.

 CD 1 Track 74

The Spaghetti Song

Do you like spaghetti?
    Yes, I do.
        I do, too.
        I do, too.
Do you like spaghetti?
    Yes, I do.
I like spaghetti, too!

Do you want spaghetti?
    Yes, I do.
        I do, too.
        I do, too.
Do you want spaghetti?
    Yes, I do.
I want spaghetti, too!

2. Practice the rhythm.

a. Introduce the song rhythmically. Have students clap to keep the beat as you model the song line by line. Have students repeat after you.

b. Play the song again. Encourage students to sing along.

3. Do the song activity.

Play the song again. This time have half of the class sing one part, and half sing the second part. Add gestures to go with the song lyrics.

4. Read the lyrics.

Have students look at the song pictures and lyrics. Ask students to point to and read words they recognize.

5. Work in groups.

Have students work in groups to create an original verse with new food vocabulary (e.g., *hamburger*, *banana*). Either provide the vocabulary or use an English picture dictionary. Then, sing the song again with the new verses.

BOOKS CLOSED

Present the verb phrases.

1. Introduce the verb phrases.

a. Say *type* with action, and repeat the action several times. Have students repeat several times with action before going on to the next phrase. Repeat with the other phrases.

b. To check understanding, say the words in random order and have students do the appropriate action.

c. Show students Teacher Cards 81–84. Have them both say the word and do the action.

d. Divide the class into two groups. Have the groups take turns saying the commands and doing the actions. Use Teacher Cards to cue the command group.

2. Introduce *Can he/she (type)?*

a. Do a quick drill of *he/she*. Point to a boy and say *he*. Point to a girl and say *she*. Point to other students and have students say *he* or *she*. Pick up speed until students are correctly indicating gender spontaneously.

b. Have the boys stand up. Have them say the action and do the gesture. Have the girls point to a boy and ask the question *Can he (type)?* Repeat with the other verbs. Repeat the entire procedure with the girls standing up and the boys asking the question *Can she (type)?*

c. Have pairs take turns asking the question as they point to a male or female student in the class. Have both students point and do the action together when they ask the question.

d. Have a boy stand up and do the gesture for *type*. Ask *Can he type?* Elicit *Yes, he can.* Have the same boy shrug his shoulders and ask the question again. Elicit *No, he can't.* Repeat with a girl. Continue with the other verbs.

e. Have pairs take turns asking *Can (he) (type)?* and answering. Students should do the gestures together.

> **Pronunciation Tip:** Model the /t/ sound at the end of *can't*. Have students practice saying *can* and *can't*.

 BOOKS OPEN

C. Let's move.

Students learn useful everyday language by combining rhythm and actions.

1. Listen and point to the verbs.

a. Play Track 75. Have students listen and point to the appropriate pictures.

 CD 1 Track 75

1. *type*
2. *wink*
3. *do a cartwheel*
4. *play Ping-Pong*

b. Play the audio again. Students listen and repeat.

2. Practice the rhythm.

a. Write the pattern on the board, or direct students' attention to their books. Play Track 76. Point to the words as students listen to the audio.

 CD 1 Track 76

Can he type?
    Yes, he can.
Can she type?
    No, she can't.

Can he type?
    Yes, he can.
Can she type?
    No, she can't.

b. Play Track 76 again. Have students clap or tap to keep the rhythm and repeat the questions and answers with the audio.

c. Have students tap or clap the rhythm and practice saying the

questions and answers without the audio.

3. Practice the questions and answers.

Play Track 77. Have students listen to the questions and answers and point to the appropriate pictures.

 CD 1 Track 77

Can he type?
    Yes, he can.
Can she wink?
    No, she can't.
Can she do a cartwheel?
    Yes, she can.
Can he play Ping-Pong?
    No, he can't.

b. Play the audio again and have students repeat the questions and answers.

c. Divide the class into question-and-answer groups and play the audio again. Each group repeats either the question or answer. Repeat with groups switching roles.

d. Have students work in pairs and take turns asking and answering questions about the pictures.

GAMES AND ACTIVITIES

1. Find Your Partner (p. 24) gives students more practice with the Let's Move vocabulary and sentence pattern. Use multiple sets of Student Cards for Units 1–3 Let's Move phrases. Students try to find another student with the same card by announcing their own. S1: *She can do a magic trick.* If the partner has the same card, S2 says *She can do a magic trick, too!* If the S2 does not have the same card, S2 says *She can't do a magic trick.*

2. I Can, He Can, She Can practices the verb phrases and *can*. Put all the verb phrase cards students have learned in a pile on the table. Divide the class into two groups. S1 picks up a card and says *I can (run).* S2 points to S1 and says *He/She can run.* Then S2 picks up a card and the game continues with the next student using *he/she.*

3. Concentration (p. 22) practices recognizing and using the vocabulary. Divide the class into pairs. Use Student Cards for Units 1–3 Let's Move phrases. Have S1 identify the first card and then flip over the second card. S1 identifies that card and if the two cards match, S1 says *I can (wink)* and keeps the pair. S2 then chooses cards. Continue until all the cards are gone.

EXTRA PRACTICE

WORKBOOK **pages 28–29**

Assign for homework or do in class. For instructions and Answer Key, see Teacher's Book page 167.

SKILLS BOOK **pages 28–29**

Assign for homework or do in class. For instructions and Answer Key, see Teacher's Book page 149.

COMPONENTS LINK

CD-ROM 2

For extra fun, students can play Unit 4, Game 1 on a computer at school or at home. Students listen and answer *Yes/No* questions about the pictures to beat the clock. This activity reinforces listening, the Unit 3 and 4 verbs, and the Unit 4 grammar pattern *Can she/he ...? Yes, she/he can. No she/he can't.*

LET'S GO TESTS AND QUIZZES

Lesson Quiz: Explain and administer the reproducible Unit 4 Let's Start quiz from *Let's Go Tests and Quizzes*, page 20. Instructions and Answer Key are also in *Let's Go Tests and Quizzes.*

LET'S CHANT LET'S SING 2

Page 23: "Do You Want a Hot Dog?"

This chant practices the question-and-answer pattern *Do you want a hot dog? Yes, I do. No, I don't.*

Let's Learn

Topic: Food

Lesson objectives: Students learn to use *wants* with *he/she.*

New grammar: *He/She wants (an omelet). What does he/she want? He/She wants (an omelet). Does he/she want (a peach)?*

Review grammar: *Yes, he/she does. No, he/she doesn't.*

New language: *an omelet, a peach, a pear, a pancake, yogurt, cereal, tea, hot chocolate*

Review language: food words from Level 1

Materials: Teacher and Student Cards 85–92, CD 1 Tracks 78–84, contraction card *(doesn't)*

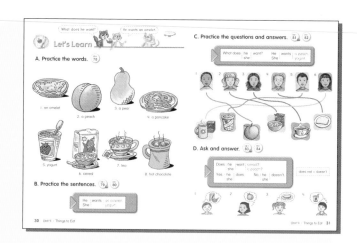

WARM UP AND REVIEW

Choose one of the following:

1. Sing the "Whose Bag Is That?" song and review the sentence patterns. Have students put their belongings in a pile on the table. Divide the class into groups or teams. One student from each group chooses an item. The rest of the groups try to be the first to identify the owner. S1: *Whose (comic book) is this?* G1: *It's (Miki's) (comic book).*

2. He/She Can practices verb phrases with *can.* Review the vocabulary from Let's Move Units 1–3, using Teacher Cards. Say the verb as you point to a student. That student acts out the verb. The rest of the class then says *(He) can (run).*

PRESENT THE LANGUAGE

📖 BOOKS CLOSED

Introduce the words.

1. Use Teacher Cards 85–88 to introduce *an omelet, a peach, a pear,* and *a pancake.* Show one Teacher Card at a time and say the word. Students repeat each word several times.

2. Conduct a quick drill of the words. Do not speak as you show the cards. Have students identify the

new foods plus all the previously learned foods. Gradually pick up speed as students get used to saying the words.

3. Use Teacher Cards 89–92 to introduce *yogurt, cereal, tea,* and *hot chocolate.* Help students to identify the difference between the two groups of foods.

4. Conduct a quick drill of all eight words. Be sure that students remember to include *a* and *an* when necessary.

> **Grammar Tip:** This lesson introduces the concept of count (a pear) and non-count (cereal) nouns. Students do not need to understand the grammar behind the concept at this level; the sentence and question-and-answer pattern works for both count and non-count food items. However, if they are curious, or you wish to explore the concept further, the general rule is as follows: Most count nouns take an *–s* ending in plural form. Most non-count nouns don't pluralize at all. When we need to count foods like cereal, we use counters such as *one box of cereal* or *three bowls of cereal.* Students will learn this grammar more explicitly in upper levels of *Let's Go.*

Introduce the sentence pattern.

1. Use Teacher Cards 85–92. Show each card and say the sentence *He wants (an omelet).* Have students repeat the sentence pattern for each word. Repeat the procedure with *She wants (yogurt).*

2. Contrast *want* and *wants* with the word card and *s.* Add *s* to *want* saying *want—s, want-s, wants,* as you bring the *s* closer and closer to the word, to help students see the difference as well as hear it.

3. Remind students of the article *an* (an omelet). Quickly drill *an apple, an orange, an eraser.* Then mix these with the other vocabulary.

4. Conduct a quick drill of the sentence pattern *(He) wants (cereal)* using Teacher Cards 89–92. Do not speak as you show the cards. Gradually pick up speed as students get used to saying the sentences.

📖 BOOKS OPEN

A. Practice the words.

1. Play Track 78. Have students listen and point to the words.

CD 1 Track 78

1. *an omelet*
2. *a peach*
3. *a pear*
4. *a pancake*
5. *yogurt*
6. *cereal*
7. *tea*
8. *hot chocolate*

2. Play the audio again and have students repeat the words.

B. Practice the sentences.

1. Listen to the sentences.

Write the patterns on the board, or direct students' attention to their books. Play Track 79. Point to the words as students listen to the audio. Then have students repeat after the audio.

 CD 1 Track 79

He wants an omelet.
She wants yogurt.

He wants an omelet.
She wants yogurt.

2. Practice the rhythm.

a. Play Track 79 again. This time, have students listen to the rhythm and intonation of the sentences.

b. Play the audio again. Have students tap or clap to match the rhythm of the audio. Have students listen to the spoken sentences to hear how the sentences match the rhythm, and then have them repeat the sentences along with the recorded rhythm.

c. Have students tap or clap the rhythm and practice saying the sentences without the audio.

3. Practice the sentences.

a. Play Track 80 and have students point to the vocabulary pictures as they listen.

 CD 1 Track 80

He wants an omelet.
She wants a peach.
He wants a pear.
She wants a pancake.
He wants yogurt.
She wants cereal.
He wants tea.
She wants hot chocolate.

b. Play Track 80 again and have students repeat the sentences.

c. Play **Slap** (p. 23) for additional reinforcement. Put the food and drink cards on the table faceup. The teacher or student says a word (*a pancake*). Have students find it, "slap" it, and say *(He) wants (a pancake)*.

📖 BOOKS CLOSED

Introduce the question forms.

1. Introduce the *Wh-* question-and-answer pattern.

a. Use student volunteers to present the question and answer *What does he want? He wants (a pancake)*. Allow a male student to select one of Teacher Cards 85–92. T: *What do you want?* S1: *I want (a pancake)*. Give the student the card selected. Model the question and answer: *What does he want? He wants (a pancake)*. Have students repeat the answer as you point to the card. Give the remaining Teacher Cards to male students and repeat the question *What does he want?* Have students answer each time.

b. Have students repeat the question *What does he want?* Practice the question several times.

c. Point to each student holding a Teacher Card and have students ask *What does he want?* The teacher answers each time.

d. Repeat steps a–c to teach the *Wh-* question-and-answer pattern with *she*.

e. Divide the class into two groups. Use Teacher Cards to cue the students. Groups take turns asking and answering questions. Use student volunteers or simple drawings of a boy and girl to cue *he* and *she*.

2. Introduce the *Yes/No* question-and-answer pattern.

a. Offer Teacher Card 86 *(a peach)* to a male student. T: *Do you want (a peach)?* Prompt the student to answer *Yes, I do* and give the card to the student, who holds it up so that the class can see. Model the question and answer *Does he want (a peach)? Yes, he does*. Have students repeat the answer as you point to the card. Give Teacher Cards to other male students and repeat the question *Does he want (a pancake)?* Have students answer *Yes, he does* each time.

b. Repeat with *No, he doesn't*. To indicate the negative answer, have students hold their Teacher Cards upside down.

c. Have students repeat the question *Does he want (a peach)?* several times. Substitute additional food vocabulary as students practice the question.

d. Point to each student holding a Teacher Card (some right-side up and others upside down) and have students ask *Does he want (a peach)?* The teacher answers each time.

e. Repeat steps a–d to teach the *Yes/No* question-and-answer pattern with *she*.

f. Divide the class into two groups. Use Teacher Cards to cue the students (right-side up to indicate *yes* and upside down to indicate *no*). Groups take turns asking and answering the questions. Use student volunteers or simple drawings of a boy and girl to cue *he* and *she*.

Let's Learn

C. Practice the questions and answers.

1. Listen to the *Wh-* question-and-answer pattern.

a. Present the pattern by writing it on the board or direct students' attention to it in the book.

b. Play Track 81. Point to the words as students listen. Have students repeat after the audio.

 CD 1 Track 81

What does he want?
*   He wants a peach.*
What does she want?
*   She wants yogurt.*

What does he want?
*   He wants a peach.*
What does she want?
*   She wants yogurt.*

2. Practice the rhythm.

a. Play Track 81 again. This time, have students listen to the rhythm and the intonation of the sentences with the audio.

b. Play the track again. Have students clap or tap to match the rhythm of the audio. Have students listen to the spoken question and answer to hear how it matches the rhythm, and then have them repeat the pattern along with the recorded rhythm.

c. Have students tap or clap the rhythm and practice saying the question and answer without the audio.

3. Practice the *Wh-* question-and-answer pattern.

a. Have students look at page 31 and describe things they see. Have them trace the lines from the boy or girl to the food item with their finger.

b. Play Track 82. Have students listen and point to the appropriate pictures.

 CD 1 Track 82

1. What does he want?
*   He wants a peach.*
2. What does she want?
*   She wants cereal.*
3. What does she want?
*   She wants tea.*
4. What does he want?
*   He wants an omelet.*
5. What does he want?
*   He wants yogurt.*
6. What does she want?
*   She wants hot chocolate.*

c. Play the audio again. Have students repeat the questions and answers.

d. Divide the class into question-and-answer groups and play the audio track again. Each group repeats either the question or the answer. Repeat, with groups switching roles.

e. Divide the class into pairs. Have students take turns asking and answering questions about the pictures and vocabulary.

D. Ask and answer.

1. Listen to the *Yes/No* question-and-answer pattern.

a. Present the pattern by writing it on the board or direct students' attention to the pattern in the book.

b. Play Track 83. Point to the words as students listen. Have students repeat after the audio.

 CD 1 Track 83

Does he want cereal?
*   Yes, he does.*
Does she want a peach?
*   No, she doesn't.*
does not = doesn't

Does she want cereal?
*   Yes, she does.*
Does he want a peach?
*   No, he doesn't.*

c. Write the explanation of the contraction on the board: *does not = doesn't*. See page 196 for how to use contraction cards to teach contractions. Have students practice saying both *No, he doesn't* and *No, he does not*.

2. Practice the rhythm.

a. Play Track 83 again and have students listen to the rhythm and intonation of the questions and answers.

b. Play the track again. Have students tap or clap to match the rhythm of the audio. Have students listen to the spoken questions and answers to hear how they match the rhythm, and then have them repeat the patterns along with the recorded rhythm.

c. Have students tap or clap the rhythm and practice saying the questions and answers without the audio.

3. Practice the *Yes/No* questions and answers.

a. Have students look at the pictures on page 31 and identify objects they recognize. Ask if each boy or girl looks happy or not.

b. Play Track 84. Have students listen and point to the appropriate pictures.

 CD 1 Track 84

1. Does he want cereal?
*   Yes, he does.*
2. Does she want a peach?
*   No, she doesn't.*
3. Does she want an omelet?
*   Yes, she does.*
4. Does he want yogurt?
*   No, he doesn't.*

b. Put students in pairs and have them ask and answer questions about the pictures.

GAMES AND ACTIVITIES

1. Matching Game practices the question and answer spontaneously. Make a cube with *He's* on three sides and *She's* on the other three sides. Have ready two sets of food cards. Put them under teacher-made *He* and *She* cards. Divide the class into teams. S1 throws the cube and asks *What does (he) want?* S2 picks up a card from the *He* pile and answers, *He wants (a peach). What about you?* S1 picks up a card from the *She* pile and says *I do, too* if it matches S2's card. If it doesn't, S1 says *I want (tea).*

2. Say It! (p. 24) practices saying vocabulary at random and spontaneously. Divide the class into several groups. Have a set of Student Cards 85–92 ready and put the cards in a line on the table. Say *Go!* One student starts at one end of the cards and says them in order: *I want a pancake, I want yogurt...* S2 starts immediately after S1, and S3 starts immediately after S2 so that everyone is moving along the cards at the same time. When all the students have finished, rearrange the cards and start again. To make this more challenging, add food Student Cards from Level 1.

3. Relay Race (p. 25) practices fluency. Divide the class into teams. Give the first player of each team a food card and a *He* or *She* card. When you say *Go!* each player asks *What does (he) want?* to the next player, who answers the question. Then that player takes the card and asks the next student. The last student must run to the first student and ask the question. When the first student finishes answering, the team sits down. The first team to sit down is the winner.

EXTRA PRACTICE

WORKBOOK pages 30–31

Assign for homework or do in class. For instructions and Answer Key, see Teacher's Book page 167.

SKILLS BOOK pages 30–31

Assign for homework or do in class. For instructions and Answer Key, see Teacher's Book page 150.

COMPONENTS LINK

LET'S GO TESTS AND QUIZZES

Lesson Quiz: Explain and administer the reproducible Unit 4 Let's Learn quiz from *Let's Go Tests and Quizzes*, page 21. Instructions and Answer Key are also in *Let's Go Tests and Quizzes*.

LET'S CHANT LET'S SING 2

Page 24: "I Want a Salad"

This chant practices the sentence pattern *I want a salad. She wants a salad. He wants a salad.*

Page 25: "Hungry Boy Chant"

This chant practices numbers and food vocabulary with the question-and-answer pattern *What does he want? He wants (one) egg.*

LET'S GO PICTURE DICTIONARY

Use pages 68–71, Fruits and Vegetables, to supplement the lesson and increase challenge.

1. Review familiar words on page 68–71, and point out new words you wish to teach.

2. Practice the words with the question-and-answer pattern *What does he/she want? He/She wants a peach. Does he/she want a peach? Yes, he/she does. No, he/she doesn't.*

Let's Learn More

Topic: Food

Lesson objectives: Students learn to talk about plural and uncountable foods with *like*.

New grammar: *He/She likes (pasta). What does he/she like? He/She likes (grapes). Does he/she like (stew)?*

Review grammar: *Yes, he/she does. No, he/she doesn't.*

New language: *grapes, pancakes, peaches, hamburgers, stew, cheese, pasta, steak*

Materials: Teacher and Student Cards 93–100, actual items, CD 1 Tracks 85–91, contraction card *(doesn't)*

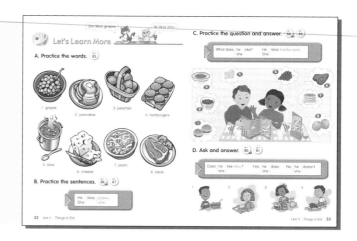

WARM UP AND REVIEW

Choose one of the following:

1. Guessing Game (p. 25) reviews vocabulary. Use Student Cards 85–92 (food). Divide the class into teams. Have one student from each team choose a Student Card. Teams ask questions to guess what a student from the opposing team has. The object is to guess the item by asking the fewest number of questions. The team that asks the fewest questions wins.

2. Use Student Cards 85–92 to practice *What does (she) want?* Divide the class into groups of three. S1 chooses a card. S2 points to S1 and asks S3 *What does (he) want?* S3 looks at the card and answers *(He) wants (a pancake).* Have students have at least three conversations so each student has a chance to say each part.

PRESENT THE LANGUAGE

📖 BOOKS CLOSED

Introduce the words.

1. Use Teacher Cards 93–96 or actual items to introduce *grapes, pancakes, peaches,* and *hamburgers.* Say the words and emphasize the final /s/, /ez/, or /z/ sound. Have students repeat each word three times before going on to the next word.

2. Conduct a quick drill of the food items after you introduce each food. Use the Teacher Cards. Don't speak as you show the cards. Have students identify the new food items plus all the previously learned foods.

3. Use Teacher Cards 97–100 to introduce *stew, cheese, pasta,* and *steak.* Help students to identify the difference between the two groups of foods (*-s* or *–es* plural vs. no change for singular or plural).

4. Conduct a quick drill of all eight words. Be sure that students remember to add an /s/, /ez/, or /z/ to the plural when necessary.

> **Pronunciation Tip:**
> Emphasize the plural ending /z/ after voiced consonants and vowels such as *hamburgers.*

> **Grammar Tip:** This lesson continues practice with count and non-count food vocabulary. The pattern works without understanding the grammar. However, if students are curious, help them explore the grammar further by producing the singular for each of the food items: *a grape, a pancake, a peach, a hamburger, stew, cheese, pasta,* and *steak.* Count nouns can be made plural; non-count nouns cannot.

Introduce the sentence pattern.

1. Use Teacher Cards 93–100. Show each card and say the sentence *He likes (grapes).* Have students repeat the sentence pattern several times. Repeat the process with *She likes (stew).*

2. Practice the pattern substituting all the words. Students should say the sentences at the same time as the teacher, not repeat after the teacher.

3. Conduct a quick drill. Show Teacher Cards 93–100 in random order and have students make sentences. Increase the speed of the drill until students are speaking at natural speed.

4. Bring a student volunteer to the front of the class. Give the student a food Teacher Card and ask the class *What does he/she like?* The class responds *He/She likes (grapes).* Continue with several more food items and volunteers.

📖 BOOKS OPEN

A. Practice the words.

1. Play Track 85. Have students listen and point to the words.

CD 1 Track 85

1. *grapes*
2. *pancakes*
3. *peaches*
4. *hamburgers*
5. *stew*
6. *cheese*
7. *pasta*
8. *steak*

2. Play the audio again and have students repeat the words.

B. Practice the sentences.

1. Listen to the sentence pattern.

Write the patterns on the board or direct students' attention to their books. Play Track 86. Point to the words as students listen to the audio. Then have students repeat after the audio.

 CD 1 Track 86

He likes grapes.
She likes stew.

He likes grapes.
She likes stew.

2. Practice the rhythm.

a. Play Track 86 again and have students listen to the rhythm and intonation of the sentences.

b. Play the track again. Have students tap or clap to match the rhythm of the audio. Have students listen to the spoken sentences to hear how they match the rhythm, and then have them repeat the sentences along with the recorded rhythm.

c. Have students tap or clap the rhythm and practice saying the sentences without the audio.

3. Practice the sentences.

a. Play Track 87 and have students point to the vocabulary pictures as they listen.

 CD 1 Track 87

She likes grapes.
She likes pancakes
She likes peaches.
He likes hamburgers.
He likes stew.
He likes cheese.
He likes pasta.
She likes steak.

b. Play Track 87 again and have students repeat the sentences.

c. Divide the class into pairs and have students practice the sentences with their books open to page 32. S1 says *She likes peaches.* S2 touches the appropriate picture and then says a different sentence.

📖 BOOKS CLOSED

Introduce the question form.

1. Introduce the *Wh-* question-and-answer pattern.

a. Use student volunteers to present the question and answer *What does he like? He likes (hamburgers).* Place Teacher Cards 93–100 on the board and ask a male student *What do you like?* Prompt the student to point to a card and answer *I like (hamburgers).* Point to the student and ask *What does he like?* Model the answer for students to repeat: *He likes (hamburgers).* Then have them repeat it in a series of three, several times. Repeat the procedure with a female student pointing to a card.

b. Have several male or female students select a card they like. Repeat the question and have students answer the question each time. Allow students to take the cards after their turn.

c. Have students repeat the questions *What does he like?* and *What does she like?* Practice the questions several times.

d. Point to each student once more and have students ask the question. The teacher answers each time.

e. Divide the class into two groups. Use Teacher Cards to cue the groups. Groups take turns asking *What does (she) like?* and answering *(She) likes (spaghetti).*

f. Have students get into groups of 3–4 and give one Student Card (93–100) to each student. S1 shows his or her card to the group saying *I like (hamburgers).* Students then ask each other questions like *What does (Megan) like?* or *What does she like?* and someone in the group responds *She likes (hamburgers).* Continue until all students have a turn.

> **Pronunciation Tip:** When asking *What does he/she like?* the stress on the words can change. Model the question first with the stress on *what* and *like*, and then with the stress on *he* or *she*. Have students guess why the question would be said different ways. (The first would be emphasizing what is liked, and the second would be emphasizing the person doing the liking.)

2. Introduce the *Yes/No* question-and-answer pattern.

a. Give Teacher Cards 93–100 to male and female students (or continue with the same students from step 1). Have some students hold their cards right-side up to indicate that they like the food pictured, and some students hold their cards upside down to indicate that they don't like the food pictured. Point to S1 and ask *Does (he) like (stew)?* Prompt students to answer *Yes, (he) does* or *No, (he) doesn't.* Point to the other students in turn and repeat the question. Students answer.

b. Have students repeat the question *Does (he) like (stew)?* several times. Substitute additional food vocabulary as students practice the question.

c. Point to each student holding a Teacher Card and have students ask *Does (she) like (grapes)?* The teacher answers each time.

d. Divide the class into two groups. Use Teacher Cards to cue the students (right-side up to indicate *yes* and upside down to indicate *no*). Groups take turns asking and answering the questions. Use volunteers or simple drawings of a boy and girl to cue *he* and *she*.

 BOOKS OPEN

C. Practice the question and answer.

1. Listen to the *Wh-* question-and-answer pattern.

a. Present the pattern by writing it on the board or direct students' attention to it in the book.

b. Play Track 88. Point to the words as students listen. Have students repeat after the audio.

 CD 1 Track 88

What does he like?
  He likes hamburgers.

What does he like?
  He likes hamburgers.

2. Practice the rhythm.

a. Play Track 88 again. Have students listen to the rhythm and intonation of the question and answer.

b. Play the audio again. Have students tap or clap to match the rhythm of the audio. Have students listen to the spoken question and answer to hear how it matches the rhythm, and then have them repeat the pattern along with the recorded rhythm.

c. Have students tap or clap the rhythm and practice the question and answer without the audio.

3. Practice the *Wh-* questions and answers.

a. Have students look at page 33 and describe the things they see.

b. Play Track 89. Have students listen and point to the pictures.

 CD 1 Track 89

1. What does he like?
  He likes hamburgers.
2. What does he like?
  He likes stew.
3. What does he like?
  He likes pasta.
4. What does he like?
  He likes cheese.
5. What does she like?
  She likes grapes.
6. What does she like?
  She likes steak.
7. What does she like?
  She likes pancakes.
8. What does she like?
  She likes peaches.

c. Have students listen to the audio again and repeat the questions and answers.

d. Divide the class into question-and-answer groups and play the audio again. Each group repeats either the question or answer. Repeat with groups switching roles.

e. Have students work in pairs and take turns asking and answering questions about the pictures.

D. Ask and answer.

1. Practice the *Yes/No* question-and-answer pattern.

a. Present the *Yes/No* question-and-answer pattern by writing it on the board or direct students' attention to the pattern in the book.

b. Play Track 90. Point to the words as students listen. Have students repeat after the audio.

 CD 1 Track 90

Does he like stew?
  Yes, he does.
Does she like stew?
  No, she doesn't.

Does he like stew?
  Yes, he does.
Does she like stew?
  No, she doesn't.

2. Practice the rhythm.

a. Play Track 90 again. This time, have students listen to the rhythm and intonation of the questions and answers.

b. Play the track again. Have students tap or clap to match the rhythm of the audio. Have students listen to the spoken questions and answers to hear how they match the rhythm, and then have them repeat the patterns along with the recorded rhythm.

c. Have students tap or clap the rhythm and practice saying the questions and answers without the audio.

3. Practice the *Yes/No* questions and answers.

a. Play Track 91. Have students listen and point to the appropriate pictures.

 CD 1 Track 91

1. Does he like stew?
  Yes, he does.
2. Does she like hamburgers?
  No, she doesn't.
3. Does she like hot chocolate?
  Yes, she does.
4. Does he like grapes?
  No, he doesn't.

b. Divide the class into pairs. Have students take turns asking and answering questions about the pictures on page 33.

GAMES AND ACTIVITIES

1. Telegram (p. 24) practices listening skills and forming sentences with *like*. Have students form rows. Give the first student a card in an envelope. S1 looks at the card and places it back in the envelope. Then S1 hands the envelope to S2 and whispers *(She) likes (peaches)*. S2 does not look at the card. He/She passes the envelope to S3 and whispers *(She) likes (peaches)*. Continue to the end of the row. The last student says the sentence aloud and then opens the envelope to see if the sentence matches the picture and if they said the same exact sentence as S1.

2. Draw It practices food vocabulary. Use Teacher Cards for food from Level 1 and Level 2. Divide the class into teams and draw a line down the center of the board. Have one student from each group choose a different card but not show it to anyone. Those students draw a picture of the food on their card while their team tries to guess what it is. The first team to guess correctly wins a point.

3. Walk and Talk (p. 26) practices the question *What does he/she like?* Have 4–5 students sit in various places around the classroom. Give each of them 2–3 food cards. Have them hold at least one of them upside down to indicate *doesn't like.* The other students walk around in pairs. Each pair must stop by one of the seated students and take turns asking each other *What does he/she like?* Continue until pairs have talked about at least two students. Then have other students sit.

4. Back-to-Back (p. 26) practices listening comprehension and speaking clearly. Use Student Cards 85–100 (singular and plural food). Divide the class into pairs. Give each student in the pair 2–3 cards. Have S1 say one of the cards once and have S2 draw it, making sure to draw two items if it's plural. Have pairs switch roles. To make this more challenging, play to a time limit and see which pair has the most correct drawings within the time limit.

EXTRA PRACTICE

WORKBOOK pages 32–33

Assign for homework or do in class. For instructions and Answer Key, see Teacher's Book page 167.

SKILLS BOOK pages 32–33

Assign for homework or do in class. For instructions and Answer Key, see Teacher's Book page 150.

REPRODUCIBLE WORKSHEET, Teacher's Book page 180

Bingo: Want and Like provides further fun and practice with food vocabulary. For instructions, see page 192.

COMPONENTS LINK

CD-ROM 2

For extra fun, students can play Unit 4, Game 2 on a computer at school or at home. In this **Concentration** game, students try to find picture-word pairs. This activity reinforces reading, listening, and the Let's Learn and Let's Learn More vocabulary

For extra fun, students can play Unit 4, Game 3 on a computer at school or at home. Students follow prompts and choose the correct objects as they pass by. This activity reinforces listening, the Let's Learn and Let's Learn More vocabulary, and the Let's Learn grammar pattern *What does she/he want? She/He wants (a/an)…*

LET'S GO TESTS AND QUIZZES

Lesson Quiz: Explain and administer the reproducible Unit 4 Let's Learn More quiz from *Let's Go Tests and Quizzes*, page 22. Instructions and Answer Key are also in *Let's Go Tests and Quizzes*.

LET'S CHANT LET'S SING 2

Page 26: "Does He Like Cookies?"

This chant practices food vocabulary with the question-and-answer pattern *Does he like cookies? Yes, he does. No, he doesn't.*

LET'S GO PICTURE DICTIONARY

Use pages 72–77, Meats and Fish, More Food, and Desserts, Snacks and Drinks to supplement the lesson and increase challenge.

1. Review familiar words on pages 72–77, and point out new words you wish to teach.

2. Practice the words with the question-and-answer patterns *What does he/she like? He/She likes ice cream. Does he/she like steak? Yes, he/she does. No, he/she doesn't.*

Let's Build

Topic: Food

Lesson objectives: Students use *like* and *want* with *he/she*.

New grammar: *Does (he) want (a pear) or (an orange)?*

Review grammar: *How many (peaches) does (she) want? (She) wants (two) (peaches).*

Review language: food, numbers

Materials: Teacher and Student Cards 85–100 and 217 (Level 1), CD 1 Tracks 92–94, beanbag, contraction card *(doesn't)*

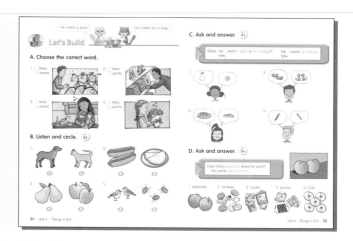

WARM UP AND REVIEW

1. Command Chain (p. 26) reviews verb phrases. Quickly show Teacher Cards 80–83 and have students say and do the actions. Then have students get into group of 8–10 students and do the command chain.

2. Concentration (p. 22) reviews plurals and practices talking about food. Play **Concentration** with double sets of Students Cards 85–100 (singular and plural food).

PRESENT THE LANGUAGE

BOOKS CLOSED

Introduce the sentence patterns.

Show Teacher Cards 85–100 (food). Have a male student come to the front of the class. Have him choose a card and show it to the class. Point to the student and say *He likes (grapes)*. Have students repeat. Now have the student rub his stomach as if he were hungry and look at the card. Say *He wants (grapes)*. Repeat the procedure with a female student.

BOOKS OPEN

A. Choose the correct word.

1. Have students look at the pictures on page 34 and describe what they see.

2. Have students check the correct word for each picture.

B. Listen and circle.

1. Have students look at the picture and describe what they see. Then play the first pair of sentences on Track 92 and circle the correct letter.

 CD 1 Track 92

1. *He doesn't want a dog.*
   He wants a cat.
2. *She doesn't want two hot dogs.*
   She wants two omelets.
3. *She doesn't like peaches.*
   She likes pears.
4. *She doesn't like spiders.*
   She likes birds.

2. Play the rest of the audio. Play the audio at least twice so that students can check their answers.

C. Ask and answer.

1. Make an *or* card. Put it between Teacher Cards 87 and 216 (Level 1) *(pear* and *orange)* on the board.

2. Ask S1 *What do you want?* S1 answers *I want (a pear)*.

3. Ask the class as you point to the cards *Does (Tom) want a pear or an orange?* Students answer *(He) wants (a pear)*.

4. Do this several times with other students and food words. Have students continue in groups of 3–4.

5. Have students look at the pictures on page 35 and describe what they see.

6. Play Track 93. Have students listen and point to the appropriate pictures. Play the track again and have students repeat after the audio.

 CD 1 Track 93

Does he want a pear or an orange?
He wants an orange.

1. *Does she want a pear or an orange?*
   She wants an orange.
2. *Does he want frogs or dogs?*
   He wants frogs.
3. *Does she want spaghetti or steak?*
   She wants steak.
4. *Does he want a blue pencil or a green pencil?*
   He wants a green pencil.

7. Have pairs look at each picture and take turns asking and answering questions.

> **Pronunciation Tip:** When asking questions that offer a choice, the intonation goes up on the first item in the question and goes down on the last item.
>
> *Does he want a pear or an orange?*

D. Ask and answer.

1. Review numbers and *How many (flowers) are there? There are (ten) flowers.*

2. Use Teacher Cards for numbers and ask *How many oranges do you want?* S1: *I want four oranges.* T: *Here you are.* S1: *Thank you.* T: *You're welcome.*

3. Play Track 94. Have students listen and point to the words and then the appropriate pictures. Play the track again and have students repeat after the audio.

 CD 1 Track 94

How many peaches does he want? He wants two peaches.

1. *How many peaches does she want?*
    She wants two peaches.
2. *How many cookies does he want?*
    He wants eight cookies.
3. *How many books does she want?*
    She wants four books.
4. *How many games does he want?*
    He wants three games.
5. *How many CDs does she want?*
    She wants five CDs.

4. Divide the class into pairs. Have students look at the pictures on page 35 and take turns asking and answering questions.

GAMES AND ACTIVITIES

1. **Beanbag Circle** (p. 24) reviews the question-and-answer pattern *What do you want/like?* Divide the class into groups. Have each group make a circle and give a beanbag to each group. S1 throws it to another student (S2) in the circle and asks *What do you want/like?* S2 answers *I want/like (peaches)* and throws it to S3 who says the name of the student: *(Miki) wants/likes (peaches).* Then S3 starts the question again.

2. **Interview** (p. 24) gives students the opportunity to use Unit 4 spontaneously. Make a class or

group chart and give one to each student. Students walk around the room asking each other what they like/want. They write down the students' names and their answers. Then in pairs, they work with each other asking what each student wants/likes: *What does Ken want? He wants a cookie.*

3. **Find the Card Race** Put food cards on the chalk rail. Students line up in teams. The last student of the team (S1) whispers what he or she likes or wants to the student in front of him or her (S2): *I like (stew).* S2 whispers to S3: *(Ken) likes (stew)* and so on up the line to the first student, who runs to the chalkboard and takes the *(stew)* card. Then he or she goes to the end of the line and starts the game again. If a card has been taken by another team, they must start again with a new sentence. The team with the most cards wins.

EXTRA PRACTICE

WORKBOOK **pages 34–35**

Assign for homework or do in class. For instructions and Answer Key, see Teacher's Book page 168.

SKILLS BOOK **pages 34–35**

Assign for homework or do in class. For instructions and Answer Key, see Teacher's Book page 151.

REPRODUCIBLE WORKSHEET, **Teacher's Book page 181**

Write, Ask, and Draw provides further fun and practice with food vocabulary. For instructions, see page 192.

COMPONENTS LINK

CD-ROM 2

For extra fun, students can play Unit 4, Game 4 on a computer at school or at home. Students look at the picture and memorize the objects, and then answer *Yes/No* questions. This activity reinforces listening, the Let's Learn and Let's Learn More vocabulary, and the Let's Build grammar pattern *What does he like? Does he want a/an…? Yes, he does. No, he doesn't.*

LET'S GO READER

Now that students have completed Unit 4, they are ready to read "You Are What You Eat." See Teacher's Book page 20 for suggestions on how to present *Readers* and incorporate them into your lesson plans.

LET'S GO TESTS AND QUIZZES

Lesson Quiz: Explain and administer the reproducible Unit 4 Let's Build quiz from *Let's Go Tests and Quizzes*, page 23. Instructions and Answer Key are also in *Let's Go Tests and Quizzes.*

Unit Test: Explain and administer the reproducible Unit 4 Test from *Let's Go Tests and Quizzes*, page 50. Instructions and Answer Key are also in *Let's Go Tests and Quizzes.*

Units 3–4 Listen and Review
Let's Learn About Months

Topic: Units 3–4 review; months

Lesson objectives: Students demonstrate comprehension of language and vocabulary taught in Units 3 and 4. Students also learn to identify the twelve months of the year.

Review grammar: *Where do you live? What's your (address)? What can he do? He can (play baseball). Where's the (bed)? It's in the (bedroom). There's a (bed) in the (bedroom). Is there a (refrigerator) in the (bedroom)? Yes, there is. No, there isn't. Are there (lamps) behind the (bed)? Yes, there are. No, there aren't. Where are the (books)? Do you want (spaghetti)? Can he (type)? Yes, he can. No, he can't. What does (Scott) want? He wants (an omelet). Does he want (cereal)? He likes (grapes). next to, behind, in front of*

Review language: food, furniture, abilities

New language: *January, February, March, April, May, June, July, August, September, October, November, December*

Materials: Teacher and Student Cards 59–112, CD 1 Tracks 95–97, contraction cards *(can't, There's, doesn't, aren't, It's)*

PART ONE: UNITS 3-4 LISTEN AND REVIEW

Review Activities

1. Let's talk/Let's sing.

Find the conversation. Give each group of students copies of the conversations for Units 3 and 4, cut into strips and mixed together. Students read the lines from the dialogues and separate them into two conversations, one about personal information and one about lunch. Then, have students take the strips from each conversation and try to arrange them in order. Finally, have students practice both conversations.

2. Let's move.

a. Find Your Partner (p. 24). Use enough sets of Student Cards 59–62 and 80–83 (verb phrases from Units 3 and 4) that every student will be able to find at least one match. Include verb phrases from Units 1 and 2 if desired. Students circulate, looking for another student who has the same verb card. They <u>can</u> do the ability shown on their student card. They <u>can't</u> do

any of the other abilities. S1 (has *use chopsticks* card): *I can use chopsticks.* S2 (has *ice-skate* card): *I can't use chopsticks. I can ice-skate.*

b. After finishing **Find Your Partner**, test students' memories by asking questions. For example, point to S1 and ask *What can he do?* Ss: *He can use chopsticks.* Point to S2 and ask *Can she ice-skate?* Ss: *Yes, she can.*

c. Make new verb phrases. Write the base verbs from Units 3 and 4 Let's Move on the board: *play, use,* and *do.* Have students work in groups to think of additional verb phrases using these base verbs (e.g., *play games, use a brush, do puzzles,* etc.) Write the new phrases on the board under each base verb. Then, have pairs or groups of students place teacher-made cards of base verbs facedown on a desk. Students turn over one card at a time and make a sentence using a new verb phrase.

3. Let's Learn/Let's Learn More

a. Use Teacher Cards for food and furniture vocabulary from Units 3 and 4. Hold up a card and ask students to tell you how to make

the object plural (e.g., *bed/beds, grape/grapes,* etc.).

b. Categories. Use Student Cards for food and furniture. Give each pair or group of students a set of Student Cards. Have students work together to separate the items into two categories as quickly as possible. For greater challenge, have students work with teacher-made word cards (without pictures), or include categories of vocabulary items from earlier units.

c. Listen and Move. Place the room cards in various locations around the classroom. Assign each student to "be" one of the furniture vocabulary items. Include duplicate pieces of furniture if necessary so that every student has one vocabulary item. Students arrange themselves according to teacher instructions. T: *There is a bed in the bedroom. There is a refrigerator in the kitchen. There's a lamp next to the bed.,* etc. Then, once all students are in place, have them answer questions about each room's arrangement. T: *Is there a chair in the bedroom?*

d. Student Interviews. In pairs, students ask and answer questions about wants and likes. The questions can be decided as a class (if the follow up will be a survey) or can be open based on Teacher Cards on the chalk rail for reference. After students have finished their questioning, have them report back to the class. S: *Amy likes salads and plums. She wants a dog.*

Introduce Listen and Review

📖 BOOKS CLOSED

1. On the board, set up a sample to resemble the activity on page 36 of the Student Book. Put three of the Teacher Cards 5–12 on the chalk rail. Draw letter *a* above the first card, letter *b* above the second, and letter *c* above the third. Have one student stand by the cards. Identify one of the cards. T: *It's a clock.* The student points to the correct card and circles the appropriate letter. Repeat as necessary until all the students understand the procedure.

2. Open your book to page 36. Show the page to the class. Have student identify the items. T: *What's this? Is this (a window)?* Have students identify the actions shown in numbers 1–6.

📖 BOOKS OPEN

A. Listen and number.

1. Play Track 95. Have students listen to the audio and number the correct pictures.

 CD 1 Track 95

1. *Where's the table?*
   It's next to the chair.
2. *Is there a table next to the chair?*
   Yes, there is.
3. *Is there a telephone in the living room?*
   No, there isn't.
   Is there a TV in the living room?
   Yes, there is. It's under the window.
4. *Are there lamps behind the sofa?*
   No, there aren't. There's one lamp. It's on the table, next to the chair.

2. Use the page for further review. Pair off students. Have partners ask each other questions about numbers 1–4 and say the commands in numbers 5–6.

B. Listen and circle.

1. Students open their books to page 36. Play Track 96. Have students listen and circle the correct picture.

 CD 1 Track 96

1. *What does he want?*
   He wants cereal.
2. *Does she want yogurt?*
   No, she doesn't. She wants hot chocolate.
3. *What does she like?*
   She likes pancakes.
4. *Does he like steak?*
   No, he doesn't. He likes hamburgers.
5. *What can she do?*
   She can ice-skate.
6. *Can he use chopsticks?*
   No, he can't.

2. Correct the test with students.

3. Use the page for further review. Pair off students. Have partners ask each other questions about numbers 1–4.

PART TWO: LET'S LEARN ABOUT THE MONTHS

📖 BOOKS CLOSED

1. Present the topic: Months

Hold up a calendar (or draw a simple calendar on the board) and ask students to tell you the names for the months in their native language. Next, ask if students know any of the English words for the months. Don't feel that you need to correct them at this point—the goal is to see what they already know about this topic.

2. Present the vocabulary.

a. Hold up a one-year calendar, or draw a simple 12-month calendar on the board (grid of 12 squares). Point to each month in turn, and say its name. Students repeat.

b. Point to the months, at random, on the calendar. Students say the appropriate name of the month.

3. Present the language pattern.

a. Point to *January,* or hold up a teacher-made word card, as you model the sentence. T: *It's January.* Students repeat. Do the same thing for each month.

b. Point to a month, or hold up a word card and model the question. T: *What month is it?* Ss: *It's January.* Have students answer for each month.

c. Ask students to repeat the question several times and correct pronunciation as needed. Have students ask the question for various months. Answer.

d. Put students into pairs or small groups, and have them practice asking and answering questions about months of the year. Have students use the calendar on the board for reference.

📖 BOOKS OPEN

4. Practice the vocabulary.

Students open their books to page 37.

a. Play the audio. Have students listen and point to the months as they listen.

CD 1 Track 97

What month is it?
    It's January.
1. *What month is it?*
    It's January.
2. *What month is it?*
    It's February.
3. *What month is it?*
    It's March.
4. *What month is it?*
    It's April.
5. *What month is it?*
    It's May.
6. *What month is it?*
    It's June.
7. *What month is it?*
    It's July.
8. *What month is it?*
    It's August.
9. *What month is it?*
    It's September.
10. *What month is it?*
    It's October.
11. *What month is it?*
    It's November.
12. *What month is it?*
    It's December.

   b. Play the audio again. Have students repeat after each word.

5. Practice the question and answer.

   a. Have students listen to the question and answer and point to the appropriate month.

   b. 1-2-3-Finished! (p. 24). In pairs, have students stand up and take turns asking and answering questions about the calendar. Each pair of students asks and answers three questions. The first pair to complete the task, say *Finished,* and sit down, wins.

GAMES AND ACTIVITIES

1. Give students more practice with months and review days of the week by **making a calendar** for the current year. Give students blank calendar forms. Have students write the names of the month and days of the week in the correct spaces at the top of the calendar, and number the squares appropriately. Allow students to decorate their calendars with illustrations, if desired.

2. Give students practice talking about the days of the week and weather by keeping a **class weather calendar**. Make a large calendar to display in your classroom. Label it with days of the week and dates. Each day, ask students *What day is it today?* and *How's the weather?* Have students take turns drawing a simple illustration for the day's weather in the appropriate square.

3. Reinforce the order of the days of the week with a **sequencing activity**. Divide the class into groups of seven, and give each student a word card with one day of the week written on it. At your signal, groups race to arrange themselves in the correct order (*Sunday* through *Saturday*). Once students are confident with this sequence, make the activity more challenging by changing the first day in the sequence (*Tuesday* through *Monday, Thursday* through *Wednesday,* etc.). For small classes, students can work together to order word cards in the correct sequence.

Do a similar sequencing activity using the months.

EXTRA PRACTICE

WORKBOOK **page 36**

Assign for homework or do in class. For instructions and Answer Key, see Teacher's Book page 168.

SKILLS BOOK **page 36**

Assign for homework or do in class. For instructions and Answer Key, see Teacher's Book page 15.

COMPONENTS LINK

CD-ROM 2

For extra fun, students can play the Review Units 3–4 game on a computer at school or at home. In this game, students spin the wheel and pick letters to spell the name of the month. This activity reinforces spelling and the Review Unit vocabulary.

LET'S GO TESTS AND QUIZZES

Units 3–4 Listen and Review Test: Explain and administer the reproducible Units 3–4 Listen and Review Test from *Let's Go Tests and Quizzes*, page 70. Instructions and Answer Key are also in *Let's Go Tests and Quizzes*.

Lesson Quiz: Explain and administer the reproducible Let's Learn About the Months quiz from *Let's Go Tests and Quizzes*, page 63. Instructions and Answer Key are also in *Let's Go Tests and Quizzes*.

Midterm Test: Explain and administer the reproducible Midterm Test from *Let's Go Tests and Quizzes*, page 78. This test covers material from Units 1–4, Let's Learn About Numbers 20–100, and Let's Learn About the Months. Instructions and Answer Key are also in *Let's Go Tests and Quizzes*.

LET'S CHANT LET'S SING 4

Page 17: "January, February, March"

This song practices vocabulary for months of the year.

Page 18: "January First"

This song practices ordinal numbers and vocabulary for months of the year.

LET'S GO PICTURE DICTIONARY

Use pages 4–5, Ordinals and Calendar, to supplement the lesson and increase challenge.

Review familiar words on page 4–5, and point out new words you wish to teach.

Unit 5 Occupations

Let's Start

Topic: Occupations; feelings; everyday activities

Lesson objectives: Students identify people they don't know, talk about how they feel, and discuss their daily activities.

New grammar: *What's the matter? I'm sick.*

Review grammar: *Who is he/she?*

New language: *Mr., teacher, nurse, wake up, get out of bed, make breakfast, get dressed, Get better soon!, maybe*

Review language: *Mrs., Miss*

Materials: Teacher and Student Cards 113–116, 126, CD 2 Tracks 2–7, puppets (optional), contraction cards (*Who's, she's, You're, don't, What's, I'm*), five labeled pictures of adults

WARM UP AND REVIEW

Choose one of the following:

1. Who? reviews asking who someone is. Have students form pairs. Stack duplicate sets of Level 1 Student Cards 106–112 (family members) facedown in front of each group. S1 picks up two cards and asks *Who's (he)?* S2 responds *(He's) my (father).*

2. Find Your Partner (p. 24) practices the question-and-answer pattern spontaneously. Use Level 1 Student Cards 106–112 (family members). Give each student a card and have them find their match. Students ask as they point to each other's card *Who's (she)?* They respond with *(She's) my (sister).*

PRESENT THE DIALOGUE

📖 BOOKS CLOSED

Present the dialogue.

1. Introduce the dialogue.

   a. Use puppets or student volunteers to introduce the dialogue. Have students identify words they already know.

   Puppet A: *What's the matter, John?*
   Puppet B: *I'm sick.*

Puppet A: *That's too bad. Maybe Mrs. Green can help you.*
Puppet B: *Who's she?*
Puppet A: *She's the new nurse.*
Puppet B: *Thanks for your help.*
Puppet A: *You're welcome. Get better soon!*

   b. Use three pictures of adults or student volunteers and label them with the names Mrs. Hill, Mr. Jones, and Mr. Lee. Point to Mrs. Hill and say *This is Mrs. Hill.* Have students repeat. Repeat with a picture of Mr. Jones and Mr. Lee. Then have the students identify Mrs. Hill, Mr. Jones and Mr. Lee by themselves.

   c. Point to yourself and then to a picture and say *I know Mrs. Hill. She's a mother.* Use gestures to help convey the meaning. Point to the class and then to the picture of Mrs. Hill and ask *Do you know (Mrs. Hill)?* Help students answer *Yes, I do. She's a mother.* Repeat with Mr. Jones.

   d. Show the picture of Mr. Lee and ask *Do you know Mr. Lee?* Help them answer *No, I don't.* Show Teacher Card 126 (*teacher*) and say *teacher.* Have students repeat three times. Then say *He's a teacher* and have students repeat. Continue the presentation with the question

Who's he? and have students respond *He's a teacher.*

> **Pronunciation Tip:** Make sure students are biting their tongues lightly when they say *thanks.*

> **Cultural Tip:** Married women are usually addressed as *Mrs.* and unmarried women as *Miss.* If you don't know if a woman is married or single, you can address her as *Ms.* Married and single men are addressed as *Mr.*

2. Introduce the dialogue question.

   a. Have students say *Who's she?* in a series of three, several times. Gradually pick up speed until they are able to say it at natural speed.

   b. Show pictures to introduce Mrs. Black and Mr. White. Then do a **Substitution Drill** (p. 21) with all the pictures. Point to a picture and ask *Do you know (Mrs. Black)?* Students answer *No, I don't. Who is she?* Answer *She's a teacher.* Repeat with Mr. White. For more practice have several volunteers point to the pictures and ask *Do you know (Mr. Black)?* The class responds.

c. Divide the class into two groups. Practice the question and answer. Group A: *Who's she?* Group B: *She's the new nurse.*

 BOOKS OPEN

A. Let's talk.

Students learn how to ask who someone is.

1. Listen to the dialogue

a. Have students look at the scene on page 38 and describe what they see.

b. Play Track 02. Have students listen to the dialogue and point to the speech bubbles. Have them identify the words they hear.

 CD 2 Track 02

Ms. Hill: *What's the matter, Scott?*
Scott: *I'm sick.*
Ms. Hill: *That's too bad.*
    Maybe Mrs. Green can help you.
Scott: *Who's she?*
Ms. Hill: *She's the new nurse.*
Scott: *Thanks for your help.*
Ms. Hill: *You're welcome. Get*
    better soon!

c. Play the dialogue again and have students repeat each line after the characters.

2. Practice the pattern.

a. Write the pattern on the board, or direct students' attention to their books. Play Track 03. Point to the words as students listen to the dialogue. Then have students repeat after the audio.

 CD 2 Track 03

Who's she?
    She's the new nurse.
Who is = Who's
She is = She's

b. Write the explanation of the contraction on the board: *She is = She's*. Follow the procedure on page 196 for how to teach contractions

with cards. Have the students practice saying both *She is the new nurse* and *She's the new nurse*. Point to the explanation on the board as they practice.

3. Practice the dialogue.

a. Ask one of the questions from the dialogue and have a volunteer answer. Repeat for the other question. Then ask the questions out of order and have volunteers answer. To make this more challenging, give one of the answers from the dialogue and have students ask the matching question.

b. Do **Conversation Lines** (p. 26) to practice the dialogue in pairs.

c. Have students practice the dialogue with several partners.

B. Let's sing.

"What's the Matter?" reinforces the language from the dialogue using rhythm and song.

1. Play and listen.

Play Track 04. Have students listen and identify the words they recognize from Let's Talk.

 CD 2 Track 04

What's the Matter?

What's the matter?
What's the matter?
What's the matter?
    I am sick.
What's the matter? Are you OK?
    I am sick today.
Oh, no!

What's the matter?
What's the matter?
What's the matter?
    I am hot.
What's the matter? Are you OK?
    I am hot today.
Oh, no!

What's the matter?
What's the matter?
What's the matter?
    I am cold.
What's the matter? Are you OK?
    I am cold today.
Oh, no!

What's the matter?
What's the matter?
What's the matter?
    I am tired.
What's the matter? Are you OK?
    I am tired today.
Oh, no!

What's the matter?
What's the matter?
What's the matter?
    I am sad.
What's the matter? Are you OK?
    I am sad today.
Oh, no!

2. Practice the rhythm.

a. Introduce the song rhythmically. Have students clap to keep the beat as you model the song line by line. Have students repeat after you.

b. Play the song again. Encourage students to sing along.

3. Do the song activity.

Play the song again. This time have half of the class sing one part and half sing the second part. Have students act out the second part. For example, have them hold their stomachs and look sick when singing *I am sick.*

4. Read the lyrics.

Have students look at the song pictures and lyrics. Ask students to point to and read words that they recognize.

5. Work in groups.

Have students work in groups to create an original verse by using a different feeling. Then, sing the song again with the new verses.

 BOOKS CLOSED

Present the verb phrases.

1. Introduce the verb phrases.

a. Say *wake up* with action, and repeat the action several times. Have students repeat several times with action before going on to the next phrase. Repeat with the other phrases.

b. To check understanding, say the phrases in random order and have students do the appropriate action.

c. Show students Teacher Cards 113–116. Have them both say the phrase and do the action.

d. Divide the class into two groups. Have the groups take turns saying the commands and doing the actions. Use Teacher Cards to cue the command group.

2. Introduce *I (wake up) every morning.*

a. Add *I* and *every morning* to each phrase and have students repeat the phrase and do the action.

b. Have pairs take turns saying a verb phrase with *every morning*. Have both students do the action together when they say the sentence.

 BOOKS OPEN

C. Let's move.
Students learn useful classroom language by combining rhythm and actions.

1. Listen and point to the verb phrases.

a. Play Track 05. Have students listen and point to the appropriate pictures.

 CD 2 Track 05

1. *wake up*
2. *get out of bed*
3. *make breakfast*
4. *get dressed*

b. Play the audio again. Students listen and repeat.

2. Practice the rhythm.

a. Play Track 06. Point to the words as the students listen.

 CD 2 Track 06

I wake up every morning.

I wake up every morning.

b. Play Track 06 again. Have students clap or tap to keep the rhythm and repeat after the audio.

c. Have students tap or clap the rhythm and practice saying the sentence without the audio.

3. Practice the sentences.

a. Play Track 07. Have student listen to the audio and point to the appropriate pictures.

 CD 2 Track 07

I wake up every morning.
I get out of bed every morning.
I make breakfast every morning.
I get dressed every morning.

b. Play the audio again and have students repeat the sentences.

c. Have students work in pairs and take turns pointing to pictures on page 39 and making sentences.

GAMES AND ACTIVITIES

1. Follow the Leader. Divide the class into small groups and have each group form a line. Designate the first student in each line the leader. Groups move around the room in their lines, following the actions of the leader (for example, get dressed, wake up, dance, sing, etc.). Play music while the students move around the classroom. When you pause the music, the first student moves to the end of the line and the next student becomes the leader.

2. Walk and Talk (p. 26) gives students practice in asking and answering questions spontaneously. Place pictures of adults around the room. Have students get into pairs and walk around the room asking and answering questions about the people in the pictures. S1: *Who's he?* S2: *He's Mr. White. He's a teacher.*

3. Rock, Paper, Scissors (p. 26) practices verb phrases. Divide the class into pairs. Have them play **Rock, Paper, Scissors.** However, tell them to change the words to *Every morning, every morning, 1, 2, 3!* to

give additional practice of the key words. The winner gives a command (*Wake up!*) and the loser must say *I wake up every morning* while doing the action. Have them play several rounds. To make this more challenging, include verb phrases from earlier lessons that can be used with the sentence pattern.

EXTRA PRACTICE

WORKBOOK **pages 38–39**

Assign for homework or do in class. For instructions and Answer Key, see Teacher's Book page 168.

SKILLS BOOK **pages 38–39**

Assign for homework or do in class. For instructions and Answer Key, see Teacher's Book page 152.

COMPONENTS LINK

LET'S GO TESTS AND QUIZZES

Lesson Quiz: Explain and administer the reproducible Unit 5 Let's Start quiz from *Let's Go Tests and Quizzes*, page 24. Instructions and Answer Key are also in *Let's Go Tests and Quizzes.*

LET'S CHANT LET'S SING 2

Page 8: "I'm Cold"

This chant reinforces the question-and-answer pattern *What's the matter? I'm cold.*

Page 9: "Hi, Jack. How Are You?"

This song recycles language from Unit 1 and practices vocabulary from the Let's Talk dialogue.

Let's Learn

Topic: Occupations

Lesson objectives: Students identify and ask about occupations with *he/she*.

New grammar: *She's Mrs. Wilson.*

Review grammar: *Who's he/she? He/She's a shopkeeper. Is he/she a farmer? Yes, he/she is. No, he/she isn't.*

New language: *a shopkeeper, a cook, a nurse, a farmer, a taxi driver, a train conductor, an office worker, a police officer, a student*

Review language: *a teacher*

Materials: Teacher and Student Cards 118–127, CD 2 Tracks 08–14, puppets (optional), contraction cards (*He's, She's, Who's, isn't*), magazine pictures

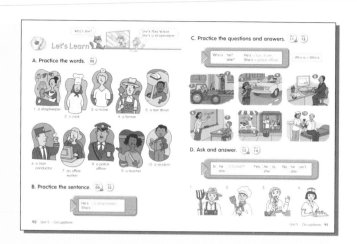

WARM UP AND REVIEW

Choose one of the following:

1. Conversation Lines (p. 26) reviews the dialogue from Let's Start. Divide the class into two parallel lines to practice the dialogue.

> Group A: *What's the matter, Scott?*
> Group B: *I'm sick.*
> Group A: *That's too bad.*
> Group A: *Maybe Mrs. Green can help you.*
> Group A: *Who's she?*
> Group B: *She's the new nurse.*
> Group A: *Thanks for your help.*
> Group B: *You're welcome. Get better soon!*

2. Every Morning practices verb phrases with *every morning*. Review the vocabulary from Let's Move, using Teacher Cards 113–116. Say the command and have students repeat and do the action together with *every morning* as quickly as possible. T: *Wake up.* Ss: *I wake up every morning.* Divide the class into two groups. Show one group the cards to cue the command and have the other group do the action with *every morning*. Reverse roles.

PRESENT THE LANGUAGE

📕 BOOKS CLOSED

Introduce the words.

1. Use Teacher Cards 118–127 to introduce the words. Show one Teacher Card at a time and say the name of the occupation. Students repeat each word several times.

2. Conduct a quick drill of the words. Do not speak as you show the cards. Have students identify the new occupation plus all the previously learned occupations. Gradually pick up speed as students get used to saying the words.

Introduce the sentence pattern.

1. Use Teacher Cards 118–127. Show each card and say the sentence *She's (a shopkeeper).* Have students repeat the sentence pattern.

2. Have students practice the sentence pattern with *She's*, substituting all the vocabulary. Students should say sentences at the same time as the teacher, not repeat after the teacher.

3. Conduct a quick drill of the sentences using Teacher Cards 118–127. Do not speak as you show the cards. Gradually pick up speed

as students get used to saying the sentences.

4. Repeat steps 1, 2, and 3 with *He's (a cook).*

5. Conduct another quick drill, but this time mix the cards so students are saying both *he's* and *she's*.

📖 BOOKS OPEN

A. Practice the words.

1. Play Track 08. Have students listen and point to the words.

🔘 CD 2 Track 08

1. *a shopkeeper*
2. *a cook*
3. *a nurse*
4. *a farmer*
5. *a taxi driver*
6. *a train conductor*
7. *an office worker*
8. *a police officer*
9. *a teacher*
10. *a student*

2. Play the audio again and have students repeat the words.

B. Practice the sentence.

1. Listen to the sentence pattern.

   a. Write the pattern on the board or direct students' attention to it in the book. Play Track 09. Point to the words as students listen to the audio. Then have students repeat after the audio.

 CD 2 Track 09

She's a shopkeeper.

She's a shopkeeper.

b. If students need to review, write the explanation of the contraction on the board: *she is = she's.* See page 196 for how to use contraction cards to teach contractions. Have students practice saying both *She is a shopkeeper* and *She's a shopkeeper.*

2. Practice the rhythm.

a. Play Track 09 again and have students listen to the rhythm and intonation of the sentences.

b. Play the track again. Have students tap or clap to match the rhythm of the audio. Have students listen to the spoken sentences to hear how the sentences match the rhythm, and then have them repeat the sentences along with the recorded rhythm.

c. Have students tap or clap the rhythm and practice saying the sentences without the audio.

3. Practice the sentences.

a. Play Track 10 and have students point to the vocabulary pictures as they listen.

 CD 2 Track 10

1. *She's a shopkeeper.*
2. *She's a cook.*
3. *She's a nurse.*
4. *He's a farmer.*
5. *He's a taxi driver.*
6. *He's a train conductor.*
7. *She's an office worker.*
8. *He's a police officer.*
9. *She's a teacher.*
10. *He's a student.*

b. Play Track 10 again and have students repeat the sentences.

c. Have students get into two parallel lines and face each other. Each student in Line 1 holds a card and the student across in Line 2 identifies the occupation: *She's (a shopkeeper).* Then each student in Line 2 moves one position to the right and identifies the next card. Continue until students return to their original positions. Then give Line 2 the cards and have Line 1 identify them.

 BOOKS CLOSED

Introduce the question forms.

1. Introduce the *Wh-* question-and-answer pattern.

a. Use puppets or student volunteers to present the question and answer.

> Puppet A: *Who's he?*
> Puppet B: *He's a taxi driver.*
> Puppet A: *Who's she?*
> Puppet B: *She's a police officer.*

b. Show Teacher Cards 118–127 and have students say the sentences *She's (a police officer).* Ask *Who's he/ she?* before you show each card.

c. Have students repeat the question. Model the question and help students with pronunciation.

d. Divide the class into teams by rows. Give S1 at the front of each row a set of Student Cards (118–127). S1 in each row turns to S2, shows a Student Card and asks *Who's he/she?* S2 responds *He/She's (a police officer).* S2 turns to S3 and repeats the question. Continue down the row asking about each card until each student has asked and answered the question.

2. Introduce the *Yes/No* question-and-answer pattern.

a. Use Teacher Cards 118–127 to present the *Yes/No* question-and-answer pattern. Show each Teacher Card and ask *Is (he) a (taxi driver)?* Students answer *Yes, (he) is* or *No, (he) isn't.* Repeat for the remaining Teacher Cards.

b. Have students repeat the question. Repeat the question several times.

c. Hold a Teacher Card so that students can't see it. Cue them with an occupation and *he* or *she.* Prompt them to ask the question *Is (he) a (taxi driver)?* Answer *Yes, (he) is* or *No, (he) isn't.* Repeat for the remaining Teacher Cards.

d. Divide the class into two groups. Have one group ask and the other group answer the questions. Cue *he* and *she* and an occupation and hold each Teacher Card so that students can't see it until after the question has been asked.

 BOOKS OPEN

C. Practice the question and answer.

1. Listen to the *Wh-* question-and-answer pattern.

a. Present the pattern by writing it on the board or direct students' attention to it in the book.

b. Play Track 11. Point to the words as students listen. Have students repeat after the audio.

 CD 2 Track 11

Who's he? He's a taxi driver.
Who's she? She's a police officer.
Who is = Who's

Who's he? He's a taxi driver.
Who's she? She's a police officer.

c. Write the explanation of the contractions on the board: *He is = He's* and *She is = She's.* See page 196 for how to use contraction cards to teach contractions. Have students practice saying both *She is a police officer* and *She's a police officer.* Point to the explanation on the board as they practice.

2. Practice the rhythm.

a. Play Track 11 again. This time, have students listen to the rhythm and intonation of the questions and answers.

b. Play the track one more time. Have students tap or clap to match the rhythm of the audio. Have students listen to the spoken questions and answers to hear how they match the rhythm, and then have them repeat the patterns along with the recorded rhythm.

c. Have students tap or clap the rhythm and practice saying the questions and answers without the audio.

3. Practice the *Wh-* questions and answers.

a. Have students look at page 41 and describe things they see.

b. Play Track 12. Have students listen and point to the appropriate pictures.

 CD 2 Track 12

1. *Who's he?*
   He's a taxi driver.
2. *Who's he?*
   He's an office worker.
3. *Who's she?*
   She's a nurse.
4. *Who's she?*
   She's a police officer.
5. *Who's she?*
   She's a cook.
6. *Who's she?*
   She's a teacher.
7. *Who's he?*
   He's a student.
8. *Who's he?*
   He's a shopkeeper.
9. *Who's he?*
   He's a farmer.
10. *Who's he?*
    He's a train conductor.

c. Play the audio again and have students repeat the questions and answers.

d. Divide the class into pairs and have students play **Slap** (p. 23) with their books open to page 41. One student points to a picture and asks *Who's she?* and the other student answers *She's (a shopkeeper).*

D. Ask and answer.

1. Listen to the *Yes/No* question-and-answer pattern.

a. Have the class look at the pictures on page 41 and describe what they see.

b. Play Track 13. Point to the words as students listen. Have students repeat the questions and answers after the audio.

 CD 2 Track 13

Is he a farmer?
   Yes, he is.
Is she a farmer?
   No, she isn't.

Is he a farmer?
   Yes, he is.
Is she a farmer?
   No, she isn't.

2. Practice the rhythm.

a. Play Track 13 again and have students listen to the rhythm and intonation of the questions and answers.

b. Play the track again. Have students tap or clap to match the rhythm of the audio. Have students listen to the spoken questions and answers to hear how they match the rhythm, and then have them repeat the patterns along with the recorded rhythm.

c. Have the students tap or clap the rhythm and practice saying the questions and answers without the audio.

3. Practice the *Yes/No* questions and answers.

a. Play Track 14. Have students listen and point to the appropriate pictures.

 CD 2 Track 14

1. *Is she a farmer?*
   Yes, she is.
2. *Is he a cook?*
   Yes, he is.
3. *Is he a police officer?*
   No, he isn't.
4. *Is she a nurse?*
   Yes, she is.

b. Divide the class into pairs. Have students take turns asking and answering questions about the pictures.

> **Grammar Tip:** Explain to students that *he is* and *she is* are never contracted in the answers *Yes, he is* and *Yes, she is.*

GAMES AND ACTIVITIES

1. Concentration (p. 22). Divide the class into small groups. Use a double set of Student Cards 118–127 (occupations) for each group. Place cards facedown in random order on a desk. Have students turn over two cards at a time and identify the occupations. S1: *(She's) (a nurse). (He's) (a taxi driver).*

2. Guess Who? practices questions and answers in a conversational way. Divide the class into small groups. Give each student a Student Card 118–127 (occupations) and tell them not to show their card. Students take turns asking about each other's pictures, using *Yes/No* questions only, for example, *Is it a man? Is it a woman? Is he/she old/young/tall/short? Is he a farmer?* Students ask one question at a time. If the answer is *Yes*, students can ask another question. If it's *No*, then the next student is questioned. Continue until the students guess all of the occupations.

3. Whisper Relay (p. 24) practices careful listening and clear pronunciation. Have students sit in several small circles. Whisper a phrase from the unit to S1: *He's a farmer. Who's she?*, etc. At your direction, have each S1 turn to S2 in her or his circle and whisper the same phrase. Continue around the circle to the last student. That student stands up and speaks the phrase.

EXTRA PRACTICE

WORKBOOK **pages 40–41**

Assign for homework or do in class. For instructions and Answer Key, see Teacher's Book page 169.

SKILLS BOOK **pages 40–41**

Assign for homework or do in class. For instructions and Answer Key, see Teacher's Book page 152.

REPRODUCIBLE WORKSHEET,
Teacher's Book page 182

Occupations Game provides further fun and practice with occupations vocabulary. For instructions, see page 192.

COMPONENTS LINK

CD-ROM 2

For extra fun, students can play Unit 5, Game 1 on a computer at school or at home. Students listen to the dialogues and choose the correct picture. This activity reinforces listening, and the Let's Learn vocabulary and grammar pattern *Who's she/he? She/He's (a)....*

For extra fun, students can play Unit 5, Game 2 on a computer at school or at home. In this word search game, students try to find the hidden words. This activity reinforces spelling and the Let's Learn vocabulary.

LET'S GO TESTS AND QUIZZES

Lesson Quiz: Explain and administer the reproducible Unit 5 Let's Learn quiz from *Let's Go Tests and Quizzes*, page 25. Instructions and Answer Key are also in *Let's Go Tests and Quizzes*.

LET'S CHANT LET'S SING 4

Page7: "The Job Chant"

This chant practices occupation vocabulary with the sentence pattern *He's a doctor.*

LET'S GO PICTURE DICTIONARY

Use pages 86–87, Occupations, to supplement the lesson and increase challenge.

1. Review familiar words on page 86–89, and point out new words you wish to teach.

2. Practice the words with the question-and-answer pattern *Is she/he a cook? Yes, she/he is. No, she/he isn't.*

Let's Learn More

Topic: Occupations

Lesson objectives: Students identify and ask about occupations with *they*.

New grammar: *Who are they? They are (Mr. and Mrs. Long). They're (teachers).*

Review grammar: *Are they (students)? Yes, they are. No, they aren't.*

New language: *teachers, police officers, doctors, pilots, engineers, train conductors, firefighters, taxi drivers, students, dentists*

Review language: *teacher, police officer, train conductor, student, taxi driver*

Materials: Teacher and Student Cards 128–137, actual items, CD 2 Tracks 15–21, contraction cards *(They're, aren't)*

WARM UP AND REVIEW

Choose one of the following:

1. Using verb phrases from Unit 1 and review verbs from Level 1, have students try to make as many sentences with *every morning* as possible.

2. **Who's She/He?** reviews occupations and the *Who's (she)? She's (a teacher)* question-and-answer pattern. Use Student Cards 118–127. Divide the class into pairs and have them ask each other *Who's he/she?* while pointing to one of the cards.

PRESENT THE LANGUAGE

BOOKS CLOSED

Introduce the words.

1. Use Teacher Cards 128–137. Practice the occupations by saying the word *(teachers)* emphasizing the final /s/ or /z/ sound. Have students repeat each word three times before going on to the next word.

2. Conduct a quick drill after you introduce each occupation. Use Teacher Cards 128–137. Don't speak as you show the cards.

Have students identify the new occupation plus all the previously learned occupations.

3. Show the cards again and have students say the singular form and then the plural form of each occupation.

Introduce the sentence pattern.

1. Use Teacher Cards 128–137. Show a card and say the sentence *They're (dentists)*. Have students repeat the sentence patterns several times before moving on to the next word.

2. Practice the pattern, substituting all the words. Students should say the sentences at the same time as the teacher, not repeat after the teacher.

3. Conduct a quick drill. Show Teacher Cards 128–137 in random order and have students make sentences. Increase the speed of the drill until students are speaking at natural speed.

📖 BOOKS OPEN

A. Practice the words.

1. Play Track 15. Have students listen and point to the words.

🔘 **CD 2 Track 15**

1. teachers
2. police officers
3. doctors
4. pilots
5. engineers
6. train conductors
7. firefighters
8. taxi drivers
9. students
10. dentists

2. Play the audio again and have students repeat the words.

B. Practice the sentence.

1. **Listen to the sentence pattern.**

  a. Write the pattern on the board or direct students' attention to it in the book.

  b. Play Track 16. Point to the words as students listen to the audio. Then have students repeat after the audio.

CD 2 Track 16

They're dentists.
They are = They're

They're dentists.

c. Write the explanation of the contraction on the board: *They are = They're*. See page 197 for how to use contraction cards to teach contractions. Have students practice saying both *They're dentists* and *They are dentists*.

2. Practice the rhythm.

a. Play Track 16 again. This time, have students listen to the rhythm and intonation of the sentences.

b. Have students tap or clap to match the rhythm of the audio. Play the track again. Have students listen to the spoken sentences to hear how the sentences match the rhythm, and then have them repeat the sentences along with the recorded rhythm.

c. Have students tap or clap the rhythm and practice saying the sentences without the audio.

3. Practice the sentences.

a. Play Track 17 and have students point to the vocabulary pictures as they listen.

 CD 2 Track 17

They're teachers.
They're police officers.
They're doctors.
They're pilots.
They're engineers.
They're train conductors.
They're firefighters.
They're taxi drivers.
They're students.
They're dentists.

b. Play Track 17 again and have students repeat the sentences.

c. Have students get into pairs and take turns pointing to the pictures on page 42 and making sentences.

📖 **BOOKS CLOSED**

Introduce the question form.

1. Introduce the *Wh-* question-and-answer pattern.

a. Hold up Teacher Card 136 and ask *Who are they?* Model the answer for students to repeat *They're students*. Then have them repeat it in a series of three, several times.

b. Ask the question showing the cards as the students answer with *They're (students)*. Have students practice the question *Who are they?* Students repeat the question several times.

c. Divide the class into two groups. Use Teacher Cards to cue students. Groups take turns asking and answering questions.

d. Further divide the two large groups into smaller groups. Use Student Cards 128–137. Give each student an occupation card to show the group while asking *Who are they?* Others in the group respond *They're (train conductors)*. Continue until all students have a turn asking a question.

> **Pronunciation Tip:** Review the pronunciation of /*th*/. Tell students to make sure their tongues are touching the back of their front teeth. Model the difference between *thanks* and *they* and have students repeat several times.

2. Introduce the *Yes/No* question-and-answer pattern.

a. Hold up Teacher Card 128 (teachers) and model the question *Are they teachers?* Prompt students to answer *Yes, they are*. Show each of the remaining Teacher Cards and ask the question. Each time, students answer *Yes, they are*.

b. Hold up Teacher Card 128 (teachers) again and ask the question *Are they pilots?* Prompt students to answer *No, they aren't*. Show all cards but 131 and ask the question. Each time, students answer *No, they aren't*.

c. Have students practice the question. They should repeat the question several times.

d. Hold the Teacher Cards so that students can't see them. Cue them to ask questions by whispering an occupation or by having them turn over Student Cards. Answer the question *Yes, they are* or *No, they aren't* each time.

e. Divide the class into two groups. Give each group a set of Student Cards (or one set of Teacher Cards and one set of Student Cards) placed facedown. One group turns over a card to cue the question. The other group turns over a card to determine their answer. Be sure both groups practice asking and answering questions.

📖 **BOOKS OPEN**

C. Practice the question and answer.

1. Listen to the *Wh-* question-and-answer pattern.

a. Present the pattern by writing it on the board or direct students' attention to the pattern in the book.

b. Play Track 18. Point to the words as students listen. Have students repeat after the audio.

 CD 2 Track 18

Who are they?
     They are Mr. Jones and Mr. Lee. They're pilots.

Who are they?
     They are Mr. Jones and Mr. Lee. They're pilots.

2. Practice the rhythm.

a. Play Track 18 again and have students listen to the rhythm and intonation of the question and answer.

Let's Learn More

b. Play the track again. Have students tap or clap to match the rhythm of the audio. Have students listen to the spoken question and answer to hear how they match the rhythm, and then have them repeat them along with the recorded rhythm.

c. Have the students tap or clap the rhythm and practice saying the question and answer without the audio.

3. Practice the *Wh-* questions and answers.

a. Have students look at page 43 and describe things they see.

b. Play Track 19. Have students listen and point to the appropriate pictures.

 CD 2 Track 19

1. *Who are they?*
   They're Ms. Adams and Mr. White. They're doctors.
2. *Who are they?*
   They're Mr. Gray and Ms. Johnson. They're students.
3. *Who are they?*
   They're Mr. and Mrs. Brown. They're dentists.
4. *Who are they?*
   They're Mr. Baker and Mr. Simmons. They're firefighters.

c. Play the audio again and have students repeat the question and answers.

d. Divide the class into question-and-answer groups and play the audio again. Each group repeats either the question or the answer. Repeat with groups switching roles.

e. Have students work in pairs and take turns asking and answering questions about the pictures.

D. Ask and answer.

1. Listen to the *Yes/No* question-and-answer pattern.

a. Present the pattern by writing it on the board or direct students' attention to the pattern in the book.

b. Play Track 20. Point to the words as students listen. Have students repeat after the audio.

 CD 2 Track 20

Are they teachers?
   Yes, they are.
Are they teachers?
   No, they aren't.

Are they teachers?
   Yes, they are.
Are they teachers?
   No, they aren't.

c. Write the explanation of the contraction on the board: *are not = aren't*. See page 196 for how to use contraction cards to teach contractions. Have students practice saying both *No, they aren't* and *No, they are not*.

2. Practice the rhythm.

a. Play Track 20 again. This time, have students listen to the rhythm and intonation of the question and answer.

b. Have students tap or clap to match the rhythm of the audio. Play the track again. Have students listen to the spoken question and answer to hear how they match the rhythm, and then have them repeat the patterns along with the recorded rhythm.

c. Have students tap or clap the rhythm and practice saying the question and answer without the audio.

3. Practice the *Yes/No* questions and answers.

a. Play Track 21. Point to the words as students listen. Have students listen and point to the appropriate pictures.

 CD 2 Track 21

1. *Are they firefighters?*
   Yes, they are.
2. *Are they engineers?*
   No, they aren't.
3. *Are they teachers?*
   No, they aren't.

b. Have students work in pairs and take turns asking and answering questions about the pictures.

> **Grammar Tip:** Tell students that *they are* is never contracted in *Yes, they are.*

GAMES AND ACTIVITIES

1. Step Away Lines (p. 26) gives students confidence in speaking in a loud voice. Give students Student Cards 128–137. Have them get into two lines and show a card as they ask *Yes/No* questions.

2. Charades (p. 22) reviews the occupations in singular and plural form. To elicit a plural answer, have two students work together to act out the occupation. For a singular answer, have one student act out the occupation.

3. Are They...? uses the pictures in the book to practice *Yes/No* questions. Use page 43 of the Student Book. Have students get into pairs and work with one book. They play **Rock, Paper, Scissors** with *Are they, are they, 1, 2, 3!* The winner asks a *Yes/No* question and the loser has to answer it correctly. Make sure students sometimes ask questions that will elicit a *No* response.

EXTRA PRACTICE

WORKBOOK pages 42–43

Assign for homework or do in class. For instructions and Answer Key, see Teacher's Book page 169.

SKILLS BOOK pages 42–43

Assign for homework or do in class. For instructions and Answer Key, see Teacher's Book page 153.

REPRODUCIBLE WORKSHEET, Teacher's Book page 183

Card Game: Occupations provides further fun and practice with occupations vocabulary. For instructions, see page 192.

COMPONENTS LINK

CD-ROM 2

For extra fun, students can play Unit 5, Game 3 on a computer at school or at home. Students answer *Yes/No* questions about the pictures. This activity reinforces listening, reading, and the Let's Learn More vocabulary and grammar pattern *Are they (teachers)? Yes, they are. No, they aren't.*

For extra fun, students can play Unit 5, Game 4 on a computer at school or at home. Students listen and choose the correct picture to move across the maze. This activity reinforces listening, and the Let's Learn More vocabulary and grammar patterns.

LET'S GO TESTS AND QUIZZES

Lesson Quiz: Explain and administer the reproducible Unit 5 Let's Learn More quiz from *Let's Go Tests and Quizzes*, page 26. Instructions and Answer Key are also in *Let's Go Tests and Quizzes*.

LET'S CHANT LET'S SING 2

Page 11: "Is He a Teacher?"

This chant practices job vocabulary while practicing the question-and-answer patterns *Is he/she a teacher? Yes, he/she is. No, he/she isn't. Are they nurses? Yes, they are. No, they aren't.*

LET'S GO PICTURE DICTIONARY

Use pages 88–89, More Occupations, to supplement the lesson and increase challenge.

1. Review familiar words on page 88–89, and point out new words you wish to teach.

2. Practice the words with the question-and-answer pattern *Are they teachers? Yes, they are. No, they aren't.*

Let's Build

Topic: Occupations

Lesson objectives: Students ask about occupations and abilities.

Review grammar: *Can (Mrs. Hill) (type)? Who is (Mr. Jones)? Is (Ms. Lee) (a teacher) or (a student)? (She's) (a student).*

Review language: numbers, occupations, *at school, use chopsticks, wink, type, make breakfast, dance, Mr., Mrs., Ms., Miss*

Materials: Teacher Cards 126–127, Student Cards 85–100, 150–158 and 216–231 from Level 1, CD 2 Tracks 22–23, contraction cards (*He's, She's, I'm*)

WARM UP AND REVIEW

Choose one of the following:

1. Do a quick review of the singular and plural occupations with Teacher Cards 118–137. Students identify the cards with complete sentences: *He's a cook. They're office workers.*

2. **Find Your Partner** (p. 24). Distribute a double set of occupations cards, one to each student, making sure there is at least one match for each student. Have students find their match. Students ask *Do you have (a farmer)?* or *Do you have (farmers)?*

PRESENT THE LANGUAGE

📖 BOOKS OPEN

A. Listen and number.

1. Have students look at the pictures on page 44 and describe what they see. Encourage them to guess what language they will hear.

2. Play Track 22. Have students listen and number the pictures in the order they hear them.

🔘 **CD 2 Track 22**

1. *a cook*
2. *police officers*
3. *train conductors*
4. *a teacher*
5. *office workers*

3. Play the audio again for students to check their answers.

B. Ask and answer.

1. Have students look at the pictures and describe what they see.

2. Play Track 23. Have students listen and repeat the questions and answers.

🔘 **CD 2 Track 23**

Who is Mr. Jones?
He's a train conductor.

1. *Who is Mr. Jones?*
   He's a train conductor.
2. *Who is Miss Black?*
   She's a teacher.
3. *Who is Ms. Smith?*
   She's a nurse.
4. *Who is Mr. White?*
   He's a pilot.
5. *Who is Mr. Lee?*
   He's a cook.

3. Divide the class into pairs. Have pairs take turns asking and answering questions about the pictures.

C. Answer the questions.

1. Make an *or* card. Put it between Teacher Cards 126 and 127 (*teacher* and *student*) on the board.

2. Ask S1 *Are you a teacher?* S1 answers *No, I'm not.*

3. Ask the class as you point to the cards *Is (Dan) a teacher or a student?* Students answer (*He's*) *a student.*

4. Have pairs of students look at the pictures on page 45 and describe what they see.

5. Keep students in pairs. Have them look at each picture and take turns asking and answering questions.

D. Look and check.

1. Review *Can you...?* and *Can he/she...?*

2. Have students look at the pictures on page 45 and describe what they see. Then read the first question and have students repeat.

3. Divide the class into pairs. Have students take turns reading the questions to each other, and check the answers together.

GAMES AND ACTIVITIES

1. **X or Y?** practices asking questions. Use Student Cards (food from Level 1 and Level 2, toys from Level 1). Divide the class into groups of three. Give each group a stack of cards. Have students take turns asking each other questions using *or*, such as *Do you want stew or pasta? Does he want stew or pasta? Do you like apples or peaches? Does she like apples or peaches?*

2. Restaurant Role Play gives students more practice talking about food. Each student takes a turn playing the waiter/waitress. Model the activity for the class.

> S1: *What do you want?*
> S2: *I want pasta.*
> S3: *I want steak.*
> S1: *Do you want milk, too?*
> S2: *Yes, I do. Thank you.*
> S3: *No, thank you.*

Encourage students to use other language they have learned to make their own dialogue.

3. Interview practices the occupation vocabulary. Make a chart for each student. Have students walk around the classroom asking each other about their parents' occupations and write them in the chart.

EXTRA PRACTICE

WORKBOOK pages 44–45

Assign for homework or do in class. For instructions and Answer Key, see Teacher's Book page 169.

SKILLS BOOK pages 44–45

Assign for homework or do in class. For instructions and Answer Key, see Teacher's Book page 153.

COMPONENTS LINK

LET'S GO TESTS AND QUIZZES

Lesson Quiz: Explain and administer the reproducible Unit 5 Let's Build quiz from *Let's Go Tests and Quizzes*, page 27. Instructions and Answer Key are also in *Let's Go Tests and Quizzes*.

Unit Test: Explain and administer the reproducible Unit 5 Test from *Let's Go Tests and Quizzes*, page 52. Instructions and Answer Key are also in *Let's Go Tests and Quizzes*.

LET'S GO READER

Now that students have completed Unit 5, they are ready to read "What's the Matter?" See Teacher's Book page 20 for suggestions on how to present *Readers* and incorporate them into your lesson plans.

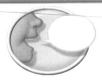

Unit 6 Locations

Let's Start

Topic: Location; everyday activities

Lesson objectives: Students ask each other about their location and afternoon activities.

New grammar: *Where are you? I'm (at home). What do you do every afternoon? I (study English) (every afternoon).*

Review grammar: *Hi, Kate. Can you (come to the park)?*

New language: *study English, talk on the telephone, watch TV, practice the piano, Sure!*

Materials: Teacher and Student Cards 138–141, CD 2 Tracks 24–29, puppets (optional), contraction cards (*I'm, She's, Where's*)

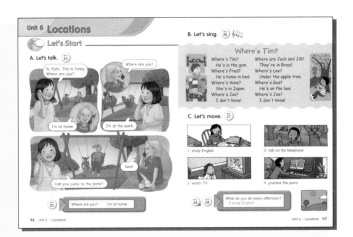

WARM UP AND REVIEW

Choose one of the following:

1. On the Telephone practices language from earlier units in a spontaneous way. Work with students to create a simple phone conversation using familiar language. Write it on the board. Erase information that could be substituted with other information. Divide the class into pairs and have them pretend to call each other. For example:

S1: *Hello. This is (Jenny).*
S2: *Hi, (Jenny). How are you?*
S1: *I'm (tired). How about you?*
S2: *I'm (hungry). Do you want (a hamburger)?*

2. Can You...? practices verb phrases with *can*. Use Student Cards featuring verb phrases from earlier lessons. Have students get in a circle. Hold up a Student Card (*run*) and point to a student (S1). S1 asks S2: *Can you run?* S2 answers. Hold up another card and have S2 ask S3. Continue quickly around the circle with the rest of the cards.

PRESENT THE DIALOGUE

📖 BOOKS CLOSED

Present the dialogue.

1. Introduce the dialogue.

a. Use puppets or student volunteers to introduce the dialogue. Ask students to identify words they hear.

Puppet A: *Hi, Kate. This is Jenny. Where are you?*
Puppet B: *I'm at home. Where are you?*
Puppet A: *I'm at the park. Can you come to the park?*
Puppet B: *Sure!*

b. Have students practice saying their names and a classmate's name with *Hi, (Kate). This is (Jenny).* Gradually pick up speed until they are able to say it at natural speed.

c. Divide the class into two groups and have them practice the dialogue.

d. Divide the class into pairs and practice the dialogue, substituting their own names.

📖 BOOKS OPEN

A. Let's talk.

Students learn how to ask about another person's location.

1. Listen to the dialogue.

a. Have students look at the scenes on page 46 and describe what they see.

b. Play Track 24. Have students listen to the dialogue and point to the speech bubbles. Have them identify words they hear.

💿 **CD 2 Track 24**

Jenny: *Hi, Kate. This is Jenny.*
    Where are you?
Kate: *I'm at home.*
    Where are you?
Jenny: *I'm at the park.*
    Can you come to the park?
Kate: *Sure!*

c. Play the dialogue again and have students repeat each line after the characters.

2. Practice the pattern.

a. Have students say *Where are you?* in a series of three, several times. Gradually pick up speed until they are able to say it at natural speed.

Write the pattern on the board, or direct students' attention to their books. Play Track 25. Point to the words as students listen to the dialogue. Then have students repeat after the audio.

CD 2 Track 25

Where are you?
    I'm at home.

b. Review *I am = I'm,* if necessary. Follow the procedure on page 196 for how to teach contractions with cards. Have the students practice saying both *I am at home* and *I'm at home.* Point to the explanation on the board as they practice.

3. Practice the dialogue.

a. Ask one of the questions from the dialogue and have a volunteer answer. Repeat for the other question. Then ask the questions out of order and have volunteers answer. To make this more challenging, give one of the answers from the dialogue and have students ask the matching question.

b. Do **Conversation Lines** (p. 26) to practice the dialogue in pairs.

c. Have students practice the dialogue with several partners, using their own names.

B. Let's sing.

"Where's Tim?" reinforces the language from the dialogue using rhythm and song.

1. Play and listen.

Play Track 26. Have students listen and identify the words they recognize from Let's talk.

CD 2 Track 26

Where's Tim?

Where's Tim?
    He's in the gym.
Where's Fred?
    He's home in bed.
Where's Anne?
    She's in Japan.
Where's Joe?
    I don't know.

Where are Jack and Jill?
    They're in Brazil.
Where's Lee?
    Under the apple tree.
Where's Gus?
    He's on the bus.
Where's Joe?
    I don't know.

2. Practice the rhythm.

a. Introduce the song rhythmically. Have students clap to keep the beat as you model the song line by line. Have students repeat after you.

b. Play the song again. Encourage students to sing along.

3. Do the song activity.

Play the song again. This time have half of the class sing one part, and half sing the second part. Add gestures to go with the song lyrics.

4. Read the lyrics.

Have students look at the song pictures and lyrics. Ask students to point to and read words that they recognize.

5. Work in groups.

Have students work in groups to create an original verse using each other's names. Then, sing the song again with the new verses.

📖 BOOKS CLOSED

Present the verb phrases.

1. Introduce the verb phrases.

a. Say *study English* with action, and repeat the action several times. Have students repeat several times with action before going on to the

next phrase. Repeat with the other phrases.

b. To check understanding, say the phrases in random order and have students do the appropriate action.

c. Show students Teacher Cards 138–141. Have them say the phrase and do the action.

d. Divide the class into two groups. Have the groups take turns saying the commands and doing the actions. Use Teacher Cards to cue the command group.

2. Introduce *What do you do every afternoon? I (study English) every afternoon.*

a. Add *every afternoon* to each verb phrase and have students repeat the phrase and do the action.

b. Have students say *What do you do every afternoon?* in a series of three, several times.

c. Use Teacher Cards 138–141. Give each student a card and ask *What do you do every afternoon?* Prompt S1 to answer based on his or her card: *I (watch TV).*

d. Have pairs ask and answer the question. Encourage students to use *How about you?*

📖 BOOKS OPEN

C. Let's move.

Students learn useful classroom language by combining rhythm and actions.

1. Listen and point to the verb phrases.

a. Play Track 27. Have students listen and point to the appropriate pictures.

CD 2 Track 27

1. *study English*
2. *talk on the telephone*
3. *watch TV*
4. *practice the piano*

b. Play the audio again. Students listen and repeat.

Let's Start

2. Practice the rhythm.

a. Play Track 28. Have students point to the words as they listen.

 CD 2 Track 28

What do you do every afternoon?
I study English.

What do you do every afternoon?
I study English.

b. Play Track 28 again. Have students clap or tap to keep the rhythm and repeat after the question and answer with the audio.

c. Have students tap or clap the rhythm and practice saying the question and answer without the audio.

3. Practice the questions and answers.

a. Play Track 29. Have students listen to the sentences and point to the appropriate pictures.

 CD 2 Track 29

What do you do every afternoon?
I study English.
What do you do every afternoon?
I talk on the telephone.
What do you do every afternoon?
I watch TV.
What do you do every afternoon?
I practice the piano.

b. Play the audio again and have students repeat the questions and answers.

c. Divide the class into question and answer groups and play the audio again. Each group repeats either the question or the answer. Repeat with groups switching roles.

d. Have students work in pairs and take turns asking and answering questions about the pictures.

GAMES AND ACTIVITIES

1. **Stand Up** helps develop listening skills. Play the song from Let's sing. When students hear the name of a place, have them stand up and sit down very quickly.

2. **Charades** (p. 22) gets students using their imaginations. Divide the class into two teams. Whisper a verb phrase and a location to S1 from each team. Each S1 has to act out the verb phrase and location. The first team to guess wins a point.

3. **Concentration** (p. 22) practices recognizing and using the verbs. Divide the class into groups of 3–4. Use Student Cards 138–141. Have S1 identify the first card and then flip over a second card. S1 identifies that card and if the two cards match, S1 says *I (study English) every afternoon* and his/her group does the action. S1 keeps the pair of cards. S2 then chooses cards. Continue until all the cards are gone.

EXTRA PRACTICE

WORKBOOK **pages 46–47**

Assign for homework or do in class. For instructions and Answer Key, see Teacher's Book page 169.

SKILLS BOOK **pages 46–47**

Assign for homework or do in class. For instructions and Answer Key, see Teacher's Book page 154.

COMPONENTS LINK

CD-ROM 2

For extra fun, students can play Unit 6, Game 1 on a computer at school or at home. Students listen and choose the correct picture to beat the clock. This activity reinforces listening and the verb pattern.

LET'S GO TESTS AND QUIZZES

Lesson Quiz: Explain and administer the reproducible Unit 6 Let's Start quiz from *Let's Go Tests and Quizzes*, page 28. Instructions and Answer Key are also in *Let's Go Tests and Quizzes*.

LET'S CHANT LET'S SING 2

Page 34: "What Do You Do in the Morning?"

This chant practices the question-and-answer pattern *What do you do (in the morning/every afternoon)? I brush my teeth. I study English.*

LET'S GO PICTURE DICTIONARY

Use pages 54–55, Playground Verbs, to supplement the Let's Move portion of the lesson.

1. Review familiar words and point out new words you wish to teach.

2. Practice the words with the question-and-answer pattern *What do you do every afternoon? I study English every afternoon.*

Let's Learn

Topic: Locations

Lesson objectives: Students ask about location with *he/she.*

New grammar: *Where is he/she? He's/She's (at school).*

Review grammar: *Is he/she (at school)? Yes, he/she is. No, he/she isn't.*

New language: *at work, at the library, at the zoo*

Review language: *at school, at home, at the park*

Materials: Teacher Cards 143–148, Student Cards 143–148, 106–112 from Level 1, CD 2 Tracks 30–36, contraction cards (*He's, She's, isn't, It's*)

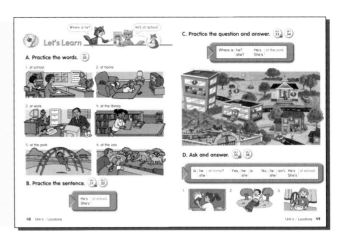

WARM UP AND REVIEW

Choose one of the following:

1. Review *at school, at home,* and *at the park.* Place all three Teacher Cards on the chalk rail (143, 144, and 147). Then, hold up various activity Teacher Cards (e.g., *play baseball, watch TV, go to sleep,* etc.) and ask students to tell you if it's something they would do at home, at school, or at the park. Place the card near the appropriate location. If students decide the activity could happen at all of the places, then place the card above the cards.

2. Review the question and answer pattern *Where's the (book)? It's (on) (the table).* After reviewing the pattern with classroom objects, ask the class *Where's the book?* and have them answer and place the correct item near the location Teacher Card (park, home, school).

PRESENT THE LANGUAGE

 BOOKS CLOSED

Introduce the words.

1. Use Teacher Cards 143–148 to introduce the locations. Show one Teacher Card at a time and say the name of the location. Students repeat each location several times.

2. Practice the words by saying the location and have students make up a gesture for it. Say all the locations

again with gestures and have students repeat. Next, just do the gestures and have students say the location as they do the gesture.

3. Conduct a quick drill of the locations. Do not speak as you show the cards. Have students identify the new location plus all the previously learned locations. Gradually pick up speed as students get used to saying the locations.

Introduce the sentence pattern.

1. Use Teacher Cards 143–148. Show each card and say the sentence *He's (at school).* Have students repeat the sentence pattern with gestures.

2. Have students practice the sentence pattern, substituting all the locations. Students should say sentences at the same time as the teacher, not repeat after the teacher.

3. Conduct a quick drill of the sentences using Teacher Cards 143–148. Do not speak as you show the cards. Gradually pick up speed as students get used to saying the sentences.

4. Use two piles of Student Cards (family and locations). Have students take turns turning over one card from each pile and making a sentence, for example, Level 1 Teacher Card 111 (*father*) and 145 (*at work*) becomes *He's at work.*

 BOOKS OPEN

A. Practice the words.

1. Play Track 30. Have students listen and point to the words.

 CD 2 Track 30

1. *at school*
2. *at home*
3. *at work*
4. *at the library*
5. *at the park*
6. *at the zoo*

2. Play the audio again and have students repeat the words.

B. Practice the sentence.

1. Listen to the sentence pattern. Write the pattern on the board or direct students' attention to their books. Play Track 31. Point to the words as students listen. Then have students repeat after the audio.

 CD 2 Track 31

She's at school.

She's at school.

2. Practice the rhythm.

a. Play Track 31 again. This time, have students listen to the rhythm and intonation of the sentences.

b. Play the audio again. Have students tap or clap to match the rhythm of the audio. Have students listen to the spoken sentences to hear how the sentences match the rhythm, and then have them repeat the sentences along with the recorded rhythm.

c. Have students tap or clap the rhythm and practice saying the sentences without the audio.

3. Practice the sentence.

a. Play Track 32 and have students point to the vocabulary pictures as they listen.

 CD 2 Track 32

He's at school.
She's at home.
He's at work.
She's at the library.
He's at the park.
She's at the zoo.

b. Play Track 32 again and have students repeat the sentences.

c. To practice the words, do a **Pass The Card** activity. Give a stack of Student Cards 143–148 (locations) to S1 in each row. Have the student say *He's (at school)* and then pass the card to S2 behind him/her. S2 says the sentence and passes the card to S3 behind him/her. Each row continues to pass all its cards until every student in the row has practiced the sentence pattern with each card.

BOOKS CLOSED

Introduce the question forms.

1. Listen to the *Wh-* question and answer.

a. Use student volunteers to present the question and answer. Place Teacher Card 147 (*at the park*) on the board. Have a male stand near the card. Model the question and answer: *Where is he? He's at the park.* Have a female student stand near Teacher Card 146 (*at the library*) and model the question and answer: *Where is she? She's at the library.*

b. Repeat the question with each location card and student volunteers. Have students repeat.

c. Have students practice asking questions. Point to students or simple drawings of a boy and girl to cue *he* and *she*. Ss: *Where is she?* Hold up a Teacher Card and answer. T: *She's at the park.*

d. Divide the class into two groups. Use Teacher Cards to cue the students. Groups take turns asking and answering questions. Group A: *Where is (he)?* Group B: *(He's) at work.*

e. Use Teacher Cards 143–148. Place them around the room. Have an identical set of Student Cards on a table. Model the activity first by instructing S1 to select one location card and stand near it. Face the class so you can't see where S1 is standing. Ask the class *Where is (David)?* Students answer *(He's at school)*. Hold up Student Card 143 (*at school*) to confirm. Repeat the activity several times with other students.

2. Introduce the *Yes/No* question and answer.

a. Have a student volunteer stand near one of the Teacher Card locations *(at school)* and ask *Is he at home?* Prompt students to answer *No, he isn't. He's at school.*

b. Repeat with other student volunteers standing in various locations. Have students practice both *Yes, (he) is* and *No, (he) isn't. (He's at home)*. Have students repeat.

c. Have students ask you questions about volunteers standing in different locations. If desired, cue the question by showing a Student Card (so that you can elicit both *yes* and *no* answers).

BOOKS OPEN

C. Practice the question and answer.

1. Listen to the *Wh-* question and answer pattern.

a. Present the pattern by writing it on the board or direct students' attention to it in the book.

b. Play Track 33. Point to the words as students listen. Have students repeat after the audio.

 CD 2 Track 33

Where is he?
  He's at the park.

Where is he?
  He's at the park.

2. Practice the rhythm.

a. Play Track 33 again. This time, have students listen to the rhythm and the intonation of the question and answer.

b. Play the track again. Have students clap or tap to keep the rhythm of the audio. Have students listen to the spoken question and answer to hear how it matches the rhythm, and then have them repeat the pattern along with the recorded rhythm.

c. Have students tap or clap the rhythm and practice saying the question and answer without the audio.

3. Practice the question-and answer-pattern.

a. Have students look at page 49 and describe things and locations they see.

b. Play Track 34. Point to the words as students listen. Have students repeat the questions and answers after the audio.

 CD 2 Track 34

1. *Where is he?*
   He's at work.
2. *Where is he?*
   He's at the zoo.
3. *Where is she?*
   She's at the park.
4. *Where is she?*
   She's at school.
5. *Where is he?*
   He's at the library.
6. *Where is he?*
   He's at home.

c. Play Track 34 again. Have students repeat the questions and answers and point to the appropriate pictures.

d. Divide the class into pairs. Have students take turns asking and answering questions about the picture and vocabulary.

D. Ask and answer.

1. Listen to the *Yes/No* question-and-answer pattern.

    a. Present the pattern by writing it on the board or direct students' attention to the pattern in the book.

    b. Play Track 35. Have students point to the words as they listen. Replay the audio as students repeat.

 CD 2 Track 35

Is he at home?
    Yes, he is.
Is she at home?
    No, she isn't. She's at school.

Is he at home?
    Yes, he is.
Is she at home?
    No, she isn't. She's at school.

2. Practice the rhythm.

    a. Play Track 35 again and have students listen to the rhythm and intonation of the questions and answers.

    b. Play the track again. Have students tap or clap to match the rhythm of the audio. Have students listen to the spoken questions and answers to hear how they match the rhythm, and then have them repeat the patterns along with the recorded rhythm.

    c. Have the students tap or clap the rhythm and practice saying the questions and answers without the audio.

3. Practice the *Yes/No* questions and answers.

    a. Play Track 36. Have students listen and point to the pictures.

 CD 2 Track 36

1. Is she at home?
    No, she isn't. She's at school.
2. Is he at the park?
    Yes, he is.
3. Is she at home?
    Yes, she is.

    b. Divide the class into pairs. Give each group one set of people Student Cards and one set of location Student Cards. Have them put the two piles facedown on a desk. S1 picks a person card and asks S2 *Is (he) at the (park)?* guessing the location. S2 picks a location card. If the card matches S1's guess, S2 answers *Yes, he is* and S1 keeps the location card. If it doesn't match, S2 returns the location card and answers *No, he isn't.* Then S2 picks a person card. Students continue until all the location cards are gone.

GAMES AND ACTIVITIES

1. Team Game (p. 25) practices the question and answer pattern. Use Teacher Cards of classroom objects, people, and locations. Place them in potential sentence pairs around the room. Ask teams to answer various questions about the objects' or people's locations. Award points for correct answers.

2. Find Your Partner (p. 24) practices the sentence pattern. Give students an object card or a location card. As you call out a sentence (*The book is in the library*), students arrange themselves in appropriate object/location pairs. After all the students are matched, practice the question-and-answer patterns. For example, *Where's the book? It's at the library. Is the elephant at school? No, it isn't. It's at the zoo.*

3. Whisper Relay (p. 24) practices listening skills and memorization. Divide the class into teams and have them stand or sit in lines. Whisper the same word to the first person in each row. Say *Go!* and have S1 whisper the word to S2, who whispers it to S3, etc., as fast as possible. The last student then runs

to the front of the class and tells the teacher the word. The first student to say the word correctly wins.

EXTRA PRACTICE

WORKBOOK pages 48–49

Assign for homework or do in class. For instructions and Answer Key, see Teacher's Book page 170.

SKILLS BOOK pages 48–49

Assign for homework or do in class. For instructions and Answer Key, see Teacher's Book page 154.

REPRODUCIBLE WORKSHEET
Teacher's Book page 184

Map Activity: Locations provides further fun and practice with the location vocabulary of the lesson. For instructions, see page 193.

COMPONENTS LINK

CD-ROM 2

For extra fun, students can play Unit 6, Game 2 on a computer at school or at home. Students put the words in order to build a sentence and beat the clock. This activity reinforces reading, prepositions, and the Let's Learn vocabulary.

LET'S GO TESTS AND QUIZZES

Lesson Quiz: Explain and administer the reproducible Unit 6 Let's Learn quiz from *Let's Go Tests and Quizzes*, page 29. Instructions and Answer Key are also in *Let's Go Tests and Quizzes.*

LET'S GO PICTURE DICTIONARY

Use pages 82–83, Stores and Buildings, to supplement the lesson and increase challenge.

1. Review familiar words and point out new words you wish to teach.

2. Practice the words with the question-and-answer patterns *Where is he/she? He's/She's at school. Is he/she at school? Yes, he/she is. No, he/she isn't.*

Let's Learn More

Topic: Locations

Lesson objectives: Students talk about location with *they.*

New grammar: *Where are they? They're (at the movies).*

Review grammar: *Are they (at the movies)? Yes, they are. No, they aren't.*

New language: *at the movies, at the store, in the restaurant, on the bus, on the train, in the taxi*

Review language: *at home, at work, at the library, at the zoo, at school, at the park*

Materials: Teacher and Student Cards 149–154, actual items, CD 2 Tracks 37–43, contraction cards (*aren't, They're*)

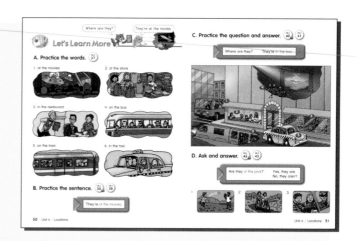

WARM UP AND REVIEW

Choose one of the following:

1. Nouns and Pronouns practices Let's Learn location words and pronouns. Put Student Cards (people, objects, animals, and locations) in two piles. Have students choose a location and a person or object and make a sentence. *My father is at the zoo. The TV is at home. The monkey is at the park.* Then have students substitute the nouns with the correct pronoun. *He is at the zoo. It is at home. It is at the park.*

2. Where Are They? practices the sentence pattern and reviews plurals. Show location and object Teacher Cards. Have students practice making sentences combining plural objects and locations: *The books are at the library.*

PRESENT THE LANGUAGE

📖 BOOKS CLOSED

Introduce the words.

1. Use Teacher Cards 149–154. Hold up one Teacher Card at a time and say the location. Students repeat each location several times. When modeling each phrase, emphasize the different prepositions.

2. Conduct a quick drill of the words after you introduce each location. Use Teacher Cards 149–154. Don't speak as you show the cards. Have students identify the new location plus all the previously learned locations. Gradually pick up speed as students get used to saying the locations with the correct prepositions.

3. Write *at, on,* and *in* on the board. Show each Teacher Card, say the phrase (*at the movies*), and put the card under the correct preposition. Take the cards down. Hold up each card again and have a volunteer say the phrase and put it under the correct preposition.

> **Grammar Tip:** Americans usually talk about being *at* a general location (*at school, at work*) and *in* a building (*in the library*). When they speak of transportation, they talk of riding *on* large vehicles (*on the bus, on the train, on the airplane*) and *in* smaller vehicles (*in the taxi, in the car*).

> **Cultural Tip:** *At the movies* means to be in a movie theater watching a movie.

Introduce the sentence pattern.

1. Use Teacher Cards 149–154. Show each card and say the sentence *They're (at the movies).* Have students repeat the sentence pattern several times before moving on to the next word.

2. Practice the pattern, substituting all the words. Students should say the sentences at the same time as the teacher, not repeat after the teacher.

3. Conduct a quick drill. Show Teacher Cards 149–154 in random order and have students make sentences. Increase the speed of the drill until students are speaking at natural speed.

4. Place each of the location cards on the chalk rail (or around the classroom). Ask two students to stand near each of the locations. Point to one of the pairs and elicit from the class *They're (at the movies).*

BOOKS OPEN

A. Practice the words.

1. Play Track 37. Have students listen and point to the phrases.

 CD 2 Track 37

1. *at the movies*
2. *at the store*
3. *in the restaurant*
4. *on the bus*
5. *on the train*
6. *in the taxi*

2. Play the audio again and have students repeat the phrases.

B. Practice the sentence.

1. Listen to the sentence pattern.
Write the pattern on the board or direct students' attention to their books. Play Track 38. Point to the words as students listen to the audio. Then have students repeat.

 CD 2 Track 38

They're at the movies.

They're at the movies.

2. Practice the rhythm.

   a. Play Track 38 again. This time, have students listen to the rhythm and intonation of the sentences.

   b. Play the track again. Have students tap or clap to match the rhythm. Have students listen to the spoken sentence to hear how it matches the rhythm, and then have them repeat the sentence along with the recorded rhythm.

   c. Have students tap or clap the rhythm and practice saying the sentences without the audio.

3. Practice the sentences.

   a. Play Track 39 and have students point to the vocabulary pictures as they listen.

CD 2 Track 39

1. *They're at the movies.*
2. *They're at the store.*
3. *They're in the restaurant.*
4. *They're on the bus.*
5. *They're on the train.*
6. *They're in the taxi.*

   b. Play Track 39 again and have students repeat the sentences.

   c. Divide the class into pairs and have students practice the sentences as they point to the pictures in the book.

📕 BOOKS CLOSED

Introduce the question forms.

1. Introduce the *Wh-* question-and-answer pattern.

   a. Review locations and prepositions. Hold up Teacher Cards 149–154 (locations) one at a time and have students say each location with the correct preposition *(in the taxi).*

   b. Place Teacher Card 149 on the board. Have two students stand near the card *(at the movies)*. Model the question and answer: *Where are they? They're at the movies.* Repeat the question with several location cards and student volunteers. Students answer the questions.

   c. Have students repeat the question. Practice the question several times.

   d. Have students practice asking questions. Ss: *Where are they?* Hold up a Teacher Card and answer. T: *They're (in the taxi).*

   e. Divide the class into two groups. Use Teacher Cards to cue the students. Groups take turns asking and answering questions.

   f. Place the Teacher Cards around the room. Have an identical set of Student Cards on a table. Have two students stand near one location. Face the class so you can't see where the students are standing. Ask *Where are they?* Students answer *They're (in the taxi).* Hold up the

matching Student Card to confirm. Then, have students take the teacher's place at the front of the room so that they are both asking and answering the question. Repeat several times.

> **Grammar Tip:** Review the difference between singular and plural pronouns by giving students four occupation Teacher Cards (*teacher* and *teachers,* and *student* and *students,* for example—one of the singular cards needs to be male and one female) and place one location card on the board. Have students place the appropriate person card next to the location card after listening to your sentence. Students will quickly figure out the difference between: *He's at the park, She's at the park,* and *They're at the park.*

2. Introduce the *Yes/No* question-and-answer pattern.

   a. Place Teacher Cards around the room and have two student volunteers stand near one of the locations *(at the movies)* and ask *Are they in the taxi?* Prompt students to answer *No, they aren't. They're at the movies.*

   b. Repeat with other student volunteers standing in various locations. Have students practice both *Yes, they are* and *No, they aren't. They're (at the store).*

   c. Have students repeat the question. Practice the question several times with various locations.

   d. Have students ask you questions about volunteers standing in different locations. If desired, cue the question by showing a Student Card (so that you can elicit both *yes* and *no* answers).

   e. Divide the class into two groups. Use Teacher Cards to cue the students. Groups take turns asking and answering questions. Group A: *Is (she) at home?* Group B: *Yes, (she) is* or *No, (she) isn't.*

Let's Learn More

 BOOKS OPEN

C. Practice the question and answer.

1. Listen to the *Wh-* question-and-answer pattern.

a. Have students look at page 51 and describe things and locations they see.

b. Play Track 40. Have students listen and point to the question and answer. Continue to play the audio, and have students listen to the questions and answers and point to the appropriate parts of the picture.

 CD 2 Track 40

Where are they?
They're in the taxi.

Where are they?
They're in the taxi.

2. Practice the rhythm.

a. Play Track 40 again and have students listen to the rhythm and intonation of the question and answer.

b. Play the track again. Have students tap or clap to match the rhythm of the audio. Have students listen to the spoken question and answer to hear how they match the rhythm, and then have them repeat the patterns along with the recorded rhythm.

c. Have the students tap or clap the rhythm and practice saying the question and answer without the audio.

3. Practice the *Wh-* questions and answers.

a. Have students look at page 51 and describe the things they see.

b. Play Track 41. Have students listen and point to the appropriate pictures.

 CD 2 Track 41

1. *Where are they?*
   They're on the bus.
2. *Where are they?*
   They're in the restaurant.
3. *Where are they?*
   They're on the train.
4. *Where are they?*
   They're at the movies.
5. *Where are they?*
   They're in the taxi.
6. *Where are they?*
   They're at the store.

c. Play the audio again and have students repeat the questions and answers.

d. Divide the class into question and answer groups and play the audio again. Each group repeats either the question or answer. Repeat with groups switching roles.

e. Have students work in pairs and take turns asking and answering questions about the pictures.

D. Ask and answer.

1. Listen to the *Yes/No* question-and-answer pattern.

a. Present the pattern by writing it on the board or direct students' attention to the pattern in the book.

b. Play Track 42. Point to the words as students listen. Have students repeat after the audio.

 CD 2 Track 42

Are they at the park?
Yes, they are.
Are they at the park?
No, they aren't.

Are they at the park?
Yes, they are.
Are they at the park?
No, they aren't.

2. Practice the rhythm.

a. Play Track 42 again and have students listen to the rhythm and

intonation of the question and answer.

b. Have students tap or clap to match the rhythm of the audio. Have students listen to the spoken question and answers to hear how they match the rhythm, and then have them repeat the patterns along with the recorded rhythm.

c. Have the students tap or clap the rhythm and practice saying the questions and answers without the audio.

3. Practice the *Yes/No* questions and answers.

a. Play Track 43. Have students listen and point to the appropriate pictures.

 CD 2 Track 43

1. *Are they at the park?*
   Yes, they are.
2. *Are they on the train?*
   No, they aren't.
3. *Are they in the car?*
   Yes, they are.

b. Divide the class into pairs. Have students look at each picture and take turns asking and answering questions using the sample question and answers. Make sure students are asking some questions that require a negative answer.

> **Grammar Tip:** Review with students that *they are* in *Yes, they are* is never contracted.

GAMES AND ACTIVITIES

1. Where Is She Now? practices the sentence pattern *She's at the movies* and memorization. Place six location cards on the board. Place two singular occupation cards (one for *he* and one for *she*) and one plural occupation card beside three location cards. Give students one minute to look at the configuration, then have them close their eyes. Move the people cards next to different locations. Tell students to open their eyes and identify what has changed. For example: *She's in the restaurant.*

2. Scrambled Sentences (p. 24) practices the sentence pattern and the prepositions. Make several sets of word cards that include locations/transportation, *he, she, they, is, are, a, the,* and the prepositions used with them in this lesson. Divide the class into groups and give each group a complete set of word cards. Set a time limit and see how many correct sentences students can make using the cards.

3. Walk and Talk (p. 26) practices using the question *Are they (at the park)?* Have three or four pairs of students sit in various places around the classroom. Give each pair a location card. The other students walk around in pairs. Walkings pairs must stop by one of the seated pairs and take turns asking each other *Are they (at the park)?* Continue until walking pairs have talked about at least two seated pairs. Make sure walking pairs practice the negative response. Then have students change roles.

EXTRA PRACTICE

WORKBOOK pages 50–51

Assign for homework or do in class. For instructions and Answer Key, see Teacher's Book page 170.

SKILLS BOOK pages 50–51

Assign for homework or do in class. For instructions and Answer Key, see Teacher's Book page 155.

REPRODUCIBLE WORKSHEET
Teacher's Book page 185

What's Different?: Locations provides further fun and practice with the location vocabulary of the lesson. For instructions, see page 193.

COMPONENTS LINK

CD-ROM 2

For extra fun, students can play Unit 6, Game 3 on a computer at school or at home. Students follow the prompts to complete the picture. This activity reinforces listening, reading, prepositions, and the Let's Learn and Let's Learn More vocabulary.

LET'S GO TESTS AND QUIZZES

Lesson Quiz: Explain and administer the reproducible Unit 6 Let's Learn More quiz from *Let's Go Tests and Quizzes,* page 30. Instructions and Answer Key are also in *Let's Go Tests and Quizzes.*

LET'S CHANT LET'S SING 2

Page 42: "Where's Penny?"

This chant practices the question-and-answer pattern *Where's Penny? She's at home.*

LET'S GO PICTURE DICTIONARY

Use pages 84–85, More Stores and Buildings, to supplement the lesson and increase challenge.

1. Review familiar words and point out new words you wish to teach.

2. Practice the words with the question-and-answer patterns *Where are they? They're in the restaurant. Are they in the restaurant? Yes, they are. No, they aren't.*

Let's Build

Topic: Locations

Lesson objectives: Students learn how to replace specific nouns (*teacher*) with pronouns (*he*) when it's clear who the pronoun refers to.

New grammar: *(The shopkeeper) is (at the store). Where's (the taxi driver)? Where are (the cooks)? Is (the police officer) (in the restaurant)? Are (the teachers) (at school)?*

Review grammar: prepositions

Review language: locations, occupations, *chair*

Materials: Teacher and Student Cards 118–127, 143–154, CD 2 Tracks 44–46, contraction cards (*Where's, They're, He's, She's, isn't, aren't*)

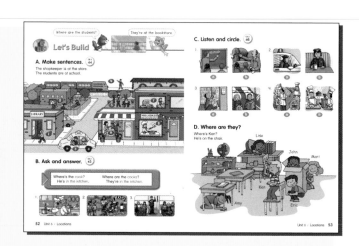

WARM UP AND REVIEW

1. Vocabulary Race (p. 24) reviews vocabulary and has students use their imaginations. Make a list of 8–10 of the locations. Divide the class into teams. Whisper the first location (*at the park*) to S1 from each team. S1s race back to their team and try to get their teammates to say the same location (by drawing pictures or arranging objects—no speaking). S2 races up to the teacher and whispers his or her guess to the teacher. If correct (including correct preposition—*in, on,* or *at*), the team moves on to the next location. The first team to guess all locations in order wins.

2. Practice substituting pronouns for nouns. Show a Teacher Card (family or occupations). Students decide whether the correct pronoun would be *he, she,* or *they*. Move through the cards quickly so that students have to respond without thinking. If students do well with people, add objects (like toys or classroom objects) and animals (which usually take *it*). For additional challenge, give students a sentence using the person or object, and have students repeat the sentence with the correct pronoun.

PRESENT THE LANGUAGE

📕 BOOKS CLOSED

Introduce the sentence patterns.

1. Show Teacher Cards 118 (*shopkeeper*) and 150 (*at the store*). Model *The shopkeeper is at the store* and have students repeat. Continue with other occupation and location cards. Review the prepositions, if necessary.

2. Show students an occupation card and a location card and have them say the sentence. Make sure they use the correct preposition.

3. Put several occupation and location cards on the board. Have a volunteer come to the board, point to one of each, and make a sentence. Continue with several volunteers.

4. Have a volunteer be the "teacher" and point to two of the cards to cue the class to make a sentence. Continue with several "teachers."

📖 BOOKS OPEN

A. Make sentences.

1. Have students look at the picture on page 52 and describe what they see. Encourage them to guess what language they will hear.

2. Play Track 44. Have students listen to the audio and point to the pictures.

 CD 2 Track 44

The shopkeeper is at the store.
The students are at school.

1. *The student is at the library.*
2. *The teacher is at school.*
3. *The taxi driver is in the taxi.*
4. *The train conductor is next to the train.*
5. *The police officer is at the park.*
6. *The shopkeeper is at the store.*
7. *The office worker is in the office.*
8. *The cook is in the restaurant.*

3. Play the audio again. Have students repeat after each sentence.

4. Do the sentence activity. Divide the class into pairs. Have students describe the pictures to each other. Have them take turns pointing to people and locations and making a sentence for each one. Ask several students for their answers.

B. Ask and answer.

1. Have students look at the pictures and describe what they see.

2. Show students how there is always more than one way to refer to a person. Point to a female student and say *She is at school.* Ask the class for a word to replace *she.*

Students answer *Amy is at school* and *The student is at school*. Repeat with a male student.

3. Have a female student stand up and hold a location Teacher Card or a room card from Unit 3. Ask the class *Where's the student?* Model the answer *She's (in the kitchen)*. Continue with several other students and cards, including *they*.

4. Play Track 45. Point to the pictures as students listen to the audio.

 CD 2 Track 45

Where's the cook?
    He's in the kitchen.
Where are the cooks?
    They're in the kitchen.

1. Where are the cooks?
    They're in the kitchen.
2. Where's the teacher?
    She's at the zoo.
3. Where are the office workers?
    They're on the train.

5. Play the audio again and have students repeat after each sentence.

6. Divide the class into pairs. Have them take turns pointing to the pictures and asking and answering a question for each one.

7. Ask students for their answers.

C. Listen and circle.

1. Have students look at the pictures and describe what they see. Then play the first question and answer of Track 46.

2. Play Track 46 and have students circle the correct letter.

 CD 2 Track 46

1. Is the teacher at the zoo?
    Yes, he is.
2. Is the police officer in the car?
    No, she isn't. She's in the restaurant.
3. Are the students on the train?
    No, they aren't. They're in the library.
4. Are the cooks in the store?
    Yes, they are.

3. Play the track again so that students can check their answers.

D. Where are they?

1. Have students look at the picture and describe what they see. Review objects in the picture, if necessary.

2. Point to Ken in the picture and ask *Where is Ken?* Model the answer *He's on the chair.* Ask about one or two of the other children in the picture and have students answer.

3. Divide the class into pairs. Have students take turns asking and answering questions about the children in the picture.

4. Have several students demonstrate the question and answer for the class.

GAMES AND ACTIVITIES

1. **Short Story** practices writing pronouns and writing several sentences together. Show students how varying nouns and pronouns helps keep language from becoming boring. Write a short story on the board.

> For example: *The train conductor is on the train. The train conductor likes trains. The train conductor is happy.*

Ask students to identify which words in each sentence repeat (*train conductor*). Explain that the first sentence in a story usually gives the most information and the other sentences use pronouns. Read the story again, substituting pronouns, to see how much better it sounds with variety. Have pairs work together to write their own short story.

2. Have students combine location vocabulary with review prepositions (*in, on, under, by, in front of, behind, next to*) and review vocabulary (family, toys, animals, furniture, rooms, etc.) to create sentences and questions involving more than one location. For example: *The teacher is in the living room at home. The teacher is on the sofa in the living room at home.* Encourage students to build long sentences.

EXTRA PRACTICE

WORKBOOK **pages 52–53**

Assign for homework or do in class. For instructions and Answer Key, see Teacher's Book page 170.

SKILLS BOOK **pages 52–53**

Assign for homework or do in class. For instructions and Answer Key, see Teacher's Book page 155.

COMPONENTS LINK

CD-ROM 2

For extra fun, students can play Unit 6, Game 4 on a computer at school or at home. Students look at the picture and answer *yes/no* questions. This activity reinforces listening, reading, the Let's Learn and Let's Learn Some vocabulary, and the Let's Build grammar pattern.

LET'S GO TESTS AND QUIZZES

Lesson Quiz: Explain and administer the reproducible Unit 6 Let's Build quiz from *Let's Go Tests and Quizzes*, page 31. Instructions and Answer Key are also in *Let's Go Tests and Quizzes*.

Unit Test: Explain and administer the reproducible Unit 6 Test from *Let's Go Tests and Quizzes*, page 54. Instructions and Answer Key are also in *Let's Go Tests and Quizzes*.

LET'S GO READER

Now that students have completed Unit 6, they are ready to read "Where Are You?" See Teacher's Book page 20 for suggestions on how to present *Readers* and incorporate them into your lesson plans.

Units 5–6 Listen and Review
Let's Learn About the Seasons

Topic: Units 5–6 Review; seasons

Lesson objectives: Students demonstrate comprehension of language and vocabulary taught in Units 5 and 6. Students also learn the names of the four seasons and talk about seasonal activities.

New language: *spring, summer, fall, winter*

Review language: daily activities, occupations, locations

Review grammar: *What's the matter? Who is (she)? Thanks for your help. You're welcome. Get better soon! I (wake up) every morning. (She's) (a shopkeeper). Is (he) (a farmer)? Yes, (he) is. No, (he) isn't. Who are they? They are (teachers). Are they (teachers)? Yes, they are. No, they aren't. Who is (Mr. Jones)? He's (a teacher). Is (he) (a teacher or a student)? Can you (make breakfast) at school? Where are you? Can you come to the park? What do you do every afternoon? I (study English) every afternoon. Where is (he)? (He's) (at school). Where are they? They're (at the movies). Are they (at the park)?*

Materials: Teacher and Student Cards 118–158, CD 2 Tracks 47–49, teacher-made cards of base verbs, contraction cards (*we're, can't, I'm, he's, she's*)

PART ONE: UNITS 5–6 LISTEN AND REVIEW

Review Activities

1. Let's talk/Let's sing.

a. Step Away Lines (p. 26). In pairs, have students personalize the Unit 5 conversation (bring in additional feelings from *Let's Go Picture Dictionary* or use student suggestions, and decide on a name for the nurse). Students stand in two lines facing each other, and take one step back after each line.

b. Telephone Conversations. Have each student take a location Student Card, or assign each student a location. Students sit facing away from a partner and practice the Unit 6 conversation (as if talking on the telephone).

c. Have students combine language from Units 5 and 6 to create an original telephone conversation. Write it on the board and have them practice in pairs.

Example:

A: *Hi, _____. We're at the park. Where are you?*
B: (sounding ill) *I'm at home.*
A: *Can you come to the park?*
B: *No, I can't.*
A: *What's the matter?*
B: *I'm sick.*
A: *That's too bad. Feel better soon!*
B: *Thanks. Good-bye.*
A: *See you later.*

2. Let's move.

a. Give pairs or groups Let's Move verb Student Cards from Units 5 and 6. Include review vocabulary from earlier lessons, if desired. Students use the cards to talk about their morning and afternoon routines. S1: *I wake up every morning. I practice the piano every afternoon. I don't watch TV every morning.*

b. Pick Up (p. 25). Place Student Cards from Units 5 and 6 facedown on the table or floor. In pairs, students play **Rock, Paper, Scissors**, saying *Morning, afternoon, 1, 2, 3!*

The winner picks up a card and makes a sentence. S: *I (get dressed) every (morning).* For added challenge, include verb cards from earlier units.

c. Make new verb phrases. Write the verbs from Unit 5 and 6 Let's move on the board: *eat, study, talk, watch,* and *practice.* Have students work in groups to think of additional verb phrases using these base verbs (e.g., *eat apples, study piano, talk to my mother, practice English,* etc.). Write the new phrases on the board under each base verb. Then, have pairs or groups of students place teacher-made cards of base verbs facedown on a desk. Students turn over one card at a time and make a sentence using a new verb phrase.

3. Let's Learn/Let's Learn More

a. Guess the Word. Students work in groups. S1 chooses one of the vocabulary words from Units 5 and 6 (occupations, locations) and writes one letter from the word on a piece of paper. The other students try to guess the word. After each round of guessing, S1 adds one additional letter to the paper.

b. Bingo (p. 22). On a bingo grid, students write nine occupation words. For greater challenge, have students listen for singular and plural forms of the occupation vocabulary.

c. Charades (p. 22). Students select a Student or Teacher Card and act out the occupation or location shown. T: *Is he a nurse? Is he at school?* etc.

d. Students work in pairs or small groups. Place location and occupation Student Cards facedown in two piles. Students turn over one card from each pile and use both words in sentences: *They're farmers. They're on the train.*

Introduce Listen and Review

 BOOKS CLOSED

1. On the board, set up a sample to resemble the activity on page 54 of the Student Book. Put three of the Teacher Cards from 118–127 on the chalk rail. Draw a letter *a* above the first card, a letter *b* above the second, and a letter *c* above the third. Have one student stand by the cards. Identify one of the cards. T: *He's a farmer.* The student points to the correct card and circles the appropriate letter. Repeat as necessary until all the students understand the procedure.

2. Open your book to page 54. Show the page to the class. Have students identify the items in numbers 1–6. Have students identify the actions shown in numbers 5–6.

📖 **BOOKS OPEN**

A. Listen and circle.

1. Students open their books to page 54. Play Track 47. Have students listen and circle the correct picture.

💿 CD 2 Track 47

1. Who's he?
    He's Mr. Jones.
    He's a train conductor.
2. Is she a taxi driver?
    No, she isn't. She's a police officer.
3. Who are they?
    They're Mr. and Mrs. Smith.
    They're firefighters.
4. Are they engineers?
    No, they aren't. They're pilots.
5. I eat breakfast every morning.
6. I practice the piano every afternoon.

B. Listen and number.

1. Play Track 48. Have students listen to the audio and number the correct pictures.

💿 CD 2 Track 48

1. Where is he?
    He's at home.
2. Where are they?
    They're on the train.
3. Where is she?
    She's at school.
4. Are they at the park?
    No, they aren't. They are at the movies.

PART TWO: LET'S LEARN ABOUT THE SEASONS

 BOOKS CLOSED

1. Present the topic: Seasons

Hold up pictures representative of each season (from a magazine, or use Teacher Cards 155–158) and ask students to tell you the names for the seasons in their native language. Next, ask if students know any of the English words for the seasons. Don't feel that you need to correct them at this point—the goal is to see what they already know about this topic.

2. Present the vocabulary.

a. Hold up the same four pictures from Step 1. Say the name for each season. Students repeat.

b. Hold up a picture, at random. Students say the appropriate name of the season.

3. Present the language pattern.

a. Hold up the picture for *spring*, or hold up a teacher-made word card, and ask students to call out activities they do during this season. Use Teacher Cards from earlier units to help them remember activity vocabulary. Place the cards on the chalk rail for later reference. Choose one of the activities and model the sentence. T: *I can fly a kite in the spring.* Students repeat. Do the same thing for each season.

b. Hold up a season picture or word card and model the question. T: *What can you do in the spring?* Ss: *I can fly a kite.* Have students answer for each season.

c. Have students repeat the question and correct pronunciation as needed. Have students practice the question for various seasons several times.

d. Put students into pairs or small groups, and have them practice asking and answering questions about things they can do in each season. Have students use the Teacher Cards on the chalk rail for reference.

e. Play the audio again. Have students repeat after each word.

4. Practice the pattern.

Students open their books to page 55.

a. Have students listen to the question and answer and point to the appropriate season.

CD 2 Track 49

What can you do in the spring?
   I can fly a kite.

1. *What can you do in the spring?*
    I can fly a kite.
2. *What can you do in the summer?*
    I can go swimming.
3. *What can you do in the fall?*
    I can play baseball.
4. *What can you do in the winter?*
    I can ice-skate.

b. 1-2-3-Finished! (p. 24). In pairs, have students take turns asking and answering questions about their activities during each season. Each pair of students stands up and asks and answers three questions. The first pair to complete the task, say *Finished*, and sit down, wins.

GAMES AND ACTIVITIES

1. Give students more practice with seasons by identifying which months belong in each season for their own part of the world. Give students both season and month vocabulary cards, and have them work together to decide which months belong in each season. Have students compare their ideas. If you want to increase international awareness, have students then change their groupings for the other hemisphere (e.g., Spring is usually March, April and May in the northern hemisphere, but September, October and November in the southern hemisphere).

2. Pick Up (p. 25). Place multiple copies of Student Cards facedown on the table or floor. Students do **Rock, Paper, Scissors** with the winner picking up a card and making a sentence *I can/can't swim in the winter.* The student with the most cards wins.

3. Make a personalized book. Fold two pieces of paper into a four-page book. Each page is for one season. Students write what they can do in each season and illustrate.

COMPONENTS LINK

CD-ROM 2

For extra fun, students can play the Review Units 5–6 game on a computer at school or at home. Students follow the prompts to match the correct picture as it goes by. This activity reinforces listening, the review vocabulary, and grammar pattern *What can you do in the (spring)? I can (fly a kite).*

LET'S GO TESTS AND QUIZZES

Units 5–6 Listen and Review Test: Explain and administer the reproducible Units 5–6 Listen and Review Test from *Let's Go Tests and Quizzes,* page 72. Instructions and Answer Key are also in *Let's Go Tests and Quizzes.*

Lesson Quiz: Explain and administer the reproducible Let's Learn About the Seasons quiz from *Let's Go Tests and Quizzes,* page 64. Instructions and Answer Key are also in *Let's Go Tests and Quizzes.*

LET'S GO PICTURE DICTIONARY

Use page 5, Calendar, and page 58–59, Sports, to supplement the lesson and increase challenge.

1. Review familiar words and point out new words you wish to teach.

2. Practice the words with the question-and-answer pattern *What can you do in the spring? I can fly a kite.*

Unit 7 Doing Things

Let's Start

Topic: Activities

Lesson objectives: Students talk about what they are doing

New grammar: *What are you doing? I'm (riding a bicycle). We're (swimming). Do you (cook dinner) every evening?*

Review grammar: *Yes, I do. No, I don't. Let's*

New language: *cook dinner, wash dishes, read e-mail, do homework, evening*

Materials: Teacher and Student Cards 159–163, CD 2 Tracks 50–55, beanbag, contraction cards (*I'm, we're, What's, He's*)

WARM UP AND REVIEW

Choose one of the following:

1. Who's He? reviews occupations. Use multiple sets of Student Cards 118–127 (occupations). Divide the class into teams and arrange them in rows. S1 in each row picks up a card and asks *Who's he/she?* to S2. S2 answers *He/She's (a taxi driver)* and then shows the card to S3 and asks the question. Continue to the end of the row. The first team to complete the question and answer wins a point. Continue with other cards.

2. Practice verb phrases from Units 1–6. Divide the class into teams. S1 from each team chooses a verb phrase card and makes a sentence with the action and either *in the morning, in the afternoon,* or *in the evening: I (talk on the telephone) in the evening.* If the sentence works, the team gets a point. If it doesn't (e.g., *I make breakfast at night*) they do not.

PRESENT THE DIALOGUE

📕 BOOKS CLOSED

Present the dialogue.

1. Introduce the dialogue.

   a. Say the first line of the dialogue and have students repeat: *Let's play a game!* Have students identify words they already know.

   b. Hold up Teacher Cards for activities from Level 1 and Level 2 Units 1–6 and have students make sentences (*Let's make a circle!*).

   c. Have students say *What are you doing?* in a series of three, several times: *What are you doing? What are you doing? What are you doing?* Pick up speed until they are able to say it at natural speed.

   d. Have two students stand up. Have S1 pretend to read a book. Have S2 ask *What are you doing?* Model the answer *I'm reading a book* and have S2 repeat. Have S1 and S2 repeat the question and answer and then switch roles.

   e. Divide the class into two groups. Have Group A pick up their books and pretend to read them. Have Group B point to Group A and ask *What are you doing?* Model the

answer *We're reading a book.* Practice several times and have groups switch roles.

   f. Divide the class into groups of three and have them practice the question and answer using *I* and *we.* Demonstrate with one group first, if necessary.

   g. Divide the class into teams. Show a Teacher Card of a verb phrase. S1 of each team says *I'm (dancing)* and does the action. S2 then says it and repeats the action. The rest of the students do the same in turn. When all of the students on a team finish saying *I'm (dancing),* they all say *(We're dancing),* do the action, and sit down.

📖 BOOKS OPEN

A. Let's talk.

Students learn how to ask what people are doing.

1. Listen to the dialogue.

   a. Have students look at the scenes on page 56 and describe what they see.

   b. Play Track 50. Have students listen to the dialogue and point to the speech bubbles. Have them identify words they hear.

Let's Start

CD 2 Track 50

Jenny: *Let's play a game!*
What are you doing?
Scott: *I'm riding a bicycle.*
Jenny: *What are you doing?*
Kate/Scott: *We're swimming.*

c. Play the dialogue again and have students repeat each line after the characters.

2. Practice the pattern.

a. Write the pattern on the board, or direct students' attention to their books. Play Track 51. Point to the words as students listen to the dialogue. Then have students repeat after the audio.

CD 2 Track 51

What are you doing?
I'm riding a bicycle.
We're swimming.

We are = We're

b. Write the explanation of the new contraction on the board: *We are = We're*. Review *I am = I'm*, if necessary. Follow the procedure on page 196 for how to teach contractions with cards. Have students practice saying both *I'm/I am* and *We're/We are*. Point to the explanation on the board as they practice.

3. Practice the dialogue.

a. Ask one of the questions from the dialogue and have a volunteer answer. Repeat for the other question. Then ask the questions out of order and have volunteers answer. To make this more challenging, give one of the answers from the dialogue and have students ask the matching question.

b. Do **Conversation Lines** (p. 26) to practice the dialogue in pairs.

c. Have students practice the dialogue with several partners, using different activities.

d. Play a **Charades** (p. 22) relay game. Divide the class into teams and have them face the front of the classroom. Whisper a different action to the last student (S1) in each team. S1 then does the action without speaking. Next S1 taps the shoulder of S2, who turns around and asks *What are you doing?* S1 does the action. S2 taps S3 on the shoulder, and so on. The answer is never said aloud. When the final student is asked, he answers by doing the gesture and saying *I'm (swimming)*. The first team to finish and correctly say and do the action wins.

B. Let's sing.

"Doing Things" reinforces the language from the dialogue using rhythm and song.

1. Play and listen.

Play Track 52. Have students listen and identify the words they recognize from Let's Talk.

CD 2 Track 52

Doing Things

What's he doing?
Reading, He's reading,
He's reading.
What's he reading?
He's reading a comic book
and talking on the telephone.

What's she doing?
Eating, She's eating,
She's eating.
What's she eating?
She's eating spaghetti and
talking on the telephone.

What are you doing?
Cooking, I'm cooking,
I'm cooking.
What are you cooking?
I'm cooking breakfast and
talking on the telephone.

2. Practice the rhythm.

a. Introduce the song rhythmically. Have students clap to keep the beat as you model the song line by line. Have students repeat after you.

b. Play the song again. Encourage students to sing along.

3. Do the song activity.

Play the song again. This time have half of the class sing one part and half sing the second part. Add gestures to go with the song lyrics. For example, students can pretend to talk on the telephone.

4. Read the lyrics.

Have students look at the song pictures and lyrics. Ask students to point to and read words that they recognize.

5. Work in groups.

Have students work in groups to create an original verse by inserting new actions using verbs from previous units. Then, sing the song again with the new verses.

 BOOKS CLOSED

Present the verb phrases.

1. Introduce the verb phrases.

a. Say *cook dinner* with an action, and repeat the action several times. Have students repeat several times with action before going on to the next phrase. Repeat with the other phrases.

b. To check understanding, say the phrases in random order and have students do the appropriate action.

c. Show students Teacher Cards 159–162. Have them both say the phrase and do the action.

d. Divide the class into two groups. Have the groups take turns saying the words and doing the actions. Use Teacher Cards to cue the speaking group.

2. Introduce *Do you (cook dinner) every evening?*

a. Add *Do you* and *every evening* to each verb phrase and have students repeat the question and do the action.

b. Hold up Teacher Card 163 and ask *Do you cook dinner every evening?* Model the answer *Yes, I do.* Hold the card upside down and ask the question again. Model the answer *No, I don't.* Practice the question and answer with different cards.

 BOOKS OPEN

C. Let's move.

Students learn useful everyday language by combining rhythm and actions.

1. Listen and point to the verb phrases.

a. Play Track 53. Have students listen and point to the appropriate pictures.

 CD 2 Track 53

1. *cook dinner*
2. *wash the dishes*
3. *read e-mail*
4. *do homework*

b. Play the audio again. Students listen and repeat.

2. Practice the rhythm.

a. Play Track 54. Have students listen to the audio.

 CD 2 Track 54

Do you cook dinner every evening?
   Yes, I do.
Do you cook dinner every evening?
   No, I don't.

Do you cook dinner every evening?
   Yes, I do.
Do you cook dinner every evening?
   No, I don't.

b. Play Track 54 again. Have students clap or tap to keep the rhythm and repeat the question and answer with the audio.

c. Have students tap or clap the rhythm and practice saying the question and answer without the audio.

3. Practice the questions and answers.

a. Play Track 55. Have students listen to the questions and answers and point to the appropriate pictures.

 CD 2 Track 55

Do you cook dinner every evening?
   Yes, I do.
Do you wash the dishes every evening?
   Yes, I do.
Do you read e-mails every evening?
   Yes, I do.
Do you do homework every evening?
   No, I don't.

b. Play the audio again and have students repeat the questions and answers.

c. Divide the class into question-and-answer groups and play the audio again. Each group repeats either the question or answer. Repeat, with groups switching roles.

d. Have students work in pairs and take turns asking and answering questions about the pictures.

GAMES AND ACTIVITIES

1. Beanbag Circle (p. 24) gives more practice with *What are you doing?* On every second or third question, say *We* to cue the student answering to hold hands with the students to the left and right. Those students answer together *We're (dancing).*

2. Find Your Partner (p. 24) reinforces the Let's Move verb phrases and question-and-answer pattern. Give each student a verb card and have them walk around the room asking *Do you (cook dinner) every evening?* Students answer with *Yes, I do* or *No, I don't.* When a student finds another student with the same card, they sit in pairs until all the students find their partners. Then each pair stands up, does the action, and says their card with a time phrase: *We cook dinner every morning/afternoon.*

3. Scrambled Sentences (p. 24) practices word order. Copy the lyrics from "Doing Things" (p. 118) onto a sheet of paper and cut it into individual sentences. In pairs or groups, have students put the sentences in order. Play the song for students to check their arrangement, and then let students sing along.

EXTRA PRACTICE

WORKBOOK **pages 56–57**

Assign for homework or do in class. For instructions and Answer Key, see Teacher's Book page 171.

SKILLS BOOK **pages 56–57**

Assign for homework or do in class. For instructions and Answer Key, see Teacher's Book page 156.

COMPONENTS LINK

LET'S GO TESTS AND QUIZZES

Lesson Quiz: Explain and administer the reproducible Unit 7 Let's Start quiz from *Let's Go Tests and Quizzes*, page 32. Instructions and Answer Key are also in *Let's Go Tests and Quizzes.*

LET'S CHANT LET'S SING 2

Page 38: "What Are You Doing?"

This song practices body vocabulary with the question-and-answer pattern *What are you doing? I'm playing a game.*

Page 39: "Long, Black Hair"

This chant practices adjectives with the question-and-answer pattern *What are you doing? I'm combing my hair.*

LET'S GO PICTURE DICTIONARY

Use pages 62–63, Outdoor Activities, to supplement the lesson and increase challenge.

1. Review familiar words and point out new words you wish to teach.

2. Practice the words with the question-and-answer pattern *Do you cook dinner every evening? Yes, I do. No, I don't.*

Let's Learn

Topic: Activities

Lesson objectives: Students ask what others are doing with *he/she*.

New grammar: *What's he/she doing? He/She is (dancing). Is he/she (running)?*

Review grammar: *Yes, he/she is. No, he/she isn't.*

New language: *dancing, fishing, sleeping, coloring a picture, singing a song, running, walking, throwing a ball*

Materials: Teacher and Student Cards 164–171, CD 2 Tracks 56–62, puppets, contraction cards (*What's, he's, she's, isn't*)

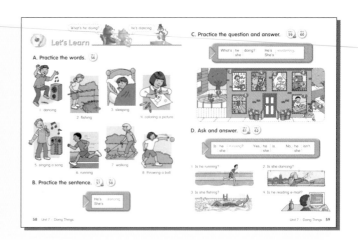

WARM UP AND REVIEW

Choose one of the following:

1. Review the sentence pattern and verb phrases from Let's Start. Divide the class into groups. Hand out several verb phrase Teacher Cards to each group. Say a sentence: *We are swimming.* Have groups choose the correct card and arrange themselves to match the sentence; they link arms to indicate *we* and hold up the *swim* card. Then they repeat the sentence. For a sentence with *I*, groups designate one student to hold up the card and repeat the sentence.

2. We're/I'm practices pronouns. Divide the class into groups. Use several sets of location Student Cards (143–154). Give a card to each student. S1 asks S2 *Where are you?* S2 answers with his or her card *I'm at the park* and so on down the line. When students find someone with the same card, they say *We're at the park.*

PRESENT THE LANGUAGE

📖 BOOKS CLOSED

Introduce the words.

1. Use Teacher Cards 164–171 to introduce the verb phrases with action. Show one Teacher Card at a time and say the verb phrase.

Students repeat each phrase several times, doing the action each time.

2. Conduct a quick drill of the words. Do not speak as you show the cards. Have students identify the new verbs plus all the previously learned verbs. Gradually pick up speed as students get used to saying the words.

3. Show a verb card, and practice saying the root and its *-ing* form. Then get into teams and pass out Student Cards to each student. In groups, have the students say their card with the two forms.

> **Teaching Tip:** In teaching the *-ing* form, contrast the root form and the *-ing* form, enunciating the difference of pronunciation when *-ing* is added: *swim = swim-ming,* not *swim-ing.* Then drill only the words with the *-ing* form, gradually picking up speed. Conduct a quick drill after you introduce the phrases. Don't speak as you show the Teacher Cards. Gradually pick up speed. When students can say them well, add the objects: *singing a song, washing the dishes,* etc.

Introduce the sentence pattern.

1. Use Teacher Cards 164–171. Show each card and say the sentence *He's (dancing).* Have students repeat the sentence pattern with gestures.

2. Have students practice with *He's/She's*, substituting all the vocabulary. Students should say sentences at the same time as the teacher, not repeat after the teacher.

3. Conduct a quick drill of the sentences using Teacher Cards 164–171. Do not speak as you show the cards. Gradually pick up speed as students get used to saying the sentences.

> **Teaching Tip:** Review *he* and *she* by showing occupation cards and having students identify them with the pronouns *He/She's a (teacher).* Show the verb phrases and practice with *He's* only: *He's dancing, He's fishing,* etc. Then practice with *She's.* Then mix the cards so that students are saying the pronoun on the cards. Conduct a quick drill. Don't speak as you show Teacher Cards. Gradually pick up speed until students can say them well.

BOOKS OPEN

A. Practice the words.

1. Play Track 56. Have students listen and point to the words.

 CD 2 Track 56

1. dancing
2. fishing
3. sleeping
4. coloring a picture
5. singing a song
6. running
7. walking
8. throwing a ball

2. Play the audio again and have students repeat the words.

B. Practice the sentence.

1. Listen to the sentence pattern.

a. Write the pattern on the board or direct students' attention to it in the book. Play Track 57. Point to the words as students listen to the audio. Then have students repeat after the audio.

 CD 2 Track 57

He's dancing.

He's dancing.

2. Practice the rhythm.

a. Play Track 57 again and have students listen to the rhythm and intonation of the sentences.

b. Play the audio again. Have students clap or tap to keep the rhythm of the audio. Have students listen to the spoken sentences to hear how the sentences match the rhythm, and then have them repeat the sentences along with the recorded rhythm.

c. Have students tap or clap the rhythm and practice saying the sentences without the audio.

3. Practice the sentences.

a. Play Track 58 and have students point to the vocabulary pictures as they listen.

 CD 2 Track 58

He's dancing
She's fishing.
He's sleeping.
She's coloring a picture.
He's singing a song.
He's running.
She's walking.
She's throwing a ball.

b. Play the audio again. Have students tap or clap to keep the rhythm as they listen and repeat the sentences.

c. Divide the class into pairs and have students do the **Slap** activity (p. 23) with their books open to page 58. One student asks *What's he doing?* and the other points to the same picture in the book and answers *He's (dancing).*

BOOKS CLOSED

Introduce the question forms.

1. Introduce the *Wh-* question-and-answer pattern.

a. Use puppets or student volunteers to present the question and answer.

Puppet A: *What's he doing?*
Puppet B: *He's swimming.*

Repeat with *she.*

b. Show Teacher Cards 164–171 and have students say the sentences *He/She's (dancing).* Ask *What's he/she doing?* before you show each card.

c. Have students practice the question several times. Model the question and help students with pronunciation.

d. Divide the class into two groups. Use Teacher Cards to cue the students. Groups take turns asking and answering questions.

e. Repeat the question-and-answer practice in pairs.

Teaching Tip: Students know already how to ask questions with *What's.* Make sure their pronunciation of /s/ is stressed, since it is usually lost when they say it. Alternately show a *boy/girl* card and have students practice saying *What's he?/What's she?* until they can say it well. Then say the question form *What's he/she doing?* Practice with *he* first, and then *she.* Finally, mix them up so that students can automatically change pronouns without hesitation.

2. Introduce the *Yes/No* question-and-answer pattern.

a. Hold up Teacher Card 169 (*running*) so that students can see it. Model the question *Is (he) running?* Prompt students to answer *Yes, (he) is.* Repeat for the remaining Teacher Cards. Students answer each time.

b. Hold up Teacher Card 169 again and ask *Is (he) singing?* Prompt students to answer *No, (he) isn't.* Repeat for the remaining Teacher Cards and have students answer.

c. Have students practice the question, repeating it several times.

d. Hold the Teacher Cards so that students can't see them. Prompt them to ask questions by either whispering an activity or by having them turn over Student Cards. Answer the question with *Yes, (he) is* or *No, (he) isn't* each time.

e. Divide the class into two groups and have them practice asking and answering questions. Give each group a set of Teacher or Student Cards facedown, and have them turn over one card at a time to cue their questions and answers.

Let's Learn

C. Practice the question and answer.

1. Listen to the *Wh-* question-and-answer pattern.

a. Present the pattern by writing it on the board or direct students' attention to it in the book.

b. Play Track 59. Point to the words as students listen. Have students repeat after the audio.

 CD 2 Track 59

What's he doing?
  He's swimming.

What's he doing?
  He's swimming.

2. Practice the rhythm.

a. Play Track 59. Have students listen to the rhythm and the intonation of the sentences with the audio.

b. Play the track again. Have students clap or tap to match the rhythm of the audio. Have students listen to the spoken question and answer to hear how they match the rhythm, and then have them repeat the pattern along with the recorded rhythm.

c. Have students tap or clap the rhythm and practice saying the question and answer without the audio.

3. Practice the *Wh-* questions and answers.

a. Have students look at page 59 and describe things they see.

b. Play Track 60. Have students listen and point to the appropriate pictures.

 CD 2 Track 60

1. *What's he doing?*
     He's swimming.
2. *What's she doing?*
     She's singing a song.
3. *What's she doing?*
     She's dancing.
4. *What's she doing?*
     She's sleeping.
5. *What's he doing?*
     He's fishing.
6. *What's he doing?*
     He's reading e-mail.
7. *What's he doing?*
     He's coloring a picture.
8. *What's she doing?*
     She's running.

c. Play the audio again. Have students repeat the questions and answers.

d. Divide the class into question-and-answer groups and play the audio again. Each group repeats either the question or answer. Repeat, with groups switching roles.

e. Have students work in pairs and take turns asking and answering questions about the pictures.

D. Ask and answer.

1. Listen to the *Yes/No* question-and-answer pattern.

a. Present the pattern by writing it on the board or direct students' attention to the pattern in the book.

b. Play Track 61. Point to the words as students listen. Have students repeat after the audio.

 CD 2 Track 61

Is he running?
  Yes, he is.
Is she running?
  No, she isn't.

Is he running?
  Yes, he is.
Is she running?
  No, she isn't.

2. Practice the rhythm.

a. Play Track 61 again and have students listen to the rhythm and intonation of the question and answer.

b. Play the track again. Have students tap or clap to match the rhythm of the audio. Have students listen to the spoken question and answer to hear how they match the rhythm, and then have them repeat the patterns along with the recorded rhythm.

3. Practice the *Yes/No* questions and answers.

a. Have students look at page 59 and describe the things they see.

b. Play Track 62. Have students listen and point to the appropriate pictures.

⏺ **CD 2 Track 62**

1. *Is he running?*
     Yes, he is.
2. *Is she dancing?*
     No, she isn't.
3. *Is she fishing?*
     No, she isn't.
4. *Is he reading e-mail?*
     Yes, he is.

c. Have students work in pairs and take turns asking and answering questions about the pictures.

GAMES AND ACTIVITIES

1. Card Game (p. 25) reviews verbs and verb phrases. Divide the class into groups and give each group some verb, object, and character Student Cards. Students take turns turning over the cards and using the characters on the cards to make sentences with *he/she/they*: *(He) (is) eating (a sandwich)*. Play to a time limit. The team with the most correct sentences wins.

2. Cube Game (p. 25) practices pronouns and verbs. Make cubes with *he/she/they/we/I/* * written on the sides. The * indicates that the student can use any pronoun or name. Divide the class into two teams and put Student Cards 164–171 facedown on the floor. One student from each team throws his or her cube, picks up a card, and makes a sentence with the pronoun on the cube and the card. If the sentence is correct, he or she keeps the card. The team with the most cards wins.

3. Pick Up (p. 25) practices the question-and-answer pattern. Place Student Cards 164–171 facedown on the floor, or on a table in the center of pairs of students. Each pair plays **Rock, Paper, Scissors**, chanting *Is he, is she, 1, 2, 3!* The winner picks up a card and asks a question. S1: *Is she dancing?* S2: *Yes, she is.* Students collect cards as they play, and the student with the most cards wins.

EXTRA PRACTICE

WORKBOOK **pages 58–59**

Assign for homework or do in class. For instructions and Answer Key, see Teacher's Book page 171.

SKILLS BOOK **pages 58–59**

Assign for homework or do in class. For instructions and Answer Key, see Teacher's Book page 156.

REPRODUCIBLE WORKSHEET, **Teacher's Book page 186**

Ask and Answer Grid: What's He Doing? provides further fun and practice with the vocabulary of the lesson. For instructions, see page 194.

COMPONENTS LINK

LET'S GO TESTS AND QUIZZES

Lesson Quiz: Explain and administer the reproducible Unit 7 Let's Learn quiz from *Let's Go Tests and Quizzes*, page 33. Instructions and Answer Key are also in *Let's Go Tests and Quizzes*.

LET'S CHANT LET'S SING 2

Page 40: "What Is He Doing?"

This chant reinforces the question-and-answer pattern *What is he doing? He's playing a game.*

LET'S GO PICTURE DICTIONARY

Use pages 54–55, Playground Verbs, to supplement the lesson and increase challenge.

1. Review familiar words and point out new words you wish to teach.

2. Practice the words with the question-and-answer patterns *What is he/she doing? He/She's singing. Is he/she singing? Yes, he/she is. No, he/she isn't.*

Let's Learn More

Topic: Activities

Lesson objectives: Students ask what others are doing with *they*.

New grammar: *What are they doing? They're (playing soccer). Are they (doing homework)?*

Review grammar: *Yes, they are. No, they aren't.*

New language: *playing soccer, flying kites, watching TV, eating apples, reading comic books, riding bicycles, studying English, talking on the telephone*

Review language: verbs

Materials: Teacher and Student Cards 172–179, actual items, CD 2 Tracks 64–69, contraction cards (*They're, aren't, We're*)

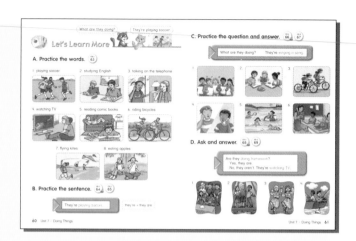

WARM UP AND REVIEW

Choose one of the following:

1. Charades (p. 22) reviews verbs. Have a student choose a verb card but not show it to the others. S1 acts out the verb. The other students guess the actions by asking *Yes/No* questions. Continue with several more student actors.

2. Slap (p. 23) practices pronouns. Use Student Cards from Let's Learn plus additional vocabulary. Have students display the cards on their desks. Call out a sentence with *I: I'm dancing.* Students race to slap the card and say the sentence with the plural pronoun *we: We're dancing.* Let students take turns being caller. For more of a challenge add *he/she* and *they.*

PRESENT THE LANGUAGE

BOOKS CLOSED

Introduce the words.

1. Use Teacher Cards 172–179 to introduce the new vocabulary with gestures. Hold up one Teacher Card at a time and say the phrase. Point to the objects on the card and have students repeat those as well. Say the phrases again and have students repeat. Encourage them to

use gestures to reinforce the verb phrases as they speak.

2. Conduct a quick drill of the phrases after you introduce each phrase. Use Teacher Cards 172–179. Don't speak as you show the cards. Have students say the new phrase plus all the previously learned phrases.

Introduce the sentence pattern.

1. Introduce *they're* using the verbs from Let's Learn. Have several students come to the front and do an action: *dance.* Students say *We're dancing.* Point to them and say *They're dancing.* Ask what the difference is between *we* and *they.*

2. Have students get into groups and decide on an action to do. As each group gets their turn they say *We're (cooking)* as they do the action. The other groups point to them and say *They're (cooking).*

3. Use Teacher Cards 172–179. Show a card and say the sentence *They're (playing soccer).* Model the question *What are they doing?* and have students repeat several times. Elicit the answer *They're (playing soccer).*

4. Hold up the other Teacher Cards. Have one group ask *What are they doing?* and the other group answer with what is on the card.

Grammar Tip: For sentences with *we're/they're* that have objects, the objects are usually said in the plural: *They're riding bicycles / We're eating cookies.*

BOOKS OPEN

A. Practice the words.

1. Play Track 63. Have students listen and point to the words.

 CD 2 Track 63

1. *playing soccer*
2. *studying English*
3. *talking on the telephone*
4. *watching TV*
5. *reading comic books*
6. *riding bicycles*
7. *flying kites*
8. *eating apples*

2. Play the audio again and have students repeat the words.

B. Practice the sentence.

1. Listen to the sentence pattern.

  a. Write the pattern on the board or direct students' attention to it in the book. Play Track 64. Point to the words as students listen to the audio. Then have students repeat after the audio.

CD 2 Track 64

They're playing soccer.

They're playing soccer.

2. Practice the rhythm.

a. Play Track 64 again and have students listen to the rhythm and intonation of the sentences.

b. Play the audio again. Have students clap or tap to keep the rhythm of the audio. Have students listen to the spoken sentences to hear how the sentence matches the rhythm, and then have them repeat it along with the recorded rhythm.

c. Have students tap or clap the rhythm and practice saying the sentence without the audio.

3. Practice the sentence.

a. Play Track 65 and have students point to the vocabulary pictures as they listen.

 CD 2 Track 65

They're playing soccer.
They're studying English.
They're talking on the telephone.
They're watching TV.
They're reading comic books.
They're riding bicycles.
They're eating apples.
They're flying kites.

b. Play Track 65 again and have students repeat the sentences.

c. Divide the class into pairs and have the students practice making sentences with their books open to page 60.

 BOOKS CLOSED

Introduce the question forms.

1. Introduce the *Wh-* question-and-answer pattern.

a. Have two students come to the front of the class and sing the song from Let's Sing or another song. Point to them as they sing and model the question *What are*

they doing? Model the answer for students to repeat *They're singing.* Then have them repeat it in a series of three, several times.

b. Ask the question *What are they doing?* Show a Teacher Card and have students answer each time. Ss: *They're (singing a song).* Repeat for the other vocabulary.

c. Have students practice the question. They should repeat the question several times.

d. Hold the Teacher Cards so that students can't see them, and have them practice asking you questions. Show them the Teacher Card each time as you answer.

e. Divide the class into two groups. Use Teacher Cards to cue the answering group. Groups take turns asking and answering questions.

 BOOKS OPEN

C. Practice the question and answer.

1. Listen to the *Wh-* question-and-answer pattern.

a. Present the pattern by writing it on the board or direct students' attention to the pattern in their books.

b. Play Track 66. Point to the words as students listen.

 CD 2 Track 66

What are they doing?
   They're singing a song.

What are they doing?
   They're singing a song.

2. Practice the rhythm.

a. Play Track 66 again and have students listen to the rhythm and intonation of the questions and answers.

b. Play the track again. Have students clap or tap to match the rhythm of the audio. Have students listen to the spoken question and answer to hear how it matches the rhythm, and then have them repeat

the pattern along with the recorded rhythm.

c. Have students tap or clap the rhythm and practice saying the question and answer without the audio.

3. Practice the *Wh-* questions and answers.

a. Have students look at page 61 and describe the things they see.

b. Play Track 67. Have students listen and point to the appropriate pictures.

 CD 2 Track 67

1. *What are they doing?*
   They're singing a song.
2. *What are they doing?*
   They're reading comic books.
3. *What are they doing?*
   They're riding bicycles.
4. *What are they doing?*
   They're talking on the telephone.
5. *What are they doing?*
   They're swimming.
6. *What are they doing?*
   They're studying English.

c. Play the audio again and have students repeat the questions and answers.

d. Divide the class into question-and-answer groups and play the audio again. Each group repeats either the question or answer. Repeat, with groups switching roles.

e. Divide the class into pairs and have students do the **Slap** activity (p. 23) with their books open to page 61. One student asks *What are they doing?* and the other points to the same picture in the book and answers *They're (dancing).*

D. Ask and answer.

1. Listen to the *Yes/No* question-and-answer pattern.

a. Present the pattern by writing it on the board or direct students' attention to the pattern in the book.

b. Play Track 68. Point to the words as students listen. Have students repeat after the audio.

CD 2 Track 68

Are they doing homework?
Yes, they are.
Are they doing homework?
No, they aren't. They're watching TV.

Are they doing homework?
Yes, they are.
Are they doing homework?
No, they aren't. They're watching TV.

2. Practice the rhythm.

a. Play Track 68 again and have students listen to the rhythm and intonation of the question and answer.

b. Play the track again. Have students tap or clap to match the rhythm of the audio. Have students listen to the spoken questions and answers to hear how they match the rhythm, and then have them repeat the patterns along with the recorded rhythm.

c. Have students tap or clap the rhythm and practice saying the question and answers.

3. Practice the *Yes/No* questions and answers.

a. Play Track 69. Point to the words as students listen. Have students repeat the questions and answers after the audio.

CD 2 Track 69

1. *Are they doing homework?*
   No, they aren't. They're watching TV.
2. *Are they singing?*
   Yes, they are.
3. *Are they dancing?*
   Yes, they are.
4. *Are they flying kites?*
   No, they aren't. They're fishing.

b. Have students work in pairs and take turns asking and answering questions about the pictures.

> **Grammar Tip:** Remind students that *they are* in *Yes, they are* is never contracted.

GAMES AND ACTIVITIES

1. Concentration (p. 22) reviews the sentence pattern. Have double sets of cards ready. Divide the class into pairs. S1 turns over a card and says *He is (playing soccer).* S2 turns over another card and says it in the singular. If the cards match, students say together *They are playing soccer.* If they do not match, the cards are turned over and two new cards are chosen.

2. Find Your Partner (p. 24) practices the question pattern and pronouns. Give Student Cards 172–179 to each student. Students walk around the class and ask each other *What are you doing?* When they find someone with the same card, they sit down. When all students have found partners, each pair says *We're (playing soccer).* The others point to them and say *They're (playing soccer).*

3. Step Away Lines (p. 26) gives students confidence in speaking in a loud voice. Give students verb Student Cards 172–179. Have them get into two lines and show a card as they ask *yes/no* questions from Let's Learn More.

4. Are They? uses the pictures in the book as reinforcement. Use page 61 of the Student Book. Have students gets into pairs and work with one book. They play **Rock, Paper, Scissors** with *Are they, are they, 1, 2, 3!* The winner asks a *yes/no* question and the loser has to answer it correctly.

EXTRA PRACTICE

WORKBOOK pages 60–61

Assign for homework or do in class. For instructions and Answer Key, see Teacher's Book page 171.

SKILLS BOOK pages 60–61

Assign for homework or do in class. For instructions and Answer Key, see Teacher's Book page 157.

REPRODUCIBLE WORKSHEET, Teacher's Book page 187

What Are They Doing? Game provides further fun and practice with the vocabulary of the lesson. For instructions, see page 194.

COMPONENTS LINK

CD-ROM 2

For extra fun, students can play Unit 7, Game 1 on a computer at school or at home. In this **Concentration** game, students try to find picture-word pairs. This activity reinforces reading, and the Let's Learn and Let's Learn More vocabulary.

For extra fun, students can play Unit 7, Game 2 on a computer at school or at home. Students follow the prompts to choose the correct picture and move across the maze. This activity reinforces listening, and the Let's Learn and Let's Learn More vocabulary.

LET'S GO TESTS AND QUIZZES

Lesson Quiz: Explain and administer the reproducible Unit 7 Let's Learn More quiz from *Let's Go Tests and Quizzes*, page 34. Instructions and Answer Key are also in *Let's Go Tests and Quizzes*.

LET'S GO PICTURE DICTIONARY

Use pages 62–63, Outdoor Activities, to supplement the lesson and increase challenge.

1. Review familiar words and point out new words you wish to teach.

2. Practice the words with the question-and-answer patterns *What are they doing? They're playing soccer. Are they playing soccer? Yes, they are. No, they aren't.*

Let's Build

Topic: Activities

Lesson objectives: Students ask and answer questions in the present progressive with third person singular and plural pronouns.

Review grammar: *He/She is/ They/We are / I am (walking). What is he/she (doing)? Is he/she (singing)? Yes, he/she is. No, he/she isn't. Are they (eating)? Yes, they are. No, they aren't.*

Review vocabulary: verb phrases

Materials: Teacher and Student Cards 171–179, 94, CD 2 Track 70

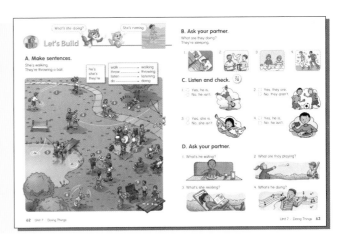

WARM UP AND REVIEW

Choose one of the following:

1. Review verb phrases from Units 1–6 and Level 1 with the progressive form. Conduct a quick drill. Hold up Teacher Cards of verbs. Have students say the verb and then the progressive form. Show each card again as you point to a student. That student does the action and says *I'm flying a kite.* The other students point to him or her and say *He/She is flying a kite.*

2. Using the same verbs as above, practice with *We're/They're (eating apples).*

PRESENT THE LANGUAGE

📖 **BOOKS OPEN**

A. Make sentences.

1. Do the sentence activity.

   a. Divide the class into pairs. Have students take turns making sentences about the pictures.

   b. Have students complete the sentences. They can either say what they are doing or make up an answer.

   c. Ask several students for their answers.

B. Ask your partner.

1. Have students look at the pictures on page 63 and describe what they

see. Encourage them to guess what language they will hear.

2. Model the question and have students repeat.

3. Divide the class into pairs. Have students look at the pictures and take turns asking and answering the question *What is he/she doing?* Ask several students for their answers.

C. Listen and check.

1. Have students look at the first picture and describe it. Then play the first question of Track 70 and check the correct box.

 CD 2 Track 70

  1. Is he doing a cartwheel?
  2. Are they playing soccer?
  3. Is she riding a bicycle?
  4. Is he eating pancakes?

2. Play the rest of the audio and have students check the correct answers. Play the audio at least twice so that students can review their answers.

D. Ask your partner.

1. Have students look at the pictures and describe what they see.

2. Hold up Teacher Card 94 (*pancakes*) and ask *What is he eating?* Model the answer *He's eating pancakes.* Practice with other Teacher Cards and verbs.

3. Divide the class into pairs. Have students take turns asking and answering questions about the pictures.

GAMES AND ACTIVITIES

1. Memory Chain practices verbs and the progressive. Divide the class into groups. S1 says *I'm (eating apples)* and does the action. S2 says *I'm (eating apples) and (dancing)* and does the actions. S3 adds another action to the sentence and so on. Have students see how long a sentence they can make until someone forgets the order of the actions.

2. Divide the class into pairs. S1 says *He's running.* S2 has to find a picture in the book that matches the sentence. Students switch roles.

EXTRA PRACTICE

WORKBOOK pages 62–63

Assign for homework or do in class. For instructions and Answer Key, see Teacher's Book page 172.

SKILLS BOOK pages 62–63

Assign for homework or do in class. For instructions and Answer Key, see Teacher's Book page 157.

Let's Build

CD-ROM 2

For extra fun, students can play Unit 7, Game 3 on a computer at school or at home. Students look at the pictures and answer *Yes/No* questions, eventually revealing the big picture at the end. This activity reinforces listening, the Let's Learn vocabulary, and the Let's Learn More vocabulary and grammar patterns.

LET'S GO TESTS AND QUIZZES

Lesson Quiz: Explain and administer the reproducible Unit 7 Let's Build quiz from *Let's Go Tests and Quizzes*, page 35. Instructions and Answer Key are also in *Let's Go Tests and Quizzes*.

Unit Test: Explain and administer the reproducible Unit 7 Test from *Let's Go Tests and Quizzes*, page 56. Instructions and Answer Key are also in *Let's Go Tests and Quizzes*.

LET'S GO READER

Now that students have completed Unit 7, they are ready to read "What Are You Doing?" See Teacher's Book page 20 for suggestions on how to present *Readers* and incorporate them into your lesson plans.

Unit 8 After School

Let's Start

Topic: After-school activities

Lesson objectives: Students learn to extend an invitation.

New grammar: *Can you come over on (Saturday)? Sorry. Do you ever (take a walk) at night?*

Review grammar: *Yes, I can. No, I can't. Yes, I do. No, I don't.*

New language: *come over, free, busy, great, See you (on Sunday), take a walk, look at stars, play outside, take a bath, night*

Review language: *Saturday, Sunday*

Materials: Teacher and Student Cards 180–184, Level 1 Cards 205–211, CD 2 Tracks 71–76, beanbag, puppets (optional), contraction cards (*don't, I'm, can't*)

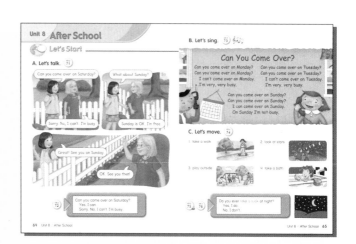

WARM UP AND REVIEW

Choose one of the following:

1. Beanbag Circle (p. 24) reviews days of the week. Have students form a circle. Toss a beanbag (or ball) to one student and call out the name of a day. T: *(Friday)*. S1 repeats, tosses the beanbag to another student, and says the name of the next day. S1: *(Friday), (Saturday)*. Continue around and across the circle. For large classes, form several circles and give each circle a beanbag.

2. To practice verb phrases, select several Teacher Cards (verb phrases from Units 1–7) and place them along the chalk rail. Divide the class into two groups. Have a student volunteer point to cards at random, one at a time. Group A says the verb phrase. Group B performs the actions. Reverse roles and continue until all the verbs have been practiced.

PRESENT THE DIALOGUE

 **BOOKS CLOSED**

Present the dialogue.

1. Introduce the dialogue.

   a. Use puppets or student volunteers to introduce the dialogue. Have students identify words they hear.

> Puppet A: *Can you come over on Saturday?*
> Puppet B: *Sorry. No, I can't. I'm busy.*
> Puppet A: *What about Sunday?*
> Puppet B: *Sunday is OK. I'm free.*
> Puppet A: *Great! See you on Sunday.*
> Puppet B: *OK. See you then!*

   b. Say the dialogue again. This time emphasize facial expressions and gestures for each sentence.

   c. Divide the class into two groups and practice the dialogue using gestures.

   d. Use Level 1 Student Cards 205–211 (days of the week). Give each student a Student Card. Have them walk around the room and practice the dialogue with as many different students as possible.

Students substitute the day on each card in the dialogue. S1: *Can you come over on (Friday)?* S2: *Sorry. No, I can't. I'm busy.* S1: *What about (Saturday)?* S2: *(Saturday) is OK.*

> **Cultural Tip:** *Come over* is an informal way of asking someone to visit you at your home. *See you* is an informal way of saying you will meet someone at some time in the near future. *I'm free* is an informal way to say that you are not busy.

📖 **BOOKS OPEN**

A. Let's talk.

Students learn how to extend an invitation and accept it or reject it politely.

1. Listen to the dialogue.

   a. Have students look at the scenes on page 64 and describe what they see.

   b. Play Track 71. Have students listen to the dialogue and point to the speech bubbles. Have them identify words they hear.

Let's Start

CD 2 Track 71

Jenny: *Can you come over on Saturday?*
Kate: *Sorry. No, I can't. I'm busy.*
Jenny: *What about Sunday?*
Kate: *Sunday is OK. I'm free.*
Jenny: *Great! See you on Sunday.*
Kate: *OK. See you then!*

   c. Play the dialogue again and have students repeat each line after the characters.

2. Practice the pattern.

   a. Write the pattern on the board, or direct students' attention to their books. Play Track 72. Point to the words as students listen to the dialogue. Then have students repeat after the audio.

CD 2 Track 72

Can you come over on Saturday?
Yes, I can.
No, I can't. Sorry. I'm busy.

   b. Review the contractions: *I am = I'm* and *cannot = can't*. Follow the procedure on page 196 for how to teach contractions with cards. Have the students practice saying both *I am / I'm* and *cannot / can't*. Point to the explanation on the board as they practice.

3. Practice the dialogue.

   a. Ask one of the questions from the dialogue and have a volunteer answer. Repeat for the other question. Then ask the questions out of order and have volunteers answer. To make this more challenging, give one of the answers from the dialogue and have students ask the matching question.

   b. Do **Conversation Lines** (p. 26) to practice the dialogue in pairs.

   c. Have students practice the dialogue with several partners, using different days of the week.

B. Let's sing.

"Can You Come Over?" reinforces the language from the dialogue using rhythm and song.

1. Play and listen.

Play Track 73. Have students listen and identify the words they recognize from Let's Talk.

CD 2 Track 73

Can You Come Over?

Can you come over on Monday?
Can you come over on Monday?
   I can't come over on Monday.
   I'm very, very busy.

Can you come over on Tuesday?
Can you come over on Tuesday?
   I can't come over on Tuesday.
   I'm very, very busy.

Can you come over on Sunday?
Can you come over on Sunday?
   I can come over on Sunday.
   On Sunday I'm not busy.

2. Practice the rhythm.

   a. Introduce the song rhythmically. Have students clap to keep the beat as you model the song line by line. Have students repeat after you.

   b. Play the song again. Encourage students to sing along.

3. Do the song activity.

Divide the class into two groups. Have the students stand in two parallel lines facing each other. Using loud voices, have one line sing the questions and the other line sing the answers. After each answer, one line moves to the right so that every student faces a new partner. Repeat until all students get back to their original partners.

4. Read the lyrics.

Have students look at the song pictures and lyrics. Ask students to point to and read words that they recognize.

5. Work in groups.

Have students work in groups to create an original verse by changing the day of the week or the adjective. Then, sing the song again with the new verses.

BOOKS CLOSED
Present the verb phrases

1. Introduce the verb phrases.

   a. Say *take a walk* with action, and repeat the action several times. Have students repeat several times with action before going on to the next phrase. Repeat with the other phrases.

   b. To check understanding, say the words in random order and have students do the appropriate action.

   c. Show students Teacher Cards 180–183. Have them both say the word and do the action.

   d. Divide the class into two groups. Have the groups take turns saying the commands and doing the actions. Use Teacher Cards to cue the command group.

2. Introduce *Do you ever (take a walk) at night?*

   a. Add *Do you ever* and *at night* to each verb phrase and have students repeat the question and do the action.

   b. Hold up Teacher Card 184 and ask *Do you ever take a walk at night?* Model the answer *Yes, I do.* Hold the card upside down and ask the question again. Model the answer *No, I don't.* Practice the question and answer with different cards.

   c. Draw a calendar of a month on the board. Put X's on random days. Say *I take a walk at night* as you point to the days with X's. Model the question *Do you ever (take a walk) at night?* Have students repeat several times.

   d. Ask a student *Do you ever take a walk at night?* Model the answers *Yes, I do* and *No, I don't.* Have the student answer.

   e. Have pairs take turns asking questions with the verbs and *Do you ever...at night?* Have both students point and do the action together when they ask the question.

Teaching Tip: Explain to students that *Do you ever...?* means doing something more than once at any time in the recent past, but not necessarily every day.

 BOOKS OPEN

C. Let's move.
Students learn useful everyday language by combining rhythm and actions.

1. Listen and point to the verbs.
a. Play Track 74. Have students listen and point to the appropriate pictures.

 CD 2 Track 74

1. *take a walk*
2. *look at stars*
3. *play outside*
4. *take a bath*

b. Play the audio again. Students listen and repeat.

2. Practice the rhythm.
a. Play Track 75. Point to the words as students listen to the audio.

CD 2 Track 75

Do you ever take a walk at night?
    Yes, I do.
Do you ever take a walk at night?
    No, I don't.

Do you ever take a walk at night?
    Yes, I do.
Do you ever take a walk at night?
    No, I don't.

b. Play Track 75 again. Have students clap or tap to keep the rhythm and repeat the question and answers with the audio.

c. Have students tap or clap the rhythm and practice saying the question and answers without the audio.

3. Practice the questions and answers.
Play Track 76. Have students listen to the questions and answers and point to the appropriate pictures.

CD 2 Track 76

Do you ever take a walk at night?
    No, I don't.
Do you ever look at stars at night?
    Yes, I do.
Do you ever play outside at night?
    No, I don't
Do you ever take a bath at night?
    Yes, I do.

b. Play the audio again and have students repeat the questions and answers.

c. Divide the class into question and answer groups and play the audio again. Each group repeats either the question or answer. Repeat with groups switching roles.

d. Have students work in pairs and take turns asking and answering questions about their own experiences.

GAMES AND ACTIVITIES

1. Have students "arrange" a day to meet several friends. Divide the class into groups of four and have members of each group ask each other *Can you come over on (Sunday)?* The students must decide on a day that works for in the whole group.

2. Interview recycles verbs from previous units and gives students practice with the *What do you do on (Mondays)?* question pattern. Give students the "Interview" reproducible worksheet (p. 188). Then have students walk around the room asking each other about their schedules. For large groups, have students ask in pairs.

3. Concentration (p. 22) practices recognizing and using the vocabulary and recycling verb and time phrases. Divide the class into pairs. Use Level 1 Student Cards 205–211 (days of the week). Have S1 identify the first card and then flip over the second card. S1 identifies

that card and if the two cards match, S1 says *I (take a walk) (after school)*. S1 keeps the pair of cards. S2 then chooses cards. Continue until all the cards are gone.

EXTRA PRACTICE

WORKBOOK pages 64–65

Assign for homework or do in class. For instructions and Answer Key, see Teacher's Book page 172.

SKILLS BOOK pages 64–65

Assign for homework or do in class. For instructions and Answer Key, see Teacher's Book page 158.

COMPONENTS LINK

CD-ROM 2

For extra fun, students can play Unit 8, Game 1 on a computer at school or at home. Students listen to the dialogues and then choose the correct picture. This activity reinforces listening, reading, and the Let's Start dialogue pattern.

LET'S GO TESTS AND QUIZZES

Lesson Quiz: Explain and administer the reproducible Unit 8 Let's Start quiz from *Let's Go Tests and Quizzes*, page 36. Instructions and Answer Key are also in *Let's Go Tests and Quizzes*.

LET'S CHANT LET'S SING 3

Page 12–13: "Busy, Busy, Busy"

This song builds on the Let's Talk dialogue and is meant for students who require extra challenge.

LET'S GO PICTURE DICTIONARY

Use pages 64–65, Indoor Activities, to supplement the lesson and increase challenge.

1. Review familiar words and point out new words you wish to teach.

2. Practice the words with the question-and-answer pattern *Do you ever take a walk at night? Yes, I do. No, I don't.*

Let's Learn

Topic: After-school activities

Lesson objectives: Students ask and answer questions about their after-school schedule of classes and activities.

New grammar: *What do you do on (Mondays)? I go to (art class).*

New language: *art class, English class, math class, dance class, karate class, soccer practice, piano class, swimming class, every Monday / on Mondays*

Review language: days of the week

Materials: Teacher and Student Cards 159–162, 164–183, 185–192, CD 2 Tracks 77–81, puppets (optional)

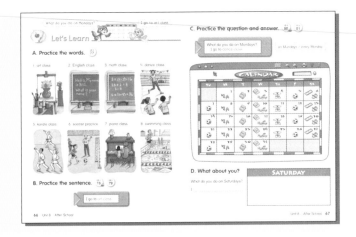

WARM UP AND REVIEW

Choose one of the following:

1. Review daily activities using Teacher Cards for activities and times of day. Place Teacher Cards at the top of the board, leaving room for other cards to be placed on the chalk rail below. Give a student volunteer an activity Teacher Card. Have the student place it under a time phrase and make a sentence (*I take a walk every evening*). This could also be done in small groups or pairs with students placing Student Cards under the appropriate time phrases.

2. Put students in groups of seven and give them Level 1 Student Cards 205–211 (days of the week). Have them quickly put the cards in order and practice saying the days of the week. This could also be done as a race.

PRESENT THE LANGUAGE

📖 BOOKS CLOSED

Introduce the words.

1. Use Teacher Cards 185–192 to introduce the activities. Show one Teacher Card at a time and say the name of the activity. Students repeat each word several times.

2. Conduct a quick drill of the activities. Do not speak as you show the cards. Have students identify the new activity plus all the previously learned activities. Gradually pick up speed as students get used to saying the words.

3. Place Teacher Cards 185–192 on the chalk rail. Point quickly to the cards, one at a time, and have the students identify each card. For a greater challenge, point to a series of cards (*swimming class, math class, computer class*) and have the class recite them in the correct sequence.

Introduce the sentence pattern.

1. Use Teacher Cards 185–192. Show each card and say the sentence *I go to (art class)*. Have students repeat the sentence pattern for each activity.

2. Conduct a quick drill of the sentences using Teacher Cards 185–192. Do not speak as you show the cards. Gradually pick up speed as students get used to saying the sentences.

📖 BOOKS OPEN

A. Practice the words.

1. Play Track 77. Have students listen and point to the words.

💿 CD 2 Track 77

1. *art class*
2. *English class*
3. *math class*
4. *dance class*
5. *karate class*
6. *soccer practice*
7. *piano class*
8. *swimming class*

2. Play the audio again and have students repeat the words.

B. Practice the sentence.

1. **Listen to the sentence pattern.**

   a. Write the pattern on the board or direct students' attention to it in the book. Play Track 78. Point to the words as students listen to the audio. Then have students repeat after the audio.

💿 CD 2 Track 78

I go to art class.

I go to art class.

2. **Practice the rhythm.**

   a. Play Track 78 again and have students listen to the rhythm and intonation of the sentences.

b. Play the audio again. Have students tap or clap to match the rhythm of the audio. Have students listen to the spoken sentence to hear how it matches the rhythm, and then have them repeat the sentence along with the recorded rhythm.

c. Have students tap or clap the rhythm and practice saying the sentences without the audio.

3. Practice the sentences.

a. Play Track 79 and have students point to the vocabulary pictures as they listen.

 CD 2 Track 79

I go to art class.
I go to English class.
I go to math class.
I go to dance class.
I go to karate class.
I go to soccer practice.
I go to piano class.
I go to swimming class.

b. Play Track 79 again and have students repeat the sentences.

c. Whisper Relay Race (p. 25). With the class in rows, have the first student of each row come to the front to get the whispered phrase (*I go to karate class*). The students return to their rows. Say *Go!* and have S1 in each row say the phrase to the next student in the row. The last student must run to the front and whisper the phrase to the teacher. The first student to say the phrase correctly wins a team point. Variation: The last student in the line writes the phrase and then hands it to the teacher. The first student to do this reads the phrase to the class when the activity is over.

 BOOKS CLOSED

Introduce the question form.

1. Write the days of the week across the board. Use puppets or student volunteers to present the question and answer.

Puppet A: *What do you do on (Mondays)?*
Puppet B: *I go to (art class).*

Place Teacher Card 185 *(art class)* on the board under *Monday.* Repeat the question for other days of the week. Hold up a Teacher Card to cue students' answers each time. Place the Teacher Card under the appropriate day.

2. Have students repeat the question. Practice the question several times.

3. Hold up Teacher Cards for days (or point to the written day on the board) and have students practice forming questions. Hold up each Teacher Card as you answer, and then place it under the appropriate day on the board. Ss: *What do you do on (Mondays)?* T: *I go to (dance class).*

4. Divide the class into two groups. Use Teacher Cards of days and activities to cue the students. Groups take turns asking and answering questions.

 BOOKS OPEN

C. Practice the question and answer.

1. Listen to the question-and-answer pattern.

a. Present the pattern by writing it on the board or direct students' attention to it in the book.

b. Play Track 80. Point to the words as students listen. Have students repeat after the audio.

 CD 2 Track 80

What do you do on Mondays?
   I go to dance class.

What do you do on Mondays?
   I go to dance class.

c. Play the audio again and have students repeat the questions and the answers.

2. Practice the rhythm.

a. Play Track 80 again. This time, have students listen to the rhythm and the intonation of the sentences with the audio.

b. Play the audio again. Have students clap or tap to match the rhythm of the audio. Have students listen to the spoken question and answer to see how it matches the rhythm, and then have them repeat the pattern along with the recorded rhythm.

c. Have students tap or clap the rhythm and practice saying the question and answer without the audio.

3. Practice the questions and answers.

a. Have students look at page 67 and describe the things they see.

b. Play Track 81. Have students listen and point to the appropriate pictures.

 CD 2 Track 81

1. *What do you do on Mondays?*
    I go to dance class.
2. *What do you do on Tuesdays?*
    I go to English class.
3. *What do you do on Wednesdays?*
    I go to math class and swimming class.
4. *What do you do on Thursdays?*
    I go to karate class.
5. *What do you do on Fridays?*
    I go to soccer practice.
6. *What do you do on Saturdays?*
    I go to art class and piano class.

c. Direct students' attention to the phrase: *every Monday = on Mondays.* Have students practice saying the sentences *I go to dance class on Mondays* and *I go to dance class every Monday.* Make sure they understand that both sentences mean the same thing.

d. Play the audio again. Have students repeat the questions and answers.

e. Divide the class into question and answer groups and play the audio again. Each group repeats either the question or the answer. Repeat with groups switching roles.

f. Divide the class into pairs. Have students take turns asking and answering questions about the picture.

D. What about you?

1. Ask several students *What do you do on Saturdays?* Help with new vocabulary, if necessary.

2. Have students write their answers in their books.

3. Divide the class into pairs. Have students tell each other what they do on Saturdays.

4. Have students practice the question with several different partners, using different days and their own activities.

GAMES AND ACTIVITIES

1. Find Your Partner (p. 24). Give each student a Student Card (activity) and have students walk around the room looking for others with the same card. Students with matching cards say their phrases to each other: *I go to (piano class).*

2. Picture Game. Divide the students into groups. Have one student from each group come to the front to get a day of the week card and an activity card. The students go back to their groups, write down the day, and start drawing a picture of the activity. Students in the group must guess the activity and then make a sentence: *I go to (dance class) on (Thursdays).*

3. Conversation Lines (p. 26). Give each student a Student Card (activities) and let them choose a day. Put students in parallel lines and have them practice the question and answer using the day of their choice: *What do you do on (Tuesdays)? I go to (dance class) on (Tuesdays).*

EXTRA PRACTICE

WORKBOOK **pages 66–67**

Assign for homework or do in class. For instructions and Answer Key, see Teacher's Book page 172.

SKILLS BOOK **pages 66–67**

Assign for homework or do in class. For instructions and Answer Key, see Teacher's Book page 158.

REPRODUCIBLE WORKSHEET, **Teacher's Book page 188**

Interview provides further fun and practice with the vocabulary of the lesson. For instructions, see page 194.

COMPONENTS LINK

CD-ROM 2

For extra fun, students can play Unit 8, Game 2 on a computer at school or at home. Students memorize the schedule and then answer questions. This activity reinforces listening, and the Let's Learn vocabulary and grammar pattern *What do you do on (Monday)? I go to (art class).*

LET'S GO TESTS AND QUIZZES

Lesson Quiz: Explain and administer the reproducible Unit 8 Let's Learn quiz from *Let's Go Tests and Quizzes*, page 37. Instructions and Answer Key are also in *Let's Go Tests and Quizzes.*

LET'S CHANT LET'S SING 3

Page 15: "What Do You Do on Monday?"

This chant reinforces school subject vocabulary and the question-and-answer pattern *What do you do on Monday(s)? I go to art class.*

Let's Learn More

Topic: After-school activities

Lesson objectives: Students ask and answer questions about other people's after-school schedule of classes and activities with *he/she*.

New grammar: *What does he/she do after school? He/She (goes to the bookstore) after school. Does he/she (do homework) after school?*

Review grammar: *Yes, he/she does. No, he/she doesn't.*

New language: *go to the bookstore, do homework, listen to music*

Review language: *ride a bicycle, take a bath, practice the piano, walk the dog, talk on the telephone*

Materials: Teacher Cards 1–4, 138–141, 159–162, 180–183, 193–200 and Student Cards 193–200, actual items, CD 2 Tracks 82–88, contraction card *(doesn't)*

WARM UP AND REVIEW

Choose one of the following:

1. Scrambled Sentences (p. 24) reviews the Let's Talk dialogue. Divide the class into pairs and give each pair the dialogue cut into one-line strips of paper. Have students put the dialogue back together and practice the conversation.

2. Elicit the names of the days of the week from the class and write them on the board. Then have students walk around the room and act out the conversation with a partner, substituting the days into the dialogue. Give a signal and have students switch partners. Continue for 1–2 minutes.

PRESENT THE LANGUAGE

BOOKS CLOSED

Introduce the words.

1. Use Teacher Cards 193–200 to introduce the new vocabulary.

2. Conduct a quick drill of the activities after you introduce each one. Use Teacher Cards 193–200. Don't speak as you show the cards. Have students identify the new verb phrases plus all the previously learned verb phrases.

3. Show one of the Teacher Cards and say just the verb (*listen*). Have students complete the phrase (*to music*). Continue with the rest of the verb phrases. Do the activity again with students divided into two groups.

Introduce the sentence pattern.

1. Say *I go, he goes, she goes*. Repeat with the other verbs. Point to a student and have him or her say *I go*. Point to that student and say *He/She goes*. Repeat with the other verbs.

2. Use Teacher Cards 193–200. Show each card and say the sentence *He (goes to the bookstore) after school*. Have students repeat the sentence pattern several times before moving on to the next word.

3. Practice the sentence pattern, substituting all the phrases. Students should say the sentences at the same time as the teacher, not repeat after the teacher.

4. Conduct a quick drill. Show Teacher Cards 193–200 in random order and have students make sentences. Increase the speed of the drill until students are speaking at natural speed.

BOOKS OPEN

A. Practice the words.

1. Play Track 82. Have students listen and point to the words.

 CD 2 Track 82

1. go to the bookstore
2. do homework
3. listen to music
4. talk on the telephone
5. practice the piano
6. ride a bicycle
7. walk the dog
8. take a bath

2. Play the audio again and have students repeat the words.

> **Pronunciation Tip:** Model the difference between *go* and *goes*. Emphasize the final /z/ in the third person singular form. Model the other verbs in the same way. Have students practice the pronunciation.

3. Play **Concentration** (p. 22). In small groups or pairs, students place Student Cards 193–200 (activities) facedown on a desk. S1 turns over two cards and identifies them with the appropriate phrase (do homework). If the cards match, S1 keeps the cards and keeps playing. If the cards don't match, the cards are turned facedown again. S2 takes a turn. Continue until all cards are matched.

B. Practice the sentence.

1. Listen to the sentence pattern.

a. Write the pattern on the board or direct students' attention to their books. Play Track 83. Point to the words as students listen to the audio. Then have students repeat after the audio.

 CD 2 Track 83

She goes to the bookstore after school.
go = goes
do = does
listen = listens
talk = talks
practice = practices
ride = rides
walk = walks
take = takes

She goes to the bookstore after school.

b. Have students practice the verbs. Say each verb. T: *I go.* Students respond with the other form of the verb. Ss: *He goes.* Repeat for each verb.

2. Practice the rhythm.

a. Play Track 83 and have students listen to the rhythm and intonation of the sentences.

b. Play the audio again. Have students clap or tap to match the rhythm of the audio. Have students listen to the spoken sentences to see how they match the rhythm, and then have them repeat the sentences along with the recorded rhythm.

c. Have students tap or clap the rhythm and practice saying the sentences without the audio.

3. Practice the sentences.

a. Play Track 84 and have students point to the vocabulary pictures as they listen.

 CD 2 Track 84

She goes to the bookstore after school.
He does homework after school.
She listens to music after school.
He talks on the telephone after school.
She practices the piano after school.
She rides a bicycle after school.
He walks the dog after school.
She takes a bath after school.

b. Play Track 84 again and have students repeat the sentences.

c. Have students work in pairs and practice the sentences with their books open to page 68. S1 says *She takes a bath after school.* S2 touches the appropriate picture and then says a different sentence.

BOOKS CLOSED

Introduce the question forms.

1. Introduce the *Wh-* question-and-answer pattern.

a. Hold up Teacher Card 193 and give it to a male student to hold. Point to the student and ask *What does he do after school?* Model the answer for students to repeat *He goes to the bookstore.* Then have them repeat the question in a series of three, several times. Repeat the procedure with a female student holding the card.

b. Divide the class into two groups. Use Teacher Cards to cue the asking group. Groups take turns asking and answering questions.

c. Further divide the two large groups into smaller groups. Use Students Cards 193–200. Give each student an activity card to show the group while saying *I (go to the bookstore).* Have students ask each other questions like *What does Megan do after school?* Or *What does she do after school?* and someone

in the group responds *He/she (goes to the bookstore).* Continue until all students have a turn. Then have students return to the two large groups and take turns asking and answering questions about members of the other group.

> **Pronunciation Tip:** When asking *What does he/she do after school?* the stress on the words can change. Model the question first with the stress on *what* and *after school,* and then with the stress on *he* or *she.* Have students guess why the question would be said different ways.

2. Introduce the *Yes/No* question-and-answer pattern.

a. Give a male student an activity Teacher Card and ask *Does he (do homework) after school?* Prompt students to answer *Yes, he does* or *No, he doesn't.* Repeat with other students and activities.

b. Repeat the question several times. Then, have students practice asking questions. Cue students with Teacher Cards. Ss: *Does she (go to the bookstore) after school?* T: *Yes, she does* or *No, she doesn't.*

c. Divide the class into two groups and have them take turns asking and answering questions. Cue the questions with Teacher Cards.

BOOKS OPEN

C. Practice the question and answer.

1. Listen to the *Wh-* question-and-answer pattern.

a. Present the pattern by writing it on the board or direct students' attention to the pattern in the book.

b. Play Track 85. Have students listen and point to the speech bubbles. Continue to play the audio, and have students listen to the question and answer and point to the appropriate pictures.

CD 2 Track 85

What does he do after school?
He goes to the bookstore.

What does he do after school?
He goes to the bookstore.

2. Practice the rhythm.

a. Play Track 85 again. This time, have students listen to the rhythm and intonation of the questions and answers.

b. Play the track again. Have students tap or clap to match the rhythm of the audio. Have students listen to the spoken question and answer to hear how they match the rhythm, and then have them repeat the question and answer along with the recorded rhythm.

c. Have students tap or clap the rhythm and practice saying the question and answer without the audio.

3. Practice the *Wh-* questions and answers.

a. Play Track 86 and have students listen and point to the appropriate pictures.

 CD 2 Track 86

1. *What does she do after school?*
   She rides a bicycle.
2. *What does he do after school?*
   He goes to the bookstore.
3. *What does he do after school?*
   He listens to music.
4. *What does she do after school?*
   She practices the piano.
5. *What does he do after school?*
   He talks on the telephone.
6. *What does she do after school?*
   She takes a bath.
7. *What does she do after school?*
   She does homework.
8. *What does he do after school?*
   He walks the dog.

b. Play the audio again. Have students repeat the questions and answers.

c. Replay the audio and have students divide into question and answer groups. Each group repeats either the question or answer. Repeat with groups switching roles.

d. Divide the class into pairs. Have students take turns asking and answering questions about the pictures.

D. Ask and answer.

1. Listen to the *Yes/No* question-and-answer pattern.

a. Play Track 87. Point to the words as students listen. Have students repeat the questions and answers after the audio.

 CD 2 Track 87

Does he do homework after school?
   Yes, he does.
Does she do homework after school?
   No, she doesn't.

Does he do homework after school?
   Yes, he does.
Does she do homework after school?
   No, she doesn't.

2. Practice the rhythm.

a. Play Track 87 again and have students listen to the rhythm and intonation of the questions and answers.

b. Play the track again. Have students tap or clap to match the rhythm of the audio. Have students listen to the spoken questions and answers to hear how they match the rhythm, and then have them repeat the patterns along with the recorded rhythm.

c. Have students tap or clap the rhythm and practice saying the questions and answers without the audio.

3. Practice the *Yes/No* questions and answers.

a. Play Track 88. Have students listen and point to the appropriate pictures.

 CD 2 Track 88

1. *Does he do homework after school?*
   Yes, he does.
2. *Does she practice the piano after school?*
   No, she doesn't.
3. *Does he go to the bookstore after school?*
   Yes, he does.
4. *Does she listen to music after school?*
   No, she doesn't.

b. Have students work in pairs and take turns asking and answering questions about the pictures.

GAMES AND ACTIVITIES

1. Telegram (p. 26) practices listening skills and forming sentences with the verb phrases. Have students form rows. Give the first student a card in an envelope. S1 looks at the card and places it back in the envelope. Then S1 hands the envelope to S2 and whispers *I go to the bookstore after school.* S2 does not look at the card. He/She passes the envelope to S3 and whispers the sentence. Continue to the end of the row. The last student says the sentence aloud and then opens the envelope to see if the sentence matches the picture and if he/she said the same sentence as S1.

2. Walk and Talk (p. 26) practices using the question *What does he/she do after school?* Have four or five students sit in various places around the classroom. Give each student two or three activity cards. Have them hold at least one of them upside down to indicate *don't.* The other students walk around in pairs. Each pair must stop by one of the seated students and take turns asking each other *What does he/she do after school?* Continue until pairs have talked about at least two students. Then rearrange pairs and let seated students walk around.

Let's Learn More

3. Charades (p. 22) practices verb phrases. Use Student Cards (all verb phrases from Units 1–8). Divide the class into teams. Have one student from each team act out a verb phrase. The first team to guess correctly wins a point.

EXTRA PRACTICE

WORKBOOK pages 68–69

Assign for homework or do in class. For instructions and Answer Key, see Teacher's Book page 172.

SKILLS BOOK pages 68–69

Assign for homework or do in class. For instructions and Answer Key, see Teacher's Book page 159.

COMPONENTS LINK

CD-ROM 2

For extra fun, students can play Unit 8, Game 3 on a computer at school or at home. In this memory chain game, students listen and follow the pattern. This activity reinforces listening and the Let's Learn More vocabulary.

LET'S GO TESTS AND QUIZZES

Lesson Quiz: Explain and administer the reproducible Unit 8 Let's Learn More quiz from *Let's Go Tests and Quizzes*, page 38. Instructions and Answer Key are also in *Let's Go Tests and Quizzes*.

LET'S CHANT LET'S SING 3

Page 16: "What Does He Do After School?"

This chant reinforces after-school activity vocabulary and practices the question-and-answer patterns *What does he/she do after school? He/She goes to the bookstore. Does he/she practice the piano? Yes, he/she does. No, he/she doesn't.*

Let's Build

Topic: After-school activities

Lesson objectives: Students talk about their own and other's after-school activities on different days of the week.

Review grammar: *I go to (English class) after school. What (does he) do on (Tuesdays)? (He goes) to (math class) on (Tuesdays). What do you do after school on (Tuesdays)? Do you ever go to (English class) after school?*

Review language: activities, days of the week

Materials: Teacher and Student Cards 185–200, CD 2 Tracks 89–90

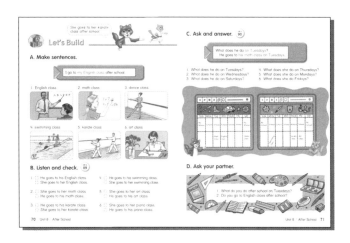

WARM UP AND REVIEW

Choose one of the following:

1. Do a quick review of activities with Teacher Cards 180–200. Students identify the cards with complete sentences, e.g., *He plays outside. She practices the piano.*

2. **Find Your Partner** (p. 24). Give each student a Student Card and ask him/her to find someone with a matching card. Students ask *What do you do?* and answer *I go to (karate class).*

PRESENT THE LANGUAGE

BOOKS CLOSED

Introduce the sentence patterns.

1. Show Teacher Cards 185–200 (activities). Hold up one card and say *I go to (English class) after school.* Have students repeat. Repeat with *he* and *she.*

2. Hold up an activity card and a day of the week card. Ask *What does she do on (Wednesdays)?* Prompt students to answer based on the activity card.

3. Ask the extended question *What does she do after school (on Wednesdays)?* Model an answer and have students repeat.

BOOKS OPEN

A. Make sentences.

1. Have students look at the pictures on page 70 and describe what they see.

2. Have students work in pairs to make sentences for each picture.

3. If desired, have students write their sentences. Ask volunteers to read their sentences to the class.

B. Listen and check.

1. Play the first sentence of Track 89 and put a checkmark in the correct box.

2. Play the rest of the audio. Play the audio at least twice so that students can check their answers.

 CD 2 Track 89

1. He goes to his English class.
2. She goes to her math class.
3. He goes to his karate class.
4. She goes to her swimming class.
5. He goes to his art class.
6. She goes to her piano class.

C. Ask and answer.

1. Have students look at the calendars on page 71. Point to the first activity and ask *What does he do on Tuesdays?* Students answer *He goes to math class on Tuesdays.*

2. Play Track 90. Have students listen and point to the appropriate pictures.

 CD 2 Track 90

What does he do on Tuesdays? He goes to his math class on Tuesdays.
1. What does he do on Tuesdays? He goes to his math class on Tuesdays.
2. What does he do on Wednesdays? He goes to his English class on Wednesdays.
3. What does he do on Saturdays? He goes to his dance class on Saturdays.
4. What does she do on Thursdays? She goes to her karate class on Thursdays.
5. What does she do on Mondays? She goes to her swimming class on Mondays.
6. What does she do on Fridays? She goes to her art class on Fridays.

3. Divide the class into pairs. Have students take turns asking and answering the questions about schedules.

4. Ask several students for their answers.

Let's Build

D. Ask your partner.

1. Ask several students *What do you do after class on Tuesdays?* and *Do you ever go to English class after school?*

2. Divide the class into pairs. Have them take turns asking and answering the extended questions.

3. Have several students report their partner's answers to the class.

GAMES AND ACTIVITIES

1. Sentence Dictation. Dictate sentences and have students write them on a piece of paper. Variation: Put students in groups of three. Have one student dictate sentences to the others. Students take turns dictating and writing sentences.

2. Use the "Bingo-After-School Activities" reproducible worksheet (p. 189). Have students arrange the activities on the grid as they like. Then put students in pairs and have S1 ask *Do you (practice soccer) on (Wednesdays)?* S2 responds according to his or her Bingo sheet. S1 and S2 take turns asking and answering questions.

3. Interview (p. 24) gives students the opportunity to use the language spontaneously. Make a class or group chart and give one to each student. Students walk around the room asking each other what they do after school or on the weekend. They write down the students' names and their answers. Then, in pairs, they work with each other asking what each student does: *What does Ken do after school on Wednesdays? He goes to the library.*

EXTRA PRACTICE

WORKBOOK pages 70–71

Assign for homework or do in class. For instructions and Answer Key, see Teacher's Book page 173.

SKILLS BOOK pages 70–71

Assign for homework or do in class. For instructions and Answer Key, see Teacher's Book page 159.

REPRODUCIBLE WORKSHEET, Teacher's Book page 189

Bingo: After-School Activities provides further fun and practice with the vocabulary of the lesson. For instructions, see page 195.

COMPONENTS LINK

CD-ROM 2

For extra fun, students can play Unit 8, Game 4 on a computer at school or at home. Students look at the schedule and answer *Yes/No* questions. This activity reinforces listening, the Let's Learn More vocabulary, and the Let's Learn More and Let's Build grammar patterns.

LET'S GO TESTS AND QUIZZES

Lesson Quiz: Explain and administer the reproducible Unit 8 Let's Build quiz from *Let's Go Tests and Quizzes*, page 39. Instructions and Answer Key are also in *Let's Go Tests and Quizzes*.

Unit Test: Explain and administer the reproducible Unit 8 Test from *Let's Go Tests and Quizzes*, page 58. Instructions and Answer Key are also in *Let's Go Tests and Quizzes*.

LET'S GO READER

Now that students have completed Unit 8, they are ready to read "Two Friends." See Teacher's Book page 20 for suggestions on how to present *Readers* and incorporate them into your lesson plans.

Units 7–8 Listen and Review
Let's Learn About Time

Topic: Units 7–8 review; time

Lesson objectives: Students demonstrate comprehension of language and vocabulary taught in Units 7 and 8. Students also learn to tell time and distinguish between a.m. and p.m. times.

New grammar: *What time is it?*

Review grammar: *Let's play a game! What are you doing? I'm (riding a bicycle). What's he (doing)? He's (dancing). Is he (running)? Yes, he is. No, he isn't. What are they doing? They're (playing soccer). Are they (doing homework)? Yes, they are. No they aren't. She is (walking). What about you? Can you come over on (Saturday)? I'm free. Sorry. No, I can't. I'm busy. See you on (Sunday). See you then! Do you ever (take a walk) at night? Yes, I do. No, I don't. What do you do (on Mondays)? I go to (art class).*

New language: *o'clock, noon, midnight, a.m., p.m.*

Review language: classes, activities, days of the week, *in the morning, in the afternoon, in the evening, at night*

Materials: Teacher and Student Cards 159–204, CD 2 Tracks 91–93, teacher-made verb cards, contraction cards *(I'm, can't, aren't, don't, it's)*

PART ONE: UNITS 7-8 LISTEN AND REVIEW

Review Activities

1. Let's talk/Let's sing.

a. Place activity Student Cards 163–179 facedown on the desk between pairs of students. Students take turns turning over the top two cards and basing a conversation on the actions shown. Students should perform the actions as they speak.

(Students turn over *run* and *dance*.)

S2: *What are you doing?*
S1: *I'm running. What about you? What are you doing?*
S2: *I'm dancing.*

Students continue until they have turned over all of the cards in their pile and used them in conversation.

b. Find Your Partner (p. 24). Assign each student a day of the week. Their task is to find another student who is free on the same day (a student holding the same day card).

S1: (has *Monday* card) *Can you come over on Monday?*
S2: (has *Sunday* card) *Sorry. No, I can't. I'm busy.*
S1: *OK. See you later.*

S1: *Can you come over on Monday?*
S3: (also has *Monday* card) *Monday is OK. I'm free.*
S1: *Great! See you on Monday.*
S3: *See you then!*

2. Let's move.

a. Pick Up (p. 25). Place Student Cards from Units 7 and 8 facedown on the table or floor. In pairs, students play **Rock, Paper, Scissors**, saying *Afternoon, evening, 1, 2, 3!* The winner picks up a card and makes a sentence. S: *I (climb trees) in the afternoon.* For added challenge, include verb cards from earlier units.

b. Class Survey. Help students create a list of survey questions including verb phrases from both Units 7 and 8 (and from earlier units, if desired). In pairs or small groups, students ask and answer the questions. S1: *Do you ever (eat apples) (at night)?* S2: *Yes, I do.* Write the questions on a large chart (or on the board) and tally the number of students in the class who answered *Yes* to each question.

c. Make new verb phrases. Write the base verbs from Unit 7 and 8 Let's Move on the board: *cook, wash, read, do, take, look,* and *play*. Have students work in groups to think of additional verb phrases using these base verbs (for example, *cook spaghetti, read books, wash the dog, do a puzzle, look at the piano, play music,* etc.). Write the new phrases on the board under each base verb. Then, have pairs or groups of students place teacher-made cards of base verbs facedown on a desk. Students turn over one card at a time and make a sentence using a new verb phrase.

3. Let's Learn/Let's Learn More

a. Charades (p. 22). Divide the class into groups. Use Student Cards for vocabulary from Units 7 and 8 to cue students. S1 selects one card and acts out the verb (or after-school lesson) shown. Students guess the vocabulary item from the actions.

b. Slap (p. 23). Call out the base verb *(dance)*. Students touch the card and say the *–ing* form of the verb *(dancing)*.

c. Assign individuals and pairs one of the verb phrases from Units 7 and 8. Have students act out their verbs, and while they are still moving, ask the class *What is he/she doing?, Is he/she (fishing)?, What are they doing?* or *Are they (fishing)?* Be sure students distinguish between *he, she,* and *they* in their answers.

d. Pairwork activity. Review the after-school activity vocabulary and place Teacher Cards on the chalk rail for reference. Give each student an empty weekly planner page for one week (Sunday through Saturday) or have students draw seven squares on a piece of paper and label them *Sunday* through *Saturday*. Have students fill in an activity for each day (one day can be "free").

Give students another blank planner page and group them in pairs. Students take turns asking and answering questions based on the weekly schedule they created. S1 writes S2's schedule on one of the blank planner pages and S2 writes S1's schedule; after they've finished, students compare pages.

📖 BOOKS CLOSED

Introduce Listen and Review

1. On the board, set up a sample to resemble the activity on page 72 of the Student Book. Put Teacher Cards 165, 168, and 169 on the chalk rail. Draw letter *a* over the first card, letter *b* over the second, and letter *c* over the third. Have one student stand by the cards. Identify one of the cards. T: *He's fishing.* The student points to the correct card and circles the appropriate letter. Repeat as necessary until all the students understand the procedure.

📖 BOOKS OPEN

A. Listen and circle.

1. Open your book to page 72. Show the page to the class. Have students

identify the actions in numbers 1–11. T: *What's he doing? He's fishing.*

2. Have student open their books to page 72. Play Track 91. Have students listen and point to the appropriate picture.

 CD 2 Track 91

1. What is he doing?
   He's fishing.
2. Is she doing homework?
   Yes, she is.
3. Are they playing soccer?
   No, they aren't. They're talking on the telephone.
4. I eat lunch every afternoon.
5. I wash the dishes every evening.
6. Do you ever do a cartwheel?
   Yes, I do.
7. What do you do on Mondays?
   I go to my English class.
8. What do you do on Tuesdays?
   I go to my math class.
9. What do you do after school on Wednesday?
   I go swimming.
10. Do you go to your piano class after school?
    Yes, I do.
11. Do you go to your art class after school?
    No, I don't. I go to the bookstore.

PART TWO: LET'S LEARN ABOUT TIME

📖 BOOKS CLOSED

Present the topic: Time

Point to the classroom clock and ask students *What time is it?* If desired, translate into students' native language. Once students understand the meaning of the question, they will probably try to answer using their knowledge of numbers. Don't feel that you need to supply the specific time vocabulary (e.g., *o'clock*) at this point—the goal is for students to realize that they'll be using the same numbers they already know to talk about this topic.

1. Introduce the words.

a. Use a clock face drawn on the board, or a clock face with movable hands (as simple as a paper plate with hands attached with a brad fastener). Move the hands and model the time.

b. To present a.m. and p.m. and link them to *morning, afternoon, evening,* and *night,* use two clock faces on the board. Have students help you identify and mark off the times of day and label as follows:

a.m./morning = 12 midnight until 12 noon
p.m./afternoon = approximately 12 noon until 5 p.m.
evening = approximately 5 p.m. until 7 p.m.
night = approximately 7 p.m. until 12 midnight

> **Teacher Tip:** Clarify for students that 12 a.m. = twelve midnight and 12 p.m. = twelve noon.

📖 BOOKS OPEN

A. What time is it?

1. Practice the vocabulary.

a. Play Track 92. Have students point to the times as they listen.

 CD 2 Track 92

What time is it?
It's three o'clock.

1. What time is it?
   It's three o'clock.
2. What time is it?
   It's six fifteen.
3. What time is it?
   It's eight thirty.
4. What time is it?
   It's ten forty-five.

b. Play the audio again. Have students repeat after each word. Put students into pairs or small groups, and have them practice asking and answering question about time.

B. Say these.

1. Practice the vocabulary.

a. Play Track 93. Have students point to the times as they listen.

 CD 2 Track 93

1. *It's 7:00 in the morning.*
   It's 7:00 a.m.
2. *It's 4:25 in the afternoon*
   It's 4:25 p.m.
3. *It's 6:43 in the evening.*
   It's 6:43 p.m.
4. *It's 9:52 at night.*
   It's 9:52 p.m.

b. Play the audio again. Have students repeat each sentence. Make sure that students understand the relationship between time of day and *a.m./p.m.* Put students into small groups and have them practice asking and answering questions about time.

GAMES AND ACTIVITIES

1. Give students more practice talking about time.

During class, stop frequently and ask students *What time is it?* If the same student(s) answers each time, ask individual students to tell you the time, but be sure every student has a chance to answer.

2. Give students practice listening and writing times.

a. Pair Dictation. In pairs, have students take turns saying and writing the times. Have them write 5–10 times on a piece of paper. For added challenge, have students add *a.m.* or *p.m.* to their times.

b. Teacher Dictation. Read a list of 5–10 times, using *in the morning/afternoon/evening* or *at night*. Students write the times, changing to *a.m.* or *p.m.* as they write.

3. Give students more practice talking about time in their personal lives.

a. Have students complete a typical daily schedule, assigning approximate times for each activity. For example:

   I wake up at 6:10 a.m.
   I get out of bed at 6:30 a.m.
   I eat breakfast at 6:35 a.m.
   I go to school at 8:12 a.m.
   I study English at 4:45 p.m.
   I watch TV at 8:30 p.m.

In pairs, have students tell each other about their days.

b. Sequencing Practice. Give each pair or group of students a series of strips of paper with a daily activity and a time printed on it (e.g., *I wash the dishes every evening at 5:45*). Students work together to put the activities in order. They will be able to use logic, time, and time words like *evening* and *p.m.* to help them order the activities. To correct students, simply pull out the strips that are in the wrong order—don't place them in the correct spot—so that students will have to reread each sentence carefully for clues.

COMPONENTS LINK

CD-ROM 2

For extra fun, students can play the Review Units 7–8 game on a computer at school or at home. Students find and match pairs of clocks. This activity reinforces listening and the Review Unit vocabulary.

LET'S CHANT LET'S SING 2

Page 32: "What Time Is It?"

This song practices the question-and-answer pattern *What time is it? It's eight o' clock. It's time for school.*

Page 33: "What Time Is It? It's Eleven O'Clock"

This chant practices the question-and-answer patterns *What time is it? It's eleven o' clock. Is it time for school? Yes, it is. No, it isn't.*

LET'S GO PICTURE DICTIONARY

Use pages 6–7, Time, to supplement the lesson and increase challenge.

1. Review familiar words and point out new words you wish to teach.

2. Practice the words with the question-and-answer pattern *What time is it? It's three o' clock.*

LET'S GO TESTS AND QUIZZES

Units 7–8 Listen and Review Test: Explain and administer the reproducible Units 7–8 Listen and Review Test from *Let's Go Tests and Quizzes,* page 74. Instructions and Answer Key are also in *Let's Go Tests and Quizzes.*

Lesson Quiz: Explain and administer the reproducible Let's Learn About Time quiz from *Let's Go Tests and Quizzes,* page 65. Instructions and Answer Key are also in *Let's Go Tests and Quizzes.*

Final Test: Explain and administer the reproducible Midterm Test from *Let's Go Tests and Quizzes,* page 84. This test covers material from Units 1–8 and the Reviews. Instructions and Answer Key are also in *Let's Go Tests and Quizzes.*

Skills Book Answer Key

Unit 1 Let's Start, pages 2–3

A. Listen and write.

Play the recording. Students listen to the conversation, and then complete the sentences.

Answers
1. Jenny: <u>Hi</u>, Kate. How <u>are you</u>?
2. Kate: I'm <u>OK</u>, thanks. <u>How</u> about you?
3. Jenny: Pretty <u>good</u>!
4. Jenny: <u>Good-bye</u>, Kate.
5. Kate: See you <u>later</u>!

 Track 02

(same as Answers)

B. Unscramble, write, and say.

Students unscramble the words, write the sentences, and say them aloud.

Answers
1. Hi, Andy. How are you?
2. <u>I'm OK, thanks. How about you?</u>
3. <u>Pretty good!</u>
4. <u>Good-bye, Andy.</u>
5. <u>See you later!</u>

C. Listen, number, and match.

Play the recording. Students listen and number the sentences. Then they draw line to match the sentences and the pictures.

 Track 03

1. I read books at school.
2. I write my name at school.
3. I erase the board at school.
4. I speak English at school.

D. Solve, write, and say.

Students write the correct letter above each number. Then they write and say the sentence.

Answer
I <u>erase the board at school</u>.

Unit 1 Let's Learn, pages 4–5

A. Unscramble, write, and match.

Students unscramble and write the words. Then they draw a line to match the words and the pictures.

Answers
1. clock   4. <u>workbook</u>
2. <u>calendar</u> 5. <u>door</u>
3. <u>picture</u>   6. <u>window</u>

B. Listen and circle.

Play the recording. Students listen to the sentences and circle the correct pictures.

Answers
1. (right)
2. (left)
3. (center)
4. (left)

 Track 04

1. That's a pencil sharpener.
2. This is a window.
3. This is a clock.
4. That's a calendar.

C. Look and write.

Students look at the pictures and complete the sentences.

Answers
1. What's this?
It's a workbook.
2. What's that?
It's <u>a door</u>.
3. What's <u>that</u>?
<u>It's</u> a calendar.
4. <u>What's this</u>?
<u>It's a window</u>.

D. Listen and number.

Play the recording. Students listen and number the pictures in the correct order.

 Track 05

1. Is it a paper clip?
Yes, it is.
2. Is it a window?
No, it isn't. It's a door.
3. Is it a clock?
Yes, it is.
4. Is it a pencil sharpener?
Yes, it is.
5. Is it a workbook?
No, it isn't. It's a calendar.
6. Is it a picture?
Yes, it is.

Unit 1 Let's Learn More, pages 6–7

A. Read and match.

Students read the words and draw a line to connect the words and the pictures.

B. Listen and check.

Play the recording. Students listen to the sentence and place a ✓ in the box next to the correct sentence.

 Track 06

1. These are workbooks.
2. Those are doors.
3. These are paper clips.
4. Those are pencil sharpeners.

C. Trace, write, and say.

Students trace the words. Then they complete the sentences and say them aloud.

Answers
1. What are these?
They're crayons.
2. What are those?
They're clocks.
3. What are these?
They're pens.
4. What are those?
They're windows.

D. Listen, trace, and write.

Play the recording. Students listen to the sentences. Then they trace the words and complete the sentences.

Answers
1. Are those pictures?
No, they aren't. They're clocks.
2. Are these pencils?
No, they aren't. They're pens.
3. Are those pencil sharpeners?
Yes, they are.

 Track 07

(same as Answers)

Unit 1 Let's Build, pages 8–9

A. Listen and check.

Play the recording. Students listen to sentences and place a ✓ next to the correct picture.

Answers
1. (left)
2. (left)
3. (right)
4. (left)

 Track 08

1. That window is big.
2. This eraser is round.
3. That kite is long.
4. This clock is square.

B. Look at A. Find, write, and say.

Students complete the sentences using the checked pictures in A and words from the word box.

Answers
1. That window is big.
2. This eraser is round.
3. That kite is long.
4. This clock is square.

C. Unscramble and write.

Students unscramble the words and write the sentences.

Answers
1. These windows are big and round.
2. Those clocks are small and square.
3. This crayon is fat and round.
4. That robot is big and new.

D. Read, check, and say.

Students read the sentences and place a ✓ next to the correct pictures. Then they say the sentences aloud.

Answers
1. (left)
2. (right)
3. (right)
4. (left)

Unit 2 Let's Start, pages 10–11

A. Listen and write.

Play the recording. Students listen to the conversation, and then complete the sentences.

Answers
1. Whose bag is that?
I don't know.
2. Is it Scott's bag?
No, it isn't his bag.
3. Is it Jenny's bag?
Yes, it is. It's her bag.

 Track 09

1. Kate: Whose bag is that?
Andy: I don't know.
2. Andy: Is it Scott's bag?
Kate: No, it isn't his bag.
3. Andy: Is it Jenny's bag?
Kate: Yes, it is. It's her bag.

B. Listen and circle.

Play the recording. Students listen to the sentences and circle the correct pictures.

Answers
1. (right)
2. (left)
3. (right)
4. (right)

 Track 10

1. She can run.
2. He can swim.
3. He can sing.
4. She can dance.

C. Write.

Students write a sentence about each child in the picture, using the words in the word box.

Answers
1. <u>She</u> can sing.
2. <u>She</u> can <u>run</u>.
3. <u>He can dance</u>.
4. <u>She</u> can <u>swim</u>.
5. <u>He can run</u>.
6. <u>He can sing</u>.

Unit 2 Let's Learn, pages 12–13

A. Find and circle.

Students find and circle the words in the word search.

B. Read, listen, and number.

Play the recording. Students listen and number the sentences in the correct order.

 Track 11

1. *I have a comic book.*
2. *I have a key.*
3. *I have a brush.*
4. *I have a candy bar.*
5. *I have a tissue.*
6. *I have a coin.*
7. *I have a comb.*
8. *I have a watch.*

C. Listen, match, and say.

Play the recording. Students listen and draw a line to connect the questions and answers.

Answers
1. d
2. a
3. f
4. b
5. e
6. c

 Track 12

1. *What do you have?*
I have a coin.
2. *What do you have?*
I have a watch.
3. *What do you have?*
I have a comic book.
4. *What do you have?*
I have a brush.
5. *What do you have?*
I have a key.
6. *What do you have?*
I have a tissue.

D. Write and say.

Students complete the questions and answers for each picture.

Answers
A.
1. Do you have a comb?
Yes, I do.
2. <u>Do you have a</u> key?
<u>No, I don't.</u>
3. <u>Do you have a</u> brush?
<u>Yes, I do.</u>

B.
1. <u>Do you have a</u> watch?
<u>No, I don't.</u>
2. <u>Do you have a</u> candy bar?
<u>Yes, I do.</u>
3. <u>Do you have a</u> brush?
<u>No, I don't.</u>

Unit 2 Let's Learn More, pages 14–15

A. Listen, number, and match.

Play the recording. Students listen to the words and number them in the correct order. Then they draw a line to match the words and the pictures.

 Track 13

1. *a camera*
2. *a key chain*
3. *a lunch box*
4. *a calculator*
5. *a train pass*
6. *a wallet*

B. Circle, trace, and write.

Students circle the correct pronoun, trace the words, and complete the sentences.

Answers
1. He has a calculator.
2. <u>She</u> has a <u>music player.</u>
3. <u>He has a camera.</u>
4. <u>She has an umbrella.</u>

C. Look and write.

Students look at the pictures and write the questions and answers.

Answers
1. What does she have?
She has a <u>key chain.</u>
2. What does <u>he have?</u>
He <u>has</u> a <u>wallet.</u>
3. What <u>does she have?</u>
<u>She has a calculator.</u>
4. <u>What does he have?</u>
<u>He has a music player.</u>

D. Look, listen, and check.

Play the recording. Students look at the picture and listen to the questions. Then they place a ✓ next to the correct answers.

Answers
1. Yes, she does.
2. No, she doesn't.
3. Yes, she does.
4. Yes, she does.

 Track 14

1. *Does she have a lunch box?*
2. *Does she have a music player?*
3. *Does she have a camera?*
4. *Does she have a wallet?*

Unit 2 Let's Build, pages 16–17

A. Read and write T for True and F for false.

Students read the sentences and look at the pictures. They write T or F next to each sentence.

Answers
1. F   2. F   3. T   4. T

B. Listen and write.

Play the recording. Students listen and complete the sentences.

Answers
1. What does she have in her hand?
She has a <u>calculator</u> in her hand.
2. What <u>does he</u> have in his bag?
He has a <u>pencil</u> in his bag.
3. What <u>does he</u> have in his <u>hand</u>?
He has a yo-yo in his <u>hand</u>.
4. What does she have in her bag?
She <u>has</u> a <u>tissue</u> in her bag.

 Track 15

(same as Answers)

C. Listen and write ✓ or ✗.

Students listen to the questions and answers. Then they place a ✓ next to the picture if it matches the answer.

 Track 16

1. *Does he have a pen?*
Yes, he does.
2. *Does he have a lunch box?*
No, he doesn't.
3. *Does he have a brush?*
No, he doesn't.
4. *Does he have a watch?*
Yes, he does.
5. *Does he have a workbook?*
No, he doesn't.
6. *Does he have a calculator?*
Yes, he does.

D. Circle and write.

Students complete sentences about themselves and a friend. Answers will vary—for example, *I have a tissue in my bag. He has a key in his bag.*

Units 1–2 Listen and Review, page 18

A. Read and write.

Students look at the pictures and answer the questions.

Answers
1. What's this?
<u>It's a comb.</u>
2. What does she have in her bag?
<u>She has a brush in her bag.</u>
3. What are those?
<u>They're paper clips.</u>
4. Does she have a key chain?
<u>No, she doesn't.</u>

B. Circle, trace, and write.

Students circle the correct verb, and then trace and write the sentences.

Answers
1. She can swim.
2. He can <u>erase the board.</u>
3. <u>He can sing.</u>
4. <u>She can read a book</u>.

Let's Learn About Numbers 20–100, page 19

A. Find and circle.

Play the recording. Students listen and circle the correct number.

 Track 17

1. *twenty-six*   5. *seventy*
2. *sixty*   6. *twenty-nine*
3. *one hundred*   7. *twenty-eight*
4. *twenty-five*   8. *twenty-three*

B. Listen and write.

Play the recording. Students listen and write the correct number.

Answers
1. twenty   6. <u>twenty-two</u>
2. <u>forty</u>   7. <u>thirty-eight</u>
3. <u>twenty-seven</u>   8. <u>sixty-three</u>
4. <u>ninety</u>   9. <u>fifty</u>
5. <u>eighty</u>   10. <u>seventy-one</u>

 Track 18

(same as Answers)

Unit 3 Let's Start, pages 20–21

A. Listen, number, and say.

Play the recording. Students listen to the conversation and number the sentences in the correct order.

 Track 19

1. Kate: *Where do you live, Jenny?*
2. Jenny: *I live in Hillsdale.*
3. Kate: *What's your address?*
4. Jenny: *It's 16 North Street.*
5. Kate: *What's your cell phone number?*
6. Jenny: *It's (798) 555-2043.*

B. Read and write.

Students complete the sentences.

Answers
1. Where do you live?
I <u>live</u> in Greenfield.
2. <u>What</u>'s your cell phone number?
<u>It's</u> 924-745-2341.
3. What's your <u>address</u>?
<u>It's</u> 202 Jones Street.

C. Look and write the letter.

Students write the letter of the correct picture next to each verb phrase.

Answers
1. <u>b</u>
2. <u>c</u>
3. <u>d</u>
4. <u>a</u>

D. Look, trace, and write.

Students look at the pictures, and then trace and complete the questions and answers.

1. What can he do?
He can use chopsticks.
2. What can he do?
He <u>can play baseball</u>.
3. What <u>can</u> she do?
She can <u>do a magic trick</u>.
4. <u>What can she do</u>?
<u>She can ice-skate</u>.

Unit 3 Let's Learn, pages 22–23

A. Write the letter.

Students write the letter of the correct word next to each picture.

Answers
1. B
2. I
3. F
4. H
5. D
6. E
7. G
8. J
9. C
10. A

B. Listen and match.

Students listen to the sentences and draw a line to match the words to the correct area of the house in the picture.

 Track 20

1. *The refrigerator is in the kitchen.*
2. *The bathtub is in the bathroom.*
3. *The telephone is in the bedroom.*
4. *The stove is in the kitchen.*
5. *The sofa is in the living room.*
6. *The bed is in the bedroom.*
7. *The TV is in the living room.*
8. *The lamp is in the bedroom.*
9. *The toilet is in the bathroom.*
10. *The sink is in the kitchen.*

C. Look and write.

Students look at the picture and complete the questions and answers.

Answers
1. Where is the bathtub?
It's in the living room.
2. <u>Where</u> is the stove?
It's <u>in</u> the <u>bedroom</u>.
3. <u>Where is the</u> TV?
<u>It's in the bathroom.</u>
4. <u>Where is the sofa/refrigerator/sink</u>?
<u>It's in the</u> kitchen.

D. Look at C. Listen and circle.

Play the recording. Students look at the picture in C, read the questions, and circle the correct answers.

Answers
1. Yes, there is.
2. Yes, there is.
3. No, there isn't.
4. No, there isn't.

Track 21

1. Is there a sofa in the kitchen?
Yes, there is.
2. Is there a bathtub in the living room?
Yes, there is.
3. Is there a telephone in the bathroom?
No, there isn't.
4. Is there a refrigerator in the bedroom?
No, there isn't.

Unit 3 Let's Learn More, pages 24–25

A. Read and match.
Students read and draw a line to match the prepositional phrases to the correct pictures.

B. Read and circle.
Students read the sentences and circle the correct prepositional phrase.

1. There are sinks next to the refrigerator.
2. There's a bed <u>in front of</u> the window.
3. There are lamps <u>behind</u> the sofa.
4. There's a bathtub <u>behind</u> the door.

C. Change the sentences.
Students write new sentences, following the model in number 1.

<u>Answers</u>
1. There are clocks next to the bed.
2. <u>There is a sink in front of the window.</u>
3. <u>There are tables behind the sofa.</u>

D. Look and check.
Students look at the picture, read the questions, and place a ✓ next to the correct answers.

<u>Answers</u>
1. Yes, there are.
2. No, there isn't.
3. Yes, there are.
4. Yes, there is.

Unit 3 Let's Build, pages 26–27

A. Listen and circle.
Play the recording. Students listen and circle the correct part of the picture.

 Track 22

1. Where are the pictures?
They're next to the door.
2. Where are the lamps?
They're behind the bed.
3. Where are the comic books?
They're under the bed.
4. Where are the candy bars?
They're in front of the lamp.

B. Trace, write, and change the sentences.
Students complete or write new sentences, changing the preposition and position of the nouns.

<u>Answers</u>
1. There is a bed in front of the lamp.
2. There is a stove <u>next to</u> the sink.
3. <u>There is a window behind the bed.</u>
4. <u>There is a door in front of the toilet.</u>
5. <u>There is a camera next to the calculator.</u>

C. Listen and circle.
Play the recording. Students listen and circle the correct picture.

<u>Answers</u>
1. (right)
2. (left)
3. (right)
4. (left)

 Track 23

1. Where's the telephone?
It's on the table behind the sofa.
2. Where's the cat?
It's on the sofa next to the TV.
3. Where's the workbook?
It's on the bed in front of the window.
4. Where's the music player?
It's in my bag next to the refrigerator.

D. Read and write.
Students look at the picture, read the questions, and write the answers.

<u>Answers</u>
1. Yes, there is.
2. <u>No, there isn't.</u>
3. <u>Yes, there is.</u>
4. <u>No, there isn't.</u>
5. <u>Yes, there is.</u>
6. <u>Yes, there is.</u>

Unit 4 Let's Start, pages 28–29

A. Read, write, and number.
Students read and complete the sentences, then number the sentences in the correct order to make a conversation.

<u>Answers</u>
1. What's for <u>lunch</u>, Mom?
2. <u>Spaghetti.</u>
3. Mmm. That's good. I <u>like</u> spaghetti.
4. I do, <u>too.</u>

B. Listen and check.
Play the recording. Students listen to the conversations and place a ✓ next to the correct picture.

Answers
1. (left)
2. (right)
3. (left)
4. (right)

 Track 24

1. Do you want spaghetti?
Yes, please.
2. Do you want pizza?
No, thank you.
3. Do you want rice?
Yes, please.
4. Do you want bread?
No, thank you.

C. Look, circle, and write.

Students look at the pictures, circle the correct pronoun, and write the answers.

Answers
1. Can she do a cartwheel?
Yes, she can.
2. Can he play Ping-Pong?
No, he can't.
3. Can he type?
Yes, he can.
4. Can she wink?
Yes, she can.

D. Listen and match.

Play the recording. Students listen to the question and answers, and then draw a line to the correct picture.

Answers
1. d
2. b
3. a
4. c

 Track 25

1. Can she type?
Yes, she can.
2. Can he do a cartwheel?
No, he can't.
3. Can she wink?
Yes, she can.
4. Can he play Ping-Pong?
Yes, he can.

Unit 4 Let's Learn, pages 30–31

A. Read and match.

Students read the words and draw a line to match the words and pictures.

Answers
1. b
2. d
3. f

4. h
5. g
6. a
7. e
8. c

B. Look at A. Listen and number.

Play the recording. Students listen and write the number next to the correct picture in A.

 Track 26

1. a pancake
2. hot chocolate
3. an omelet
4. tea
5. cereal
6. a pear
7. a peach
8. yogurt

C. Read, trace, and write.

Students trace, complete, or write the questions and answers.

Answers
1. What does he want?
He wants a pear.
2. What does she want?
She wants an omelet.
3. What does he want?
He wants a pancake.
4. What does he want?
He wants cereal.
5. What does she want?
She wants a peach.
6. What does she want?
She wants hot chocolate.

D. Listen and number.

Play the recording. Students listen to the questions and answers, and then number the pictures in the correct order.

 Track 27

1. Does she want tea?
Yes, she does.
2. Does he want an omelet?
No, he doesn't.
3. Does he want a peach?
Yes, he does.
4. Does she want hot chocolate?
No, she doesn't.

Unit 4 Let's Learn More, pages 32–33

A. Look and write.

Students look at the pictures and write the correct words in the crossword puzzle.

Answers
ACROSS: 1. grapes
           2. hamburgers
           3. stew
           4. pancakes
DOWN: 5. peaches
           6. steak
           7. cereal
           8. cheese

B. Listen and match.

Play the recording. Students listen and then draw a line to people and foods.

Answers
1. c
2. a
3. d
4. b

 Track 28

1. She likes cheese.
2. He likes grapes.
3. She likes steak.
4. He likes stew.

C. Read and write.

Students look at the pictures. Then they complete or write the sentences.

Answers
1. What does she like?
She likes hamburgers.
2. What <u>does he like</u>?
He likes <u>stew</u>.
3. <u>What does he like</u>?
<u>He likes grapes.</u>
4. <u>What does she like</u>?
<u>She likes pancakes.</u>

D. Listen and circle.

Play the recording. Students listen and circle the correct picture.

Answers
1. (right)
2. (left)
3. (right)
4. (left)

 Track 29

1. Does she like stew?
No, she doesn't.
2. Does he like cheese?
Yes, he does.
3. Does he like steak?
No, he doesn't.
4. Does she like pancakes?
Yes, she does.

A. Listen and circle.

Play the recording. Students listen and circle the correct picture.

Answers
1. (right)
2. (left)
3. (right)
4. (left)

 Track 30

1. She likes pancakes.
2. He wants a peach.
3. He likes hamburgers.
4. She wants tea.

B. Look and write.

Students look at the pictures and then complete or write the sentences.

Answers
1. She doesn't want a peach. She wants a pear.
2. He doesn't want a hamburger. He <u>wants steak</u>.
3. <u>She doesn't want grapes.</u> <u>She wants cheese.</u>
4. <u>He doesn't want cereal.</u> <u>He wants an omelet.</u>

C. Read and check.

Students read the questions and answers, and then place a ✓ next to the correct picture.

Answers
1. (right)
2. (left)
3. (right)
4. (left)

D. Listen and circle.

Play the recording. Students listen and circle the correct number of food items.

 Track 31

1. How many hamburgers does she want?
She wants two hamburgers.
2. How many pancakes does he want?
He wants five pancakes.
3. How many oranges does he want?
He wants three oranges.
4. How many pears does she want?
She wants one pear.
5. How many dogs does she want?
She wants four dogs.
6. How many omelets does he want?
He wants two omelets.
7. How many steaks does he want?
He wants nine steaks.
8. How many peaches does she want?
She wants six peaches.

Units 3–4 Listen and Review, page 36

A. Read and match.
Students read the questions and draw a line to the correct answers.

Answers
1. b   5. a
2. f   6. g
3. h   7. c
4. d   8. e

B. Listen and number the answer.
Play the recording. Students listen to the questions and number the answers.

Answers
1. She wants an orange.
2. It's on the table next to the sofa.
3. He likes hamburgers.
4. Yes, there is.

 Track 32

1. What does she want?
2. Where's the telephone?
3. What does he like?
4. Is there a sink next to the refrigerator?

Let's Learn About the Months, page 37

A. Write the name next to the number.
Students write the name of the month next to the number.

Answers
Month 1 = January
Month 8 = August
Month 3 = March
Month 11 = November
Month 5 = May
Month 9 = September

B. Listen and write the month.
Play the recording. Students listen to the questions and write the answers.

Answers
1. What month is it?
It's February.
2. What month is it?
It's September.
3. What month is it?
It's December.
4. What month is it?
It's July.

 Track 33

(same as Answers)

Unit 5 Let's Start pages 38–39

A. Listen and number.
Play the recording. Students listen to the conversation and number the sentences in the correct order.

 Track 34

1. Kate: *What's the matter, Scott?*
2. Scott: *I'm sick.*
3. Kate: *That's too bad.*
4. Kate: *Maybe Mrs. Green can help you.*
5. Scott: *Who's she?*
6. Kate: *She's the new nurse.*
7. Scott: *Thanks for your help.*
8. Kate: *You're welcome. Get better soon!*

B. Read and write.
Students read and complete the sentences.

Answers
1. Who's she?
2. She's the new nurse.
3. What's the matter?
4. That's too bad.
5. Get better soon!

C. Look and write the letter.
Students write the letter of each picture next to the correct verb phrase.

Answers
1. c
2. a
3. d
4. b

D. Look and write.
Students look at the pictures and write the sentence.

Answers
1. I get out of bed every morning.
2. I get dressed every morning.
3. I wake up every morning.
4. I make breakfast every morning.

Unit 5 Let's Learn, pages 40–41

A. Find and circle.
Students find and circle the words in the word search.

B. Listen and match.
Play the recording. Students listen and draw a line to match people with the tools of their occupations.

Answers
1. d
2. c
3. b
4. e
5. a

Track 35

1. She's a nurse.
2. He's a farmer.
3. She's a shopkeeper.
4. He's a cook.
5. She's an office worker.

C. Look and write.

Students look and answer the questions.

Answers
1. Who's she? She's Mrs. Smith. She's a taxi driver.
2. Who's he? <u>He's Mr. Brown.</u> <u>He's a police officer.</u>

D. Match and write.

Students follow the lines to the pictures, and then they write the answers.

Answers
1. No, he isn't.
2. Yes, he is.
3. Yes, she is.
4. No, she isn't.
5. No, he isn't.

Unit 5 Let's Learn More, pages 42–43

A. Listen and check.

Play the recording. Students listen and place a ✓ next to the correct picture.

Answers
1. (left)   3. (right)
2. (left)   4. (right)

 Track 36

1. three students
2. two teachers
3. two train conductors
4. four police officers

B. Look and write.

Students look at the pictures and write the sentences.

Answers
1. They're teachers.
2. <u>They're engineers.</u>
3. <u>They're dentists.</u>
4. <u>They're firefighters.</u>

C. Read, write, and say.

Students read the questions, write the answers, and say them aloud.

Answers
1. Who are they?
They're Mr. and Mrs. Cross. They're farmers.
2. Who are they?
<u>They're Mr. and Mrs. Long.</u> <u>They're teachers.</u>
3. Who are they?
<u>They're Mr. and Mrs. White.</u> <u>They're doctors.</u>

D. Listen and check.

Play the recording. Students listen to the questions and place a ✓ next to the correct answers.

Answers
1. Yes, they are.
2. <u>Yes, they are.</u>
3. <u>Yes, they are.</u>
4. <u>No, they aren't.</u>

 Track 37

1. Are they dentists?
2. Are they firefighters?
3. Are they students?
4. Are they engineers?

Unit 5 Let's Build, pages 44–45

A. Look and write.

Students look at the pictures and write the sentences.

Answers
1. I'm a nurse.
2. I'm <u>a pilot.</u>
3. <u>I'm a firefighter.</u>
4. <u>I'm a dentist.</u>
5. <u>I'm an engineer.</u>
6. <u>I'm a teacher.</u>

B. Listen and check.

Play the recording. Students listen and place a ✓ next to the correct pictures.

Answers
1. (left)
2. (right)
3. (right)
4. (left)

 Track 38

1. Who is Mr. Jones?
He's a pilot.
2. Who is Miss Smith?
She's a student.
3. Who is Mr. Kim?
He's a police officer.
4. Who is Mrs. Lee?
She's a cook.

C. Look, read, and write.

Students look at the pictures, and then complete the questions and answers.

Answers
1. Is Miss Smith a teacher or a student?
She's a teacher.
2. Is Mr. Jones a doctor or a dentist?
<u>He's a doctor.</u>
3. Is Mr. Lee a cook or <u>a taxi driver</u>?
<u>He's a taxi driver.</u>

D. Read and write.

Students read the questions and write the answers.

Answers
1. No, he can't.
2. Yes, she can.
3. Yes, they can.
4. No, he can't.

Unit 6 Let's Start, pages 46–47

A. Read, write, and listen.

Play the recording. Students listen and complete the sentences.

Answers
1. Jenny: Hi, Kate. This is Jenny. Where are you?
2. Kate: I'm at home. Where are you?
3. Jenny: I'm at the park. Can you come to the park?
4. Kate: Sure!

 Track 39

(same as Answers)

B. Read, listen, and number.

Students listen to the sentences and number them in the correct order.

 Track 40

1. Hi, Kate. This is Jenny.
2. Where are you?
3. I'm at home. Where are you?
4. I'm at the park.
5. Can you come to the park?
6. Sure.

C. Match and write.

Students connect the lines to match the pictures and verb phrases. Then they write sentences.

Answers
1. I practice the piano.
2. I talk on the telephone.
3. I watch TV.
4. I study English.

D. Look and write.

Students look at the pictures and write sentences.

Answers
1. I talk on the telephone.
2. I study English.
3. I watch TV.

Unit 6 Let's Learn, pages 48–49

A. Look and write.

Students look at the pictures and write the correct locations.

Answers
1. at work
2. at home
3. at school
4. at the library
5. at the park
6. at the zoo

B. Listen and draw a line.

Play the recording. Students listen and draw a line to match the people with the correct locations.

 Track 41

1. She's at the library.
2. He's at the park.
3. She's at the zoo.
4. He's at home.
5. She's at school.
5. He's at work.

C. Read and write.

Students look at the pictures, and then read and complete the questions and answers.

Answers
1. Where is he?
He's at the park.
2. Where is she?
She's at the zoo.
3. Where is she?
She's at the library.
4. Where is he?
He's at home.

D. Listen and match.

Play the recording. Students listen and draw a line to match the people and locations.
Answers
1. b
2. d
3. a
4. c

 Track 42

1. Is she at home?
Yes, she is.
2. Is she at work?
No, she isn't. She's at the park.
3. Is he at school?
No, he isn't. He's at the zoo.
4. Is she at school?
Yes, she is.

Unit 6 Let's Learn More, pages 50–51

A. Listen and number.

Play the recording. Students listen and number the pictures.

 Track 43

1. at the store
2. on the train
3. in the taxi
4. at the movies
5. on the bus
6. in the restaurant

B. Look and write.

Students look at the pictures and write the sentences.

Answers
1. They're at the movies.
2. They're at the store.
3. They're in the restaurant.

C. Read and match.

Students read the sentences and draw a line to match the sentences and pictures.

D. Listen and check.

Play the recording. Students listen and place a ✓ next to the correct picture.

Answers
1. (left)
2. (right)
3. (right)
4. (left)

 Track 44

1. Where are they?
They're in the taxi.
2. Where are they?
They're at the movies.
3. Where are they?
They're on the train.
4. Where are they?
They're in the restaurant.

E. Look, read, and write.

Students look at the pictures, read the questions, and write the answers.

Answers
1. Are they at school?
No, they aren't. They're at the movies.
2. Are they on a train?
No, they aren't. They're at the store.

Unit 6 Let's Build, pages 52–53

A. Look and write.

Students look at the pictures, read the questions, and write the answers.

Answers
1. They're at the zoo.
2. He's at work.
3. They're at the movies.
4. They're in the restaurant.
5. She's at work.
6. He's at the library.

B. Look at A. Listen and check.

Play the recording. Students look at the pictures in A, listen, and place a ✓ next to the correct answers.

Answers
1. Yes, she is.
2. Yes, she is.
3. Yes, they are.
4. No, they aren't.
5. No, he isn't.
6. Yes, he is.

 Track 45

1. Is the teacher at the zoo?
Yes, she is.
2. Is the shopkeeper at the store?
Yes, she is.
3. Are the doctors at the restaurant?
Yes, they are.
4. Are the police officers at work?
No, they aren't.
5. Is the farmer in a taxi?
No, he isn't.
6. Is the office worker at work?
Yes, he is.

C. Listen and match.

Play the recording. Students listen to the sentences and then draw a line to match the people and locations.

Answers
1. b
2. a
3. d
4. c

 Track 46

1. The teachers are at school.
2. The cook is in the kitchen.
3. The train conductor is on the train.
4. The engineers are at work.

D. Read and draw.

Students read the sentences and draw in the boxes.

Units 5–6 Listen and Review, page 54

A. Listen and number.

Play the recording. Students listen and then number the sentences in the correct order.

 Track 47

1. She's a teacher.
2. He's at school.
3. Are they at the movies? Yes, they are.
4. I practice the piano every afternoon.
5. They're in the kitchen.
6. They're Mr. and Mrs. Long. They're teachers.

B. Write a sentence about the picture.

Students write a sentence about each picture. Answers will vary; for example, *I wake up every morning. I go to the park every afternoon.*

Let's Learn About the Seasons, page 55

A. Match.

Students draw a line to match the words and pictures.

B. Look and write.

Students look at the picture and write the season.

Answers
1. summer
2. winter
3. spring
4. fall

Unit 7 Let's Start, pages 56–57

A. Listen and number.

Play the recording. Students listen and number the sentences.

 Track 48

1. Let's play a game.
2. I'm riding a bicycle.
3. We're swimming.
4. What are you doing?

B. Look and write.

Students complete the conversation.

Answers
What's he doing? He's riding a bicycle.
What's she doing? She's swimming.
What are they doing? They're playing a game.

C. Read and match.

Students read the questions and look at the pictures. Then they draw a line matching the pictures to the answers.

Answers
1. b. I'm swimming.
2. c. I'm riding a bicycle.
3. a. We're playing a game.

D. Write.

Students write the correct verb phrase under each picture.

Answers
read e-mail
cook dinner
do homework

E. Listen and match.

Play the recording. Students listen to the questions and answers. Then they draw a line to the correct pictures.

 Track 49

1. Do you read e-mail every evening?
Yes, I do.
2. Do you cook dinner every evening?
No, I don't. I wash the dishes every evening.
3. Do you do homework every evening?
Yes, I do.
4. Do you wash the dishes every evening?
No, I don't. I cook dinner every evening.

Unit 7 Let's Learn, pages 58–59

A. Read, listen, and number.

Play the recording. Students listen and number the pictures in the correct order.

 Track 50

1. dancing
2. throwing a ball
3. running
4. singing a song
5. fishing
6. walking
7. coloring a picture
8. sleeping

B. Look and write.

Students look at the pictures and write sentences.

Answers
1. He's throwing a ball.
2. She's coloring a picture.
3. He's sleeping.
4. She's dancing.
5. She's running.
6. He's fishing.

C. Listen and match.

Play the recording. Students listen and then draw a line to the correct pictures.

Track 51

1. What's he doing?
He's sleeping.
2. What's she doing?
She's throwing a ball.
3. What's he doing?
He's singing a song.
4. What's she doing?
She's walking.
5. What's he doing?
He's dancing.
6. What's she doing?
She's fishing.

D. Listen and check.

Play the recording. Students listen and place a ✓ next to the correct answer.

Answers
1. Yes, she is.
2. No, he isn't.
3. Yes, she is.
4. No, he isn't.

 Track 52

1. Is she coloring a picture?
2. Is he throwing a ball?
3. Is she running?
4. Is he fishing?

Unit 7 Let's Learn More, pages 60–61

A. Look and write.

Students write the correct verb phrase below each picture.

Answers
1. eating apples
2. playing soccer
3. riding bicycles
4. flying kites
5. studying English
6. talking on the telephone

B. Listen and match.

Play the recording. Students listen to the sentences and then draw a line to match the pictures to the sentences.

 Track 53

1. They're playing soccer.
2. They're watching TV.
3. They're studying English.
4. They're reading comic books.

C. Listen and match.

Play the recording. Students listen and then draw a line to match the people to the activities.

 Track 54

1. What are they doing?
They're flying kites.
2. What are they doing?
They're riding bicycles.
3. What are they doing?
They're talking on the telephone.
4. What are they doing?
They're singing a song.

D. Write.

Students look at the pictures, read the questions, and write the answers.

Answers
1. No, they aren't. They're watching TV.
2. Yes, they are.
3. No, they aren't. They're riding bicycles.
4. Yes, they are.

Unit 7 Let's Build, pages 62–63

A. Listen and number.

Play the recording. Students listen to the sentences and number the pictures in the correct order.

 Track 55

1. He's walking.
2. She's cooking dinner.
3. They're coloring a picture.
4. She's fishing.
5. He's running.
6. They're throwing a ball.

B. Read, look, and circle.

Students read the questions, look at the pictures, and circle the correct answers.

Answers
1. He's sleeping.
2. She's doing homework.
3. They're running.
4. I'm studying English.

C. Read and write.

Students read the questions, look at the pictures, and write the correct answers.

Answers
1. No, she isn't. She's coloring a picture.
2. Yes, they are.
3. No, he isn't. He's playing soccer.

D. Listen and circle.

Play the recording. Students listen to the questions and answers. Then they circle the correct picture.

Answers
1. (peaches)   3. (comic book)
2. (bat and ball)   4. (dishes in a sink)

Track 56

1. What are they eating?
They're eating peaches.
2. What are they playing?
They're playing baseball.
3. What is she reading?
She's reading comic books.
4. What is he doing?
He's washing the dishes.

Unit 8 Let's Start, pages 64–65

A. Unscramble and write. Then listen and number.

Students first unscramble and write the sentences. Then, play the recording. Students listen and number the sentences in order.

Answers
Great! See you on Sunday!
Can you come over on Saturday?
What about Sunday?
Sorry. No, I can't. I'm busy.
Sunday is OK. I'm free.
OK. See you then!

 Track 57

1. Can you come over on Sunday?
2. Sorry. No, I can't. I'm busy.
3. What about Sunday?
4. Sunday is OK. I'm free.
5. Great! See you on Sunday!
6. OK. See you then!

B. Look and write.

Students look at the picture, read the questions, and write the correct answers based on the choices in the box.

Answers
1. Yes, I can.
2. No, I can't. I'm busy.
3. No, I can't. I'm busy.

C. Match.

Students match the verb phrases to the correct pictures.

Answers
1. c
2. d
3. b
4. a

D. Write.

Students look at the pictures, read the questions, and write the answers.

Answers
1. Yes, I do.
2. No, I don't.

E. Listen and check.

Play the recording. Students listen and place a ✓ next to the correct picture.

Answers
1. (right)   3. (right)
2. (left)   4. (left)

 Track 58

1. Do you ever take a walk at night?
No, I don't.
2. Do you ever take a bath at night?
Yes, I do.
3. Do you ever look at stars at night?
No, I don't.
4. Do you ever play outside at night?
Yes, I do.

Unit 8 Let's Learn, pages 66–67

A. Look and number.

Students look at the picture and write the correct number by each class.

B. Listen and match.

Play the recording. Students listen and draw a line to match the people and activities.

Answers
1. c
2. d
3. b
4. a

 Track 59

1. I go to math class.
2. I go to art class.
3. I go to English class.
4. I go to karate class.

C. Listen and number.

Play the recording. Students look at the daily planner and number the days/activities in the correct order.

Answers
1. Tuesday/piano class
2. Friday/math class
3. Monday/ English class
4. Wednesday/soccer practice
5. Saturday/swimming class
6. Thursday/art class

Track 60

1. What do you do on Tuesdays?
I go to piano class.
2. What do you do on Fridays?
I go to math class.
3. What do you do on Mondays?
I go to English class.

4. What do you do on Wednesdays?
I go to soccer practice.
5. What do you do on Saturdays?
I go to swimming class.
6. What do you do on Thursdays?
I go to art class.

D. Write three sentences.

Students write three sentences using the example as a model. Answers may vary; for example, *I go to piano class on Mondays.*

Unit 8 Let's Learn More, pages 68–69

A. Listen and number.

Play the recording. Students listen and number the pictures.

 Track 61

1. *go to the bookstore*
2. *listen to music*
3. *walk the dog*
4. *do homework*
5. *practice the piano*
6. *take a bath*
7. *ride a bicycle*
8. *talk on the telephone*

B. Look and write.

Students look at the pictures and write sentences.

Answers
1. He walks the dog.
2. He goes to the bookstore.
3. He rides a bicycle.
4. She listens to music.

C. Read and match.

Students read the questions and answers. Then they draw a line to match them to the correct pictures.

D. Listen and check.

Play the recording. Students listen and place a ✓ next to the correct pictures.

Answers
1. (left)
2. (left)
3. (left)
4. (right)

 Track 62

1. *Does she practice the piano after school?*
No, she doesn't. She walks the dog.
2. *Does he ride a bicycle after school?*
Yes, he does.
3. *Does she do homework after school?*
Yes, she does.
4. *Does he study English after school?*
No, he doesn't. He goes to the bookstore.

Unit 8 Let's Build, pages 70–71

A. Write.

Students look at the pictures and write sentences.

Answers
1. I go to my math class after school.
2. I go to my dance class after school.
3. I go to my karate class after school.
4. I go to my art class after school.

B. Listen and circle.

Play the recording. Students listen to the sentences and circle the correct pronouns.

Answers
1. She goes to her English class.
2. She goes to her art class.
3. He goes to his karate class.
4. She goes to her math class.
5. He goes to his English class.
6. She goes to her dance class.

 Track 63

(same as Answers)

C. Listen and circle.

Play the recording. Students listen and then circle the correct activity on the day indicated.

 Track 64

1. *What does she do on Tuesdays?*
She goes to her piano class on Tuesdays.
2. *What does he do on Fridays?*
He goes to his art class on Fridays.
3. *What does she do on Wednesdays?*
She goes to the bookstore on Wednesdays.
4. *What does he do on Mondays?*
He goes to his English class on Mondays.
5. *What does she do on Thursdays?*
She practices the piano on Thursdays.
6. *What does he do on Thursdays?*
He goes to his soccer practice on Thursdays.

D. Write.

Students read the questions and write the answers. Answers will vary.

Units 7–8 Listen and Review, page 72

A. Match.

Students draw a line to match the questions and answers.

Answers
1. d
2. c
3. a
4. f
5. b
6. e

B. Listen and number the answer.

Play the recording. Students listen to the questions and number the answers.

Answers
1. No, she isn't. She's singing a song.
2. I go to my piano practice after school on Tuesdays.
3. Yes, they are.
4. He listens to music.

 Track 65

1. *Is she dancing?*
2. *What do you do after school on Tuesdays?*
3. *Are they watching TV?*
4. *What does he do after school?*

Let's Learn About Time, page 73

A. Match.

Students draw a line to match the times.

Answers
1. c
2. d
3. b
4. f
5. e
6. a

B. Listen, write, and circle.

Students listen to the sentences, write the numbers on the clocks, and circle *a.m.* or *p.m.*

 Track 66

1. *It's 8:30 a.m.*
2. *It's 9:45 at night.*
3. *It's 3:04 p.m.*
4. *It's 12:00 noon.*
5. *It's 6:00 in the morning.*
6. *It's 2:15 in the afternoon.*

Extra Practice

Page 74

A. Listen and circle.

Play the recording. Students listen to the conversations and circle the correct items in the pictures.

Answers
1. a comic book, a watch
2. a coin, a key, a candy bar, a comic book

 Track 67

1. *Jenny: Hi, Andy! How are you?*
Andy: I'm OK.
Jenny: What do you have in your bag?
Andy: I have a comb.
Jenny: Do you have a watch?
Andy: Yes, I do.
Jenny: I'm hungry. Do you have a candy bar?
Andy: No, I don't. Sorry.

2. *Scott: Is it your bag?*
Kate: Yes, it is. It's my bag.
Scott: Do you have a tissue?
Kate: No, I don't.
Scott: Do you have a calculator?
Kate: No, I don't.
Scott: What do you have in your bag?
Kate: I have a coin, a key, a candy bar, and a comic book.

B. Look and write.

Students write sentences about the objects in their bags. Answers will vary—for example, *I have a wallet. I have a comb.*

Page 75

A. Listen and check.

Play the recording. Students listen and place a ✓ next to the correct answer. Then students complete the sentence for the Extra question.

Answers
1. It's in the living room.
2. lamps, TV, bed
Extra: Where are the lamps? They're <u>on the table next to the bed.</u>

 Track 68

1. Boy: *Where's the telephone?*
Girl: *It's in the kitchen.*
Boy: *No, it isn't. It isn't in the kitchen.*
Girl: *Is it in the bedroom?*
Boy: *No, it isn't in the bedroom.*
Girl: *Is it in the living room?*
Boy: *Aha! Yes, here it is. It's in the living room.*

2. Girl *1: Is this your bedroom?*
Girl 2: *Yes, it is.*
Girl 1: *Is there a TV in your bedroom?*
Girl 2: *Yes, there is. It's next to the door.*
Girl 1: *Is there a refrigerator in your bedroom?*
Girl 2: *No, there isn't.*
Girl 1: *Are there lamps in your bedroom?*
Girl 2: *Yes, there are.*
Girl 1: *Where are the lamps?*
Girl 2: *They're on the table next to the bed.*

B. Read and draw.

Students read and then illustrate the sentences.

Page 76

A. Listen and write.

Play the recording. Students listen and then complete the answers.

Answers
1. She likes <u>hamburgers</u>. She doesn't like <u>stew and pancakes</u>.
2. He wants <u>yogurt</u>, a <u>peach</u>, a <u>pear</u>, and <u>cereal</u>.

 Track 68

1. Mom: Hello?
Daughter: Hi, Mom. Can Jenny come for lunch?
Mom: Sure. Does she like pancakes?
Daughter: No, she doesn't like pancakes.
Mom: Does she like stew?
Daughter: No, she doesn't like stew.
Mom: What does she like?
Daughter: She likes hamburgers.
Mom: OK. Hamburgers for lunch!

2. Boy 1: Are you hungry? I'm going to the store.
Boy 2: No, I'm not hungry. But John is hungry.
Boy 1: What does he want?
Boy 2: He wants yogurt.
Boy 1: OK. Yogurt.
Boy 2: He wants a peach and a pear.
Boy 1: A peach and a pear…
Boy 2: And he wants cereal.
Boy 1: He wants cereal, too? He's hungry!

B. Write and draw.

Students write sentences about foods they like and draw pictures of them. Answers will vary—for example, *I like grapes and stew. I like peaches.*

Page 77

A. Listen and match.

Play the recording. Students listen and draw a line to match the names and the occupations. For number 2, students connect Mr. Hill to the correct occupation and activity.

Answers
1. Mrs. Johnson: shopkeeper, Mr. Smith: police officer, Miss Lee: teacher
2. Mr. Hill, office worker, He can talk on the telephone.

 Track 70

1. Girl 1: Who's she?
Girl 2: She's Mrs. Johnson. She's a shopkeeper.
Girl 1: Who's he?
Girl 2: He's Mr. Smith
Girl 1: Is he a farmer?
Girl 2: No, he isn't. He's a police officer.
Girl 1: Who's she?
Girl 2: She's Miss Lee.
Girl 1: Is she a teacher?
Girl 2: Yes, she is!

2. Boy 1: Who's he?
Boy 2: He's Mr. Hill.
Boy 1: Is he a shopkeeper or an office worker?
Boy 2: He's an office worker.
Boy 1: Can he type at work?
Boy 2: Yes, he can.
Boy 1: Can he talk on the telephone at work?
Boy 2: Yes, he can.
Boy 1: Can he study English at work?
Boy 2: No, he can't. He's very busy at work!

B. Write.

Students write sentences about what they want to be. Answers will vary; for example, *I want to be a farmer.*

Page 78

A. Listen and number.

Play the recording. Students listen and then number the locations.

Answers
1. (home)
2. (library)
3. (school)
4. (zoo)

 Track 71

1. Boy: What do you do every afternoon?
Girl: I practice the piano and study English.
Boy: Where?
Girl: At home.
2. Girl: Are the students on the bus?
Boy: No, they aren't. They're at the library.
3. Girl 1: Is Miss Lee a student or a teacher?
Girl 2: She's a teacher.
Girl 1: Is she at school?
Girl 2: No, she isn't. She's at the movies.
4. Boy 1: Who are they?
Boy 2: They're Mr. and Mrs. Jones.
Boy 1: Are they shopkeepers?
Boy 2: No, they aren't. They're farmers.
Boy 1: Are they at the store?
Boy 2: No, they aren't. They're at the zoo.

B. Make sentences.

Students look at the pictures and write sentences.

Answers
1. She's at the <u>library</u>.
2. They're <u>at the park</u>.
3. <u>He's at school</u>.

Page 79

A. Listen and write.

Play the recording. Students listen and then write sentences.

Answers
He's reading e-mails.
They're watching TV.
He's fishing.
Jenny is fishing.

 Track 72

Jenny: What are you doing? Are you doing homework? Let's play a game!
Andy: No, I'm reading e-mails.
Jenny: I'm bored. What are Kate and Sarah doing?
Andy: They're watching TV.
Jenny: I don't want to watch TV. What about Scott? Is he playing soccer?
Andy: No, he isn't. He's fishing.
Jenny: Fishing? Oh, that sounds like fun! I'm going fishing, too.

B. Write.

Students write sentences about what they and a friend are doing. Answers will vary; for example, *I'm fishing. My friend is sleeping.*

Page 80

A. Listen and match.

Play the recording. Students listen and then match the activities they hear in the conversation to the correct days.

> Answers
> Monday/karate class, Wednesday/soccer practice, Tuesday/English class, Thursday/math class
> Extra: What day can she come over? <u>Saturday</u>

 Track 73

Kate: Can you come to my house on Monday?
Jenny: No, I can't. I go to karate class on Mondays. How about Wednesday?
Kate: No, I can't. I go to soccer practice on Wednesdays. How about Tuesday?
Jenny: No, I can't. I go to English class on Tuesdays. How about Thursday?
Kate: I go to math class.
Jenny: Oh, no! What day can I come over?
Kate: Can you come over on Saturday?
Jenny: Saturday is OK. I'm free!
Kate: Great! See you then!

B. Write four activities.

Students write four sentences about their after-school activities. Answers will vary—for example, I go to karate class after school.

Workbook Answer Key

Unit 1 Let's Start, pages 2–3

A. Read, trace, and write.
Students read, trace the words, and complete the conversations in the speech bubbles.

Answers
Hi, Andy. How are you?
Pretty good, thanks. How about you?
I'm OK.
Good-bye, Andy.
See you later!

B. Look, unscramble, and write.
Students look at the picture, unscramble the words, and write the verb phrases.

Answers
1. erase the board
2. write my name
3. read books
4. speak English

C. Look and write.
Students look at the pictures, and then complete or write sentences.

Answers
1. I write my name at school.
2. I speak English at school.
3. I read books at school.
4. I erase the board at school.

Unit 1 Let's Learn, pages 4–5

A. Trace and match.
Students trace the words and draw a line to match the words and pictures.

B. Read and circle.
Students read the sentences and circle the correct pictures.

Answers
1. (left)
2. (left)
3. (right)
4. (left)

C. Trace and write.
Students trace the words, and then complete or write the sentences.

Answers
1. What's this? It's a paper clip.
2. What's that? It's a picture.

3. What's that? It's a door.
4. What's this? It's a calendar.

D. Read, trace, and write.
Students read the questions, and then trace or write the answers.

Answer
1. Yes, it is.
2. No, it isn't.
3. No, it isn't.
4. Yes, it is.

Unit 1 Let's Learn More, pages 6–7

A. Look and write.
Students look at the pictures and write sentences.

Answers
1. Those are clocks.
2. These are paper clips.
3. Those are windows.
4. These are pencil sharpeners.
5. Those are calendars.
6. These are pictures.

B. Write.
Students write new sentences, following the model in numbers 1 and 2.

Answers
1. These are windows.
2. Those are calendars.
3. These are doors.
4. Those are pictures.

C. Read and match.
Students read the questions and answers. Then they draw a line to match them to the correct picture.

D. Connect, trace, and write.
Students follow the lines to connect each question and answer to a picture. Then they trace and complete the questions and answers.

Answers
1. Are these windows? No, they aren't.
2. Are those paper clips? Yes, they are.
3. Are those pencil sharpeners? Yes, they are.
4. Are those pictures? Yes, they are.

Unit 1 Let's Build, pages 8–9

A. Circle and write.

Students circle either *This* or *That*. Then students circle and write the correct adjectives to complete the sentences.

Answers
1. This door is little.
2. That window is round.
3. This workbook is old.
4. That picture is long.

B. Read and match.

Students read, then draw a line to match the sentences to the correct pictures.

C. Look and check.

Students look at the pictures and check the correct sentences.

Answers
1. This bicycle is long.
2. Those erasers are square.

D. Unscramble and write.

Students unscramble and write the sentences.

Answers
1. Those clocks are big.
2. This rabbit is small.
3. These pencils are long.
4. That door is square.
5. This picture is new.
6. Those calendars are round.

Unit 2 Let's Start, pages 10–11

A. Read and write.

Students read and complete the conversations.

Answers
1. Whose bag is that?
It's his bag.
2. Whose bag is that?
It's her bag.

B. Look and write.

Students read and complete the questions and answers.

Answers
1. Whose bag is that? It's Scott's bag.
2. Whose bag is that? It's Jenny's bag.

C. Read and match.

Students read the sentences, then draw a line to match the sentences and pictures.

D. Look and write.

Students look at the pictures and write sentences.

Answers
1. He can dance.
2. She can swim.
3. She can sing.
4. He can run.

Unit 2 Let's Learn, pages 12–13

A. Look and write.

Students write the correct word under each picture.

Answers
1. a tissue
2. a key
3. a watch
4. a brush
5. a coin
6. a comb

B. Draw and write.

Students read the question, and draw and write their answer.

Answers will vary; for example, *I have a watch.*

C. Trace and write.

Students trace the words and write sentences.

Answers
A.
1. I have a candy bar.
2. I have a comb/tissue.
3. I have a tissue/comb.

B.
1. I have a comic book.
2. I have a brush/coin.
3. I have a coin/brush.

D. Read and circle.

Students read the questions and circle the answers.

Answers
1. Yes, I do.
2. No, I don't.
3. No, I don't.
4. Yes, I do.

Unit 2 Let's Learn More, pages 14–15

A. Unscramble and write.

Students unscramble and write the words.

Answers
1. calculator
2. wallet
3. umbrella
4. lunch box
5. key chain
6. train pass
7. camera
8. music player

B. Connect and write.

Students follow the lines connecting people and objects. Then they write sentences.

Answers
1. She has a camera.
2. He has a key chain.
3. She has a calculator.
4. He has an umbrella.
5. She has a music player.

C. Trace and write.

Students trace and write the sentences.

Answers
1. What does she have? She has a lunch box.
2. What does he have? He has a wallet.
3. What does she have? She has a train pass.

D. Trace, write, and check.

Students trace and complete the questions. Then they place a ✓ next to the correct answer.

Answers
1. Does he have a lunch box? Yes, he does.
2. Does she have a comb? No, she doesn't.
3. Does he have a music player? No, he doesn't.
4. Does she have a calculator? Yes, she does.

Unit 2 Let's Build, pages 16–17

A. Trace and write.

Students trace and complete the sentences.

Answers
1. She has a coin in her bag.
2. He has a key in his bag.

B. Trace and write.

Students trace and complete the questions and answers.

Answers
1. What does she have in her hand? She has a comic book in her hand.
2. What does he have in his hand? He has a comb in his hand.
3. What does she have in her hand? She has a brush in her hand.
4. What does he have in his hand? He has a music player in his hand.

C. Read and check.

Students read the questions and place a ✓ next to the correct answers.

Answers
1. No, he doesn't.
2. Yes, he does.
3. Yes, she does.
4. No, she doesn't.

D. Draw and write.

Students read the question, and then write and draw three answers. Answers will vary; for example, *I have a comic book in my bag.*

Units 1–2 Listen and Review, page 18.

A. Read and match.

Students draw a line to match the questions with pictures and answers.

Answers
1. What are these?   They're windows.
2. What does he have   He has a train pass in
   in his hand?   his hand.
3. Does she have a watch?   Yes, she does.
4. Whose bag is that?   It's his bag.

B. Read and circle.

Students read and circle the correct verb or verb phrase.

Answers
1. He can swim.
2. I speak English at school.
3. She can run.
4. I erase the board at school.

Let's Learn About Numbers 20–100, page 19

A. Match.

Students match the written and Arabic numbers.

B. Count and write.

Students count the dots and write the numbers.

Answers
1. *29* twenty-nine
2. *36* thirty-six
3. *40* forty
4. *14* fourteen
5. *70* seventy

Unit 3 Let's Start, pages 20–21

A. Trace and write.

Students trace and complete the conversations.

Answers
1. Where do you live? I live in Hillsdale.
2. What's your address? It's 16 North Street.
3. What's your cell phone number? It's (798) 555-2043.

B. Write.

Students answer the question. Answers will vary—for example, *I live in Greenfield.*

C. Read and check.

Students read the questions and place a ✓ next to the correct answers.

Answers
1. He can do a magic trick.
2. She can play baseball.
3. He can ice-skate.
4. She can use chopsticks.

D. Draw and write.

Students read the question, and then draw and write two answers. Answers will vary; for example, *I can use chopsticks*.

Unit 3 Let's Learn, pages 22–23

A. Look and write.

Students write the words in the crossword puzzle.

Answers
ACROSS 1. stove, 2. bed, 3. sofa, 4. TV, 5. refrigerator
DOWN 6. toilet, 7. sink, 8. bathtub

B. Look, trace, and write.

Students look at the pictures, and trace or write the sentences.

Answers
1. The lamp is in the bedroom.
2. The stove is in the kitchen.
3. The telephone is in the living room.

C. Read and check.

Students read and check the correct pictures.

Answers
1. (right)
2. (left)

D. Look and write.

Students look at the picture, read the questions, and write the answers.

Answers
1. Yes, there is.
2. Yes, there is.
3. No, there isn't.
4. No, there isn't.

Unit 3 Let's Learn More, pages 24–25

A. Write.

Students write the correct prepositional phrase under each picture.

Answers
1. next to
2. in front of
3. behind

B. Read and check.

Students read the sentences and place a ✓ next to the correct pictures.

Answers
1. (right)
2. (left)
3. (left)
4. (left)

C. Look, read, and write.

Students look at the pictures, read the questions, and write the answers.

Answers
1. No, there isn't.
2. No, there isn't.
3. Yes, there is.
4. Yes, there is.

D. Look, read, and check.

Students look at the picture, read the questions, and place a ✓ next to the correct answer.

Answers
1. Yes, there are.
2. Yes, there are.
3. No, there aren't.

Unit 3 Let's Build, pages 26–27

A. Unscramble and write.

Students unscramble and write the questions and answers.

Answers
1. Where are the books? They are under the table.
2. Where are the cats? They are on the sofa.

B. Match.

Students draw a line to match sentences with the same meaning.

Answers
1. There's a stove next to the refrigerator.
    There's a refrigerator next to the stove.
2. There's a toilet behind the door.
    There's a door in front of the toilet.
3. There's a bed in front of the window.
    There's a window behind the bed.
4. There's a cat on the bed.
    There's a bed under the cat.

C. Read and write.

Students read the questions and complete the answers by writing in the prepositions.

Answers
1. It's on the table behind the sofa.
2. It's in the box next to the refrigerator.
3. It's in the sink next to the stove.
4. It's on the bed under the window.

D. Read and check.

Students read the questions and place a ✓ next to the correct answers.

Answers
1. No, there isn't.
2. Yes, there is.
3. No, there isn't.

Unit 4 Let's Start, pages 28–29

A. Read and trace.

Students read and trace the conversation.

B. Look, read, and check.

Students look at the pictures, read the questions, and place a ✓ next to the correct answers.

Answers
1. Yes, please.
2. No, thank you.
3. Yes, please.
4. No, thank you.

C. Read and match.

Students read the questions and answers, then draw a line to match them with the correct pictures.

D. Look, trace, and write.

Students trace and write the questions and answers.

Answers
1. Can he do a cartwheel? Yes, he can.
2. Can he play Ping-Pong? No, he can't.
3. Can she type? No, she can't.
4. Can she wink? Yes, she can.

Unit 4 Let's Learn, pages 30–31

A. Look and write.

Students write the correct word under each food item.

Answers
1. hot chocolate
2. tea
3. a peach
4. cereal
5. yogurt
6. an omelet
7. a pancake
8. a pear

B. Unscramble and write.

Students unscramble and write the sentences.

Answers
1. He wants a pear.
2. She wants an omelet.
3. She wants tea.
4. He wants yogurt.

C. Read, connect, and write.

Students read the questions, follow the lines connecting the questions and pictures, and write the answers.

Answers
1. She wants tea.
2. She wants an omelet.
3. He wants yogurt.
4. She wants a pancake.
5. He wants a peach.
6. He wants a pear.

D. Look and check.

Students read the questions and place a ✓ next to the correct answers.

Answers
1. No, she doesn't.
2. Yes, he does.

Unit 4 Let's Learn More, pages 32–33

A. Find and circle.

Students find and circle the words in the word search.

Answers
1. grapes
2. pancakes
3. peaches
4. hamburgers
5. stew
6. cheese
7. spaghetti
8. steak

B. Look and write.

Students look at the pictures and write sentences.

Answers
1. He likes hamburgers.
2. She likes pancakes.

C. Read and match.

Students read the questions and answers, then draw a line to match them to the correct pictures.

D. Look, read, and write.

Students look at the pictures, and complete or write the questions and answers.

Answers
1. Does she like pancakes? Yes, she does.
2. Does he like cheese? No, he doesn't.
3. Does she like pasta? No, she doesn't.
4. Does he like steak? Yes, he does.

Unit 4 Let's Build, pages 34–35

A. Look and circle.
Students look at the picture and circle the correct verb in the sentence.

Answers
1. likes
2. wants
3. wants
4. doesn't like

B. Trace and write.
Students trace and write the sentences.

Answers
1. He doesn't want a dog. He wants a cat.
2. She doesn't want a rabbit. She wants a frog.
3. He doesn't want a bird. He wants a turtle.

C. Look, read, and write.
Students look at the pictures, read the questions, and write the answers.

Answers
1. She wants a peach.
2. She wants a giraffe.
3. He wants a camera.
4. He wants a cookie.

D. Count and write.
Students count the food items in the pictures, read the questions, and write the answers.

Answers
1. She wants three eggs.
2. He wants six pancakes.
3. She wants two sandwiches.
4. He wants four milkshakes.

Units 3–4 Listen and Review, page 36

A. Read and write.
Students write the answers to the questions based on the choices in the text box.

Answers
1. It's in the bedroom.
2. He likes cereal.
3. It's next to the lamp.
4. He wants grapes.

B. Look and write the question.
Students look at the pictures, read the answers, and write the questions.

Answers
1. Where's the stove?
2. What does she want?
3. What does he like?
4. What does she want?

Let's Learn About the Months, page 37

A. Trace and number.
Students trace the months and number them in order.

Answers
1. January
2. February
3. March
4. April
5. May
6. June
7. July
8. August
9. September
10. October
11. November
12. December

B. Look and write.
Students look at the pictures and answer the questions.

Answers
1. It's February.
2. It's July.
3. It's October.
4. It's May.

Unit 5 Let's Start, pages 38–39

A. Write.
Students complete the conversation based on the choices in the text box.

Answers
What's the matter, Scott?
I'm sick.
That's too bad.
Maybe Mrs. Green can help you.
Who's she?
She's the new nurse.
Thanks for your help.
You're welcome. Get better soon!

B. Read and connect.
Students read and connect the sentences.

Answers
1. What's the matter?   I'm sick.
2. Who's she?   She's the new nurse.
3. I'm sick.   That's too bad.
4. Thanks for your help.   You're welcome.

C. Look and number.
Students look at the pictures and number the sentences in the correct order.

Answers
1. I get out of bed every morning.
2. I get dressed every morning.
3. I wake up every morning.
4. I make breakfast every morning.

D. Trace and check.

Students trace the sentences and place a ✓ next to the correct pictures.

Answers
1. (right)
2. (right)

Unit 5 Let's Learn, pages 40–41

A. Look and write.

Students look at the pictures, and then write the answer based on the choices in the text box.

Answers
1. She's a nurse.
2. She's a police officer.
3. She's a taxi driver.
4. She's a farmer.
5. He's a shopkeeper.
6. He's an office worker.
7. He's a cook.
8. He's a train conductor.

B. Connect and write.

Students follow the lines to connect the people and the occupations. Then they write sentences.

Answers
1. She's Ms. Lee. She's a nurse.
2. He's Mr. Brown. He's a police officer.
3. She's Mrs. Smith. She's an office worker.
4. He's Mr. Jones. He's a train conductor.

C. Read and match.

Students read the questions and answers and draw a line to match them to the correct pictures.

Unit 5 Let's Learn More, pages 42–43

A. Look and write.

Students look at the pictures and write the correct words in the crossword puzzle.

Answers
1. firefighters
2. doctors
3. students
4. dentists
5. taxi drivers
6. engineers
7. teachers
8. pilots

B. Trace and write.

Students trace or write the sentences.

Answers
1. They're teachers.
2. They're pilots.

C. Look and write.

Students look at the pictures and write sentences.

Answers
1. They're Mr. and Mrs. Smith. They're police officers.
2. They're Jack and Billy Thompson. They're students.
3. They're Ms. Long and Ms. Park. They're teachers.

D. Read and circle.

Students read and circle the correct answer.

Answers
1. No, they aren't.
2. Yes, they are.
3. No, they aren't.
4. No, they aren't.

Unit 5 Let's Build, pages 44–45

A. Match.

Students match the speech bubbles to the people.

B. Look and write.

Students look at the pictures, and then trace and write the questions and answers.

Answers
1. Who is Mr. Ray? He's a doctor.
2. Who is Ms. Church? She's a student.
3. Who is Mr. Bond? He's a teacher.
4. Who is Mrs. Mann? She's a dentist.

C. Read and check.

Students read the questions and place a ✓ next to the correct answers.

Answers
1. She's an office worker.
2. He's a police officer.
3. He's a firefighter.

D. Look and write.

Students look at the pictures and answer the questions.

Answers
1. No, she can't.   3. Yes, they can.
2. Yes, he can.   4. No, he can't.

Unit 6 Let's Start, pages 46–47

A. Trace and write.

Students trace or complete the sentences based on the choices in the text box.

Answers
1. Hi, Kate. This is Jenny.
2. Where are you?
I'm at home.
3. Where are you?
I'm at the park.
4. Can you come to the park?
Sure!

B. Connect and write.

Students follow the lines to connect the people and activities. Then they write sentences.

Answers
1. I talk on the telephone.
2. I practice the piano.
3. I study English.
4. I watch TV.

C. Unscramble and write.

Students unscramble and write the questions and answers.

Answers
1. What do you do every afternoon?
2. I practice the piano.
3. What do you do every afternoon?
4. I study English.

Unit 6 Let's Learn, pages 48–49

A. Look and write.

Students look at the picture and write the location phrases in the blanks based on the choices in the text box.

Answers
1. at school   4. at the zoo
2. at home   5. at the park
3. at work   6. at the library

B. Trace and write.

Students trace and complete the sentences.

Answers
1. He's at the library.
2. She's at work.
3. He's at school.
4. She's at the zoo.

C. Find and write.

Students look at the picture, find the people, and write sentences.

Answers
1. She's at school.
2. He's at the park.
3. She's at the zoo.
4. He's at home.
5. She's at the store.
6. He's at the library.

D. Look at C. Read and check.

Students look at the picture in C. Then they read the questions and place a ✓ next to the correct answers.

Answers
1. No, she isn't. She's at school.
2. Yes, he is.
3. No, she isn't. She's at the store.
4. No, he isn't. He's at home.

Unit 6 Let's Learn More, pages 50–51

A. Look and write.

Students look at the picture, find the numbered people, and then trace and write the sentences.

Answers
1. They're on the train.
2. They're at the movies.
3. They're in the restaurant.
4. They're in the taxi.
5. They're at the store.
6. They're on the bus.

B. Read and write.

Students read the questions and write the answers.

Answers
1. They're at the store.
2. They're at the movies.
3. They're on the train.
4. They're in the restaurant.

C. Read, look, and circle.

Students read the questions, look at the pictures, and circle the correct answers.

Answers
1. Yes, they are.
2. No, they aren't.
3. No, they aren't.
4. No, they aren't.

Unit 6 Let's Build, pages 52–53

A. Read and match.

Students read the sentences and then draw a line to match the people and the locations.

B. Read and number

Students read and then number the pictures in the correct order.

C. Look, trace, and write.

Students read the questions, and then trace and write the answers.

Answers
1. No, he isn't. He's at home.
2. No, they aren't. They're on the bus.
3. No, they aren't. They're at work.
4. No, she isn't. She's in the bedroom.

D. Read and match.

Students read the questions and answers, then draw a line to match them to the pictures.

Units 5–6 Listen and Review, page 54

A. Read and match.

Students read the questions, then draw a line to match the pictures to the correct answers.

Answers
1. Who's she? She's Mrs. Jones. She's the new nurse.
2. Where is he? He's at the library.
3. Who are they? They're Mr. and Mrs. Cross. They're farmers.
4. Are they doctors? No, they aren't. They're police officers.
5. Is he at the park? Yes, he is.

B. Write.

Students write the sentences.

Answers
1. I get dressed every morning.
2. I watch TV every afternoon.
3. She's at the library.
4. He's at home.

Let's Learn About the Seasons, page 55

A. Trace and write.

Students trace and write the correct season under each picture.

Answers
1. spring   spring
2. summer   summer
3. fall   fall
4. winter   winter

B. Write.

Students look at the pictures, then answer the questions.

Answers
1. I can go sailing.
2. I can go skiing.
3. I can fly a kite.
4. I can go hiking.

Unit 7 Let's Start, pages 56–57

A. Write.

Students look at the pictures, then complete the conversation.

Answers
1. Let's play a game.
2. What are you doing?
I'm riding a bicycle.
3. What are you doing?
We're swimming.

B. Look and write.

Students read the questions and write the answers.

Answers
1. We're playing baseball.
2. I'm doing a cartwheel.

C. Trace and match.

Students trace the verb phrases and draw a line to match them to the pictures.

D. Read, trace, and write.

Students read, and then trace or write the questions and answers.

Answers
1. No, I don't.
2. Yes, I do.
3. Do you read e-mail every evening?
4. Do you cook dinner every evening?

Unit 7 Let's Learn, pages 58–59

A. Read and number.

Students read the sentences and number the pictures.

B. Read and write.

Students read the questions and write the answers.

Answers
1. He's sleeping.
2. She's fishing.
3. She's throwing a ball.
4. He's coloring a picture.

C. Connect and write.

Students follow the lines to connect the questions to the correct pictures, then write the answers.

Answers
1. Yes, he is.
2. No, he isn't.
3. Yes, she is.
4. No, she isn't.

Unit 7 Let's Learn More, pages 60–61

A. Read and match.

Students read the verb phrases and draw a line to connect them to the correct pictures.

B. Trace and match.

Students trace the sentences and match them to the correct pictures.

C. Write.

Students write the questions and answers.

Answers
1. What are they doing? They're riding bicycles.
2. What are they doing? They're watching TV.
3. What are they doing? They're playing soccer.
4. What are they doing? They're eating apples.

D. Read and check.

Students read the questions and place a ✓ next to the correct answers.

> Answers
> 1. No, they aren't. They're studying English.
> 2. Yes, they are.
> 3. No, they aren't. They're watching TV.

Unit 7 Let's Build, pages 62–63

A. Look and write.

Students look at the pictures and write sentences.

> Answers
> 1. They're riding bicycles.
> 2. He's <u>playing soccer</u>.
> 3. <u>She's reading a comic book</u>.
> 4. <u>They're singing a song</u>.

B. Read and write the question.

Students read the answers and write the questions.

> Answers
> 1. <u>What's he doing</u>?
> 2. <u>What's she doing</u>?
> 3. <u>What are they doing</u>?
> 4. <u>What are they doing</u>?

C. Read and circle.

Students look at the pictures, read, and then circle the correct answers.

> Answers
> 1. No, she isn't.
> 2. Yes, he is.
> 3. No, they aren't.
> 4. No, he isn't.

D. Match.

Students read the questions and answers, then draw a line to match them to the correct pictures.

Unit 8 Let's Start, pages 64–65

A. Read and number.

Students read the conversation and number the sentences in order.

> Answers
> 1. Can you come over on Saturday?
> 2. Sorry. No, I can't. I'm busy.
> 3. What about Sunday?
> 4. Sunday is OK. I'm free.
> 5. Great! See you on Sunday!
> 6. OK. See you then!

B. Read and match.

Students read the questions and match them to the correct answers.

> Answers
> 1. Can you come over Monday?
>   Yes, I can. I'm free on Monday.
> 2. Can you come over on Thursday?
>   No, I can't. I'm busy on Thursday.
> 3. Can you come over on Sunday?
>   Yes, I can. I'm free on Sunday.
> 4. Can you come over on Saturday?
>   No, I can't. I'm busy on Saturday.

C. Write.

Students write the correct verb phrase under each picture based on the choices in the text box.

> Answers
> 1. take a bath
> 2. <u>take a walk</u>
> 3. <u>play outside</u>
> 4. <u>look at stars</u>

D. Read and check.

Students read the questions and answers, then place a ✓ next to the correct picture.

> Answers
> 1. (right)
> 2. (left)
> 3. (right)
> 4. (left)

Unit 8 Let's Learn, pages 66–67

A. Match.

Students draw a line to match the classes with the pictures.

B. Trace and write.

Students look at the picture, then trace and complete the answers.

> Answers
> 1. I go to <u>art class.</u>
> 2. I go to <u>karate class.</u>

C. Look and write.

Students look at the planner and write the questions and answers.

> Answers
> 1. I go to math class.
> 2. <u>I go to karate class.</u>
> 3. <u>I go to English class.</u>
> 4. <u>What do you do on Wednesdays</u>?
> 5. <u>What do you do on Saturdays</u>?
> 6. <u>What do you do on Sundays</u>?

D. How about you? Write.

Students answer the questions with personal information. Answers will vary—for example, *I go to art class on Saturdays. I go to math class on Tuesdays.*

Unit 8 Let's Learn More, pages 68–69

A. Look and write.

Students write the correct verb phrase under each picture based on the choices in the text box.

Answers
1. walk the dog
2. take a bath
3. do homework
4. go to the bookstore

B. Read and match.

Students read the sentences and match them to the pictures.

C. Look and write.

Students look at the pictures and write the questions and answers.

Answers
1. What does she do after school? She takes a bath.
2. What does he do after school? He goes to the bookstore.
3. What does she do after school? She does homework.
4. What does he do after school? He walks the dog.

D. Look and check.

Students look at the picture, read the question, and place a ✓ next to the correct answer.

Answers
1. No, he doesn't.
2. Yes, she does.

Unit 8 Let's Build, pages 70–71

A. Read and draw a line.

Students read the speech bubbles and draw a line to connect them to the correct location.

B. Look and write.

Students complete and write the sentences.

Answers
1. He goes to his math class after school.
2. She goes to her piano class after school.
3. He goes to his soccer practice after school.

C. Look and write.

Students look at the planners, read the questions, and write the answers.

Answers
1. He goes to English class.
2. He goes to math class.
3. She goes to karate class.
4. She goes to dance class.

D. What about you? Write.

Students answer the questions with personal information. Answers will vary for *1.* and *2.*; for example, *I go to dance class on Mondays.* For *3., Yes, I do./ No, I don't.*

Units 7–8 Listen and Review, page 72

A. Write.

Students look at the pictures and answer the questions.

Answers
1. Yes, they are.
2. Yes, she is.
3. He goes to soccer practice.
4. They're riding bicycles.

B. Match.

Students draw a line to match the verb phrases with the correct pictures.

Let's Learn About Time, page 73

A. Read and write.

Students rewrite the times.

Answers
1. It's two-fifteen. It's 2:15.
2. It's twelve-thirty. It's 12:30.
3. It's four o'clock. It's 4:00.
4. It's nine forty-five. It's 9:45.
5. It's twelve midnight. It's 12:00.
6. It's twelve noon. It's 12:00.

B. Read, write, and check.

Students read the sentences, write the times, and place a ✓ next to *a.m.* or *p.m.*

Answers
1. 8:00 a.m.
2. 2:30 p.m.
3. 5:00 p.m.
4. 7:45 p.m.
5. 3:30 a.m.
6. 11:00 p.m.

Unit 1
Classroom Objects

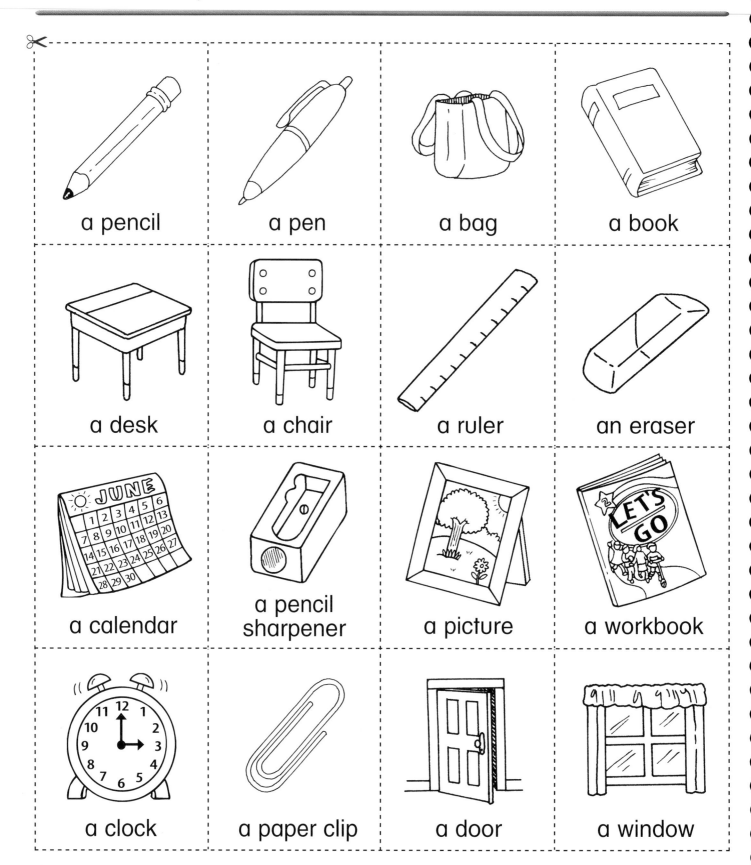

a pencil	a pen	a bag	a book
a desk	a chair	a ruler	an eraser
a calendar	a pencil sharpener	a picture	a workbook
a clock	a paper clip	a door	a window

See instructions on page 190.

Unit 1
Singular/Plural Game

See instructions on page 190.

Unit 2
Do You Have...? Interview

A. Match.

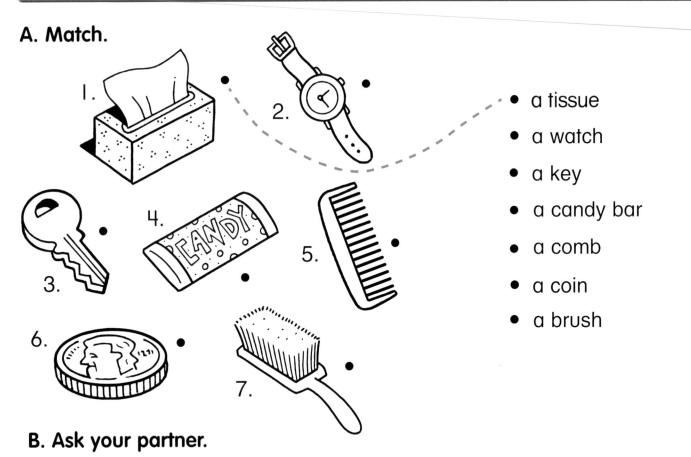

1.
2.
3.
4.
5.
6.
7.

- a tissue
- a watch
- a key
- a candy bar
- a comb
- a coin
- a brush

B. Ask your partner.

Do you have a tissue?

Yes, I do.

No, I don't.

Do you have...?	Yes	No	Name
a tissue			
a watch			
a key			
a candy bar			
a comb			
a coin			
a brush			

See instructions on page 190.

Unit 2

Do You Have...? Cards

a lunch box	a key	a candy bar	a comic book
a comb	a coin	a brush	a tissue
a watch	a camera	a key chain	a music player
a calculator	a train pass	an umbrella	a wallet

See instructions on page 191.

Unit 3
Address Book

Write.

Name _____

Town _____

Address _____

Telephone _____

Name _____

Town _____

Address _____

Telephone _____

See instructions on page 191.

Unit 3

Look, Listen, and Circle

A.

next to

in front of

behind

B.

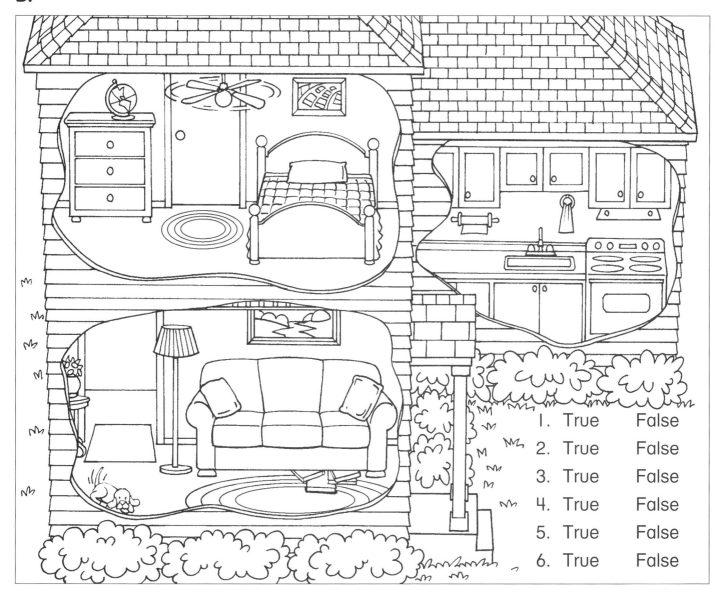

1. True   False
2. True   False
3. True   False
4. True   False
5. True   False
6. True   False

See instructions on page 191.

Unit 4
Bingo: Want and Like

omelet	peach	pear	pancake
yogurt	cereal	tea	hot chocolate
stew	cheese	pasta	hamburgers
steak	grapes	peaches	pancakes

See instructions on page 192.

Oxford University Press. Permission granted to reproduce for instructional use.

Unit 4
Write, Ask, and Draw

A. Label.

B. Ask and draw.

See instructions on page 192.

Unit 5
Occupations Game

See instructions on page 192.

Unit 5
Card Game: Occupations

Mr. and Mrs. Bond

Mr. and Mrs. Long

Sue and Ben Lee

Mark and Joy Jones

Bob and Bill Smith

John and Steve White

Mr. and Mrs. Wong

Ms. Dane and Ms. Mack

See instructions on page 192.

Unit 6
Map Activity: Locations

See instructions on page 193.

Unit 6
What's Different?: Locations

A.

B.

See instructions on page 193.

Unit 7
Ask and Answer Grid: *What's He Doing?*

Tom   Sue   Lee   Bob

Mike   Jane   May   Cole

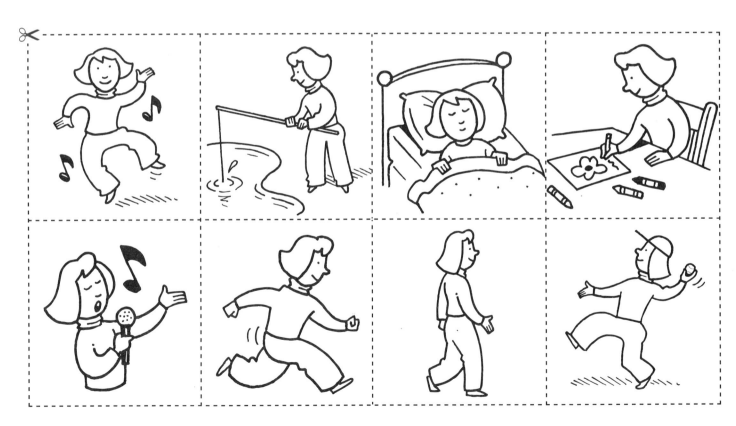

See instructions on page 193.

Unit 7

What Are They Doing? Game

See instructions on page 194.

Unit 8
Interview

What Do You Do On...

Day	Activity	Name
	Go to art class	
	Go to English class	
	7-3=4 Go to math class	
	Go to dance class	
	Go to karate class	
	Go to soccer practice	
	Go to piano class	
	Go to swimming class	

See instructions on page 194.

Unit 8

Bingo: After-School Activities

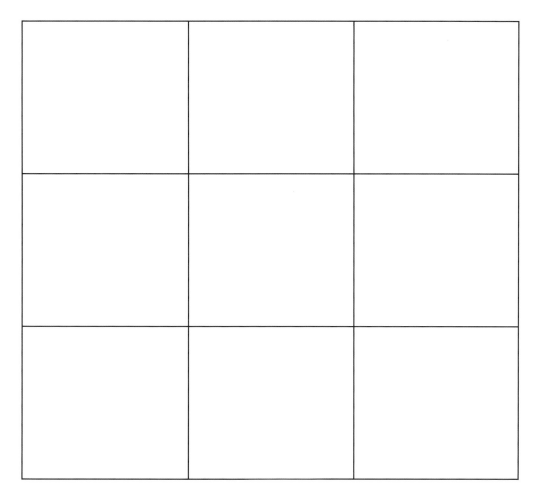

See instructions on page 195.

Reproducible Worksheet Instructions

UNIT 1

Classroom Objects (page 174)

Use with the Let's Learn lesson.

Activity summary: Students turn over cards and ask and answer questions in pairs. The activity reinforces classroom vocabulary and the question-and-answer patterns *What's this/that? It's (a pencil sharpener)* and *Is this/that (a pencil sharpener)? Yes, it is. No, it isn't.*

Steps:

1. Give one set of cards to each student.

2. Model the activity with one pair of students as others watch.

 a. Have S1 and S2 place their stacks of cards on the table, facedown in front of them.

 b. Prompt S1 to turn over the top card, show it, and ask *What's this?* S2 answers *It's (a pencil).* Next, have S2 turn over a card and ask S1 *What's this?* S1 answers. In the next round, students should turn over a card, place it on the other side of the desk, and point to it when they ask *What's that?*

3. When students understand the activity, have them work in pairs and ask questions and give answers using the cards.

Variations:

1. Have students make a grid with nine numbered squares. Students place one of their cards in each square. Call out a number at random. T: *Number 1. Is this (a calendar)?* All students with a *Yes* answer should answer aloud and turn over the card. After you've asked about all nine squares, the student with the most turned-over cards wins.

2. Use multiple sets of cards to play **Concentration**.

3. Use the uncut page to play **Bingo**. Have students cross out (or cover) two squares on their own pages. Play **Bingo**, calling out the vocabulary words. Crossing out two squares in the beginning increases the number of times that students will get Bingo.

UNIT 1

Singular/Plural Game (page 175)

Use with the Let's Learn More lesson.

Activity summary: Groups of students play a board game and make sentences with classroom objects. The game reinforces *these/those, this/that,* classroom vocabulary, and singular and plural objects.

Steps:

1. Display an enlarged copy of the game board at the front of the room.

2. Model the activity.

 a. Roll a die. Move a magnet/marker that number of spaces on the game board and make a sentence about the object(s) in the space. *This is a clock. Those are books.*

 b. If the sentence is correct, the player's marker remains in that square. If a player lands on an arrow square, the player moves the indicated number of spaces and then makes a sentence. If either sentence is incorrect, the marker returns to the position at the start of that turn. Have the other players help make a correct sentence.

3. Put students in groups of three or four and give each group a game board, markers, and a die.

Variations:

1. Play as an entire class in three teams, using one large game board at the front of the room.

2. Play the game again, having students ask and answer questions about the objects such as *What's this/that? What are these/those? Is this/that (a window)?*

UNIT 2

Do you have...? Interview (page 176)

Use with the Let's Learn lesson.

Activity summary: Students circulate, interviewing each other about personal possessions. The activity reinforces *have* and the question *Do you have...?*

Steps:

1. Distribute one page to each student.

2. Model the activity with an enlarged copy.

 a. Point to the tissue. Match and elicit the word. Along with students, trace the dotted line between the picture and the word. Have students draw lines between the remaining pictures and words. For non-readers, read each word aloud and have students find the corresponding picture and draw a line between the two.

 b. Ask S1 *Do you have a tissue?* S1 answers *Yes, I do/ No, I don't.* Point to *a tissue* in the chart at the bottom of the page and ask students what it says. If necessary, show students how they can use the matching exercise to help them "read" the words in the chart. Then, place a check mark in the yes or no column next to *a tissue.* Tell students to write the other student's name next to the item they were asked about.

3. Students circulate, asking and answering questions about possessions. Make sure they ask a different student about each item on the chart. Remind students to mark their partner's answers, not their own.

Variations:

1. When students finish, have them write out sentences about their own possessions using each of the seven words.

2. Have students make a similar interview grid using their own choice of possessions from Units 1–5.

UNIT 2

Do you have...? Cards

Use with the Let's Learn More lesson.

Activity summary: Students work in groups to play a variation of **Card Game / Go Fish** to find a match. The activity reinforces *Do you have (a wallet)?* and personal possessions vocabulary.

Steps:

1. Divide the class into groups of 3–4 students. Give each group a set of cards.

2. Play **Go Fish**. Model with one group as other students watch.

　　a. Have students choose equal numbers of facedown cards at random. They don't show their cards to the other students. Keep some cards in a pile facedown in the center of the group.

　　b. Students look at their own cards and put aside any matches. Then S1 asks S2 *What do you have?* S2 chooses one of his or her cards and says *I have a (a tissue).* If S1 also has a *(tissue),* he or she takes S2's card and puts the match aside. If S1 doesn't have a *(tissue)* card, he or she must pick a new card from the remaining pile. Then S2 repeats the procedure with S3. The first student to get matches of all their cards wins.

3. When students understand the activity, have them work in groups and play the game.

Variations:

1. Play **Slap** in small groups. Place the cards faceup in the center. As you call out one of the items, students race to touch the picture card and make a sentence: *I have (a candy bar).*

2. When less time is available, have students play **Concentration** without making sentences.

3. Play this game like a more traditional **Go Fish** game, but with students playing in pairs. One student in the pair holds the cards. Pairs take turns asking the questions.

UNIT 3

Address Book (page 178)

Use with the Let's Start lesson.

Activity summary: Students work in pairs, interviewing each other to find out address information. The activity reinforces personal information questions.

Steps:

1. Distribute one page to each student.

2. Model the activity on the board.

　　a. Say *I live in (Amity). My address is (1521 Hatcher Street),* as you write the information on the board. Continue with your phone number.

　　b. Ask a student *Where do you live? What is your address? What is your telephone number?* Write the student's information on the board.

　　c. Have students walk around and ask two students for their personal information and write it on their own worksheets.

Variation:

When students finish, have them write out sentences about their classmates' information.

UNIT 3

Look, Listen, and Circle (page 179)

Use with the Let's Learn More lesson.

Activity summary: In this activity, you read a sentence and students circle True or False after looking at the illustration. The activity reinforces house vocabulary and prepositions.

Steps:

1. Distribute one page to each student.

2. Review the prepositions and room names.

　　a. Look at A. Point to each picture and say the preposition it illustrates: *next to, in front of, behind.* Have students repeat.

　　b. Look at the picture in B. Point to each room and say its name: *bedroom, kitchen, living room.* Have students repeat.

3. Read the sentences below. Have students look at the picture in B, decide whether the sentence is True or False, and circle accordingly.

　　1. There's a lamp next to the sofa. (True)
　　2. There's a bathtub in the kitchen. (False)
　　3. There's a stove next to the sink. (True)
　　4. There's a toilet behind the bed in the bedroom. (False)
　　5. There are books under the sofa. (True)
　　6. There's a TV in front of the sofa in the living room. (False)

Variation:

Have students write one true sentence and one false sentence about the picture in B. Then have them read their sentences aloud and have the class decide whether they are true or false. This can also be done in small groups.

Bingo: Want and Like (page 180)

Use with the Let's Learn More lesson.

Activity summary: Students play **Bingo** using food items. The activity reinforces food vocabulary and the questions *What do you like?* and *What do you want?*

Steps:

1. Make a set of cue cards by cutting out the cards and putting them in a bag.

2. Give each student the worksheet and have them cut out the squares. Review the vocabulary.

3. Have students make Bingo grids by arranging their cards as they like in a 4x4 grid.

4. Choose a student volunteer. Ask the student *What do you want/like?* Have the student draw a cue card from the bag and answer *I want/like (a peach)*. Students playing should turn over their own (*peach*) cards. The first to get Bingo says *Bingo!* and is the next helper.

5. Check the winning student's squares by asking the student to make sentences about the food on the overturned squares (e.g., *I like steak. I want a peach.*).

Variation:

Play **Letter-shape Bingo**, where students cover squares so that the cards form specific alphabet letters in order to win. Capital letters that work especially well for this **Bingo** variation include *C, I, H, O, T,* and *X*.

UNIT 4

Write, Ask, and Draw (page 181)

Use with the Let's Build lesson.

Activity summary: Students label objects, and then work in pairs to ask and answer questions and draw the answers. The activity reinforces the question-and-answer pattern *Do you want (a peach) or (steak)? I want (a peach)*.

Steps:

1. Model the activity in part A of the worksheet.

    a. Point to the first object and ask *What is it?* Students can guess or answer *I don't know*. Say the name of the object. Ask the question again. This time students can answer correctly. Continue until all objects are identified.

    b. Label the objects.

2. Model the B (draw) activity in part B of the worksheet on an enlarged copy.

    a. Give one page and crayons or colored pencils to each student.

    b. Ask S1 *Do you want a peach or a pancake?* S1 answers *I want a peach.*

    c. Draw a picture of a peach in the first square.

    d. When students understand the activity, have them work in pairs, ask questions and give answers, and draw.

Variations:

Have two pairs get together and ask questions about each other's pictures *Does he/she want a peach or steak? He/She wants steak.*

UNIT 5

Occupations Game (page 182)

Use with the Let's Learn lesson.

Activity summary: In this activity, groups of three or four play a board game. The game reinforces occupations vocabulary, pronouns, and the patterns *He/She's (a shopkeeper)* and *Is he/she (a farmer)? Yes, he/she is. No, he/she isn't.*

Steps:

1. Display an already-colored copy of the game board at the front of the room. Choose two students to help you model the activity.

2. Model the activity.

    a. Have S1 roll a die. Move a magnet/marker that number of spaces on the game board, and ask S1 a question about the object in the space he or she lands on. *Is he/she (a farmer)?*

    b. If S1 answers the question correctly, S1's marker remains in that square, or, in the case of arrow squares, he or she moves the marker the indicated number of spaces. If S1 answers incorrectly, the marker returns to the space at which S1 started the turn.

    c. Next, have S2 roll the die and S1 ask the question. When S2's turn is finished, he or she asks the question to the next student.

3. Put students in groups of three or four and give a game board, crayons, markers, and a die to each group. Set a time limit for coloring the game squares and then begin play.

Variations:

1. This game can be played as an entire class in three teams, using one large game board at the front of the room.

2. Have students play **Slap** in groups of three with one board. S1 makes a statement to describe one of the people on the board saying *He/She's (a nurse).* S2 and S3 race to touch the correct square. The first to touch makes the next statement.

UNIT 5

Card Game: Occupations (page 183)

Use with the Let's Learn More lesson.

Activity summary: Students turn over cards and ask and answer questions in pairs. The activity reinforces plural occupation vocabulary and the question-and-answer patterns *Who are they? They're (Mr. and Mrs. Wong). They're (dentists)* and *Are they (teachers)? Yes, they are. No, they aren't.*

Steps:

1. Give two sets of cards to each student.

2. Model the activity with one pair of students as other students watch.

    a. Have S1 and S2 place their stacks of cards facedown in front of them.

    b. Prompt S1 to turn over the top card and ask, *Who are they?* S2 answers, *They're (Mr. and Mrs. Wong). They're (dentists).* Next, have S2 turn over a card from his or her stack. If the card is the same, S2 asks *Are they dentists?* and S1 answers *Yes, they are.* If the card is different, S2 still asks *Are they teachers?* but S1 answers *No, they aren't. They're (engineers).*

    c. The pair then starts the procedure over, with S2 turning over a card and asking *Who are they?*

3. When students understand the activity, have them work in pairs and ask questions and give answers using the cards.

Variations:

1. Have students make a grid with nine numbered squares. Students place one of the cards in each square (leaving one blank). Call out a number at random. T: *Number 3. Are they (teachers)?* All students with a *Yes* answer should answer aloud and turn over their card. After you've asked about all nine squares, the student with the most facedown cards wins.

2. Use duplicate sets of cards to play **Concentration**.

3. Do all of the above activities with the singular question-and-answer patterns, having students point to single people in the illustrations.

UNIT 6

Map Activity: Locations (page 184)

Use with the Let's Learn lesson.

Activity summary: Students listen to sentences and place characters in the correct location. The activity reinforces location vocabulary and the question-and-answer patterns *Where is he/she? He/She's at (school).*

Steps:

1. Give students copies of the town map worksheet. Have them cut out the characters.

2. Model the activity with one student.

    a. Hold up one of the characters and say *He's at (the park).* Have S1 put the character in the correct location on the map.

    b. After saying five more locations for the other characters, point to one of the characters and ask *Where is he?* S1 answers *He's at (the park).* Continue with the other characters.

3. When students understand the activity, arrange the characters on your map, and read the six sentences to the class. Have students place their own characters in the correct locations. Check maps together.

4. Have them work in pairs using their own maps.

Variation:

Do a **Back-To-Back** activity. Have students sit back-to-back. Pairs should agree on names for their characters (both members of the pair should use the same names). S1 places the characters on his or her map and then describes it to S2 saying *(Sue's) at (the zoo).* S2 puts the characters on his or her map to match. Then students look at each other's maps to see if they match. Reverse roles.

UNIT 6

What's Different?: Locations (page 185)

Use with the Let's Learn More lesson.

Activity summary: Students compare two similar scenes and identify differences in the locations of people. The activity reinforces location vocabulary and the question-and-answer patterns *Where is he/she? He/She's (at the movies). Where are they? They're (on a bus). Is he/she (at the movies)? Yes, he/she is. No, he/she isn't. Are they (on a bus)? Yes, they are. No, they aren't.*

Steps:

1. Give one page to each student.

2. Model the activity with a student and an enlarged page.

    a. Point to one of the characters or couples in scene A and ask *Where is he?* or *Where are they?* Have S1 answer *He's/They're (on a bus).*

    b. Point to the same character or couple in scene B and ask if the character/couple is in the same location as before: *Is he/Are they (on a bus)?* S1 answers *Yes* or *No.*

3. When students understand the activity, have them work in pairs and ask questions and give answers to find the differences in the scenes.

Variation:

Have students write sentences to describe the differences, e.g. A: *He's on the bus.* B: *He's in a taxi.*

UNIT 7

Ask and Answer Grid: What's He Doing? (page 186)

Use with the Let's Learn lesson.

Activity summary: Students ask and answer questions in pairs. The activity reinforces progressive form, verb phrases, and the question-and answer-pattern *What's he doing? He's (swimming).*

Steps:

1. Give one page to each student.

2. Model the activity with one student as others watch. Have a grid prepared with the eight verb cards already cut out and taped over the face cards. Don't show students your page until the end of the activity.

a. Display an enlarged copy of the top half of the page on the board, and give S1 eight cut-out cards from the bottom of the page.

b. Prompt S1 to ask a question about one of the squares: *What's Tom doing?* Answer *He's (sleeping).* S1 should place (tape) the *sleeping* card on the Tom square. Continue for the remaining verbs.

c. Once all of the cards have been placed on the page, show the class your original and have them see if S1 put the verbs in the correct locations.

3. When students understand the activity, have them work in pairs and ask questions and place the verb cards correctly. Either have students sit back-to-back, sit with a screen between them, or work inside file folders so that they can't see their partner's pages. Have S1 prepare his or her page and S2 ask questions, then switch.

Variations:

1. Have students place the verbs on the faces, and then write a sentence for each (e.g., *Sue is running.*).

2. Play the game with three students. S1 sits on one side of the room, and places the verbs on the page. S2 sits on the other side of the room and asks questions. S3 moves between S1 and S2, carrying information from one student to the other. S2: *What is Tom doing?* S3 to S1: *What is Tom doing?* S1: *He's sleeping.* S3 to S2: *He's sleeping.* Then they compare pages to see if they match.

UNIT 7

What Are They Doing? Game (page 187)

Use with the Let's Learn More lesson.

Activity summary: Groups of students play a board game and ask and answer questions with verb phrases. The game reinforces *they,* verb phrases, progressive form, and the patterns *What are they doing? They're (watching TV).*

Steps:

1. Display an enlarged copy of the game board at the front of the room. Choose a student to help you model the activity.

2. Model the activity.

a. Have S1 roll a die and move a magnet/marker that number of spaces on the game board. Ask *What are they doing?* S1 answers according to the picture in the space.

b. If the sentence is correct, the player's marker remains in that square. If a player lands on an arrow square, the player moves forward or back the indicated number of spaces, and then makes a sentence. If either sentence is incorrect, the marker returns to the position at the start of that turn. Have the class help make a correct sentence.

3. Put students in groups of three or four, and give each group a game board, markers, and a die.

Variations:

1. Play as an entire class in three teams, using one large game board at the front of the room.

2. Have pairs use each picture to ask and answer questions. Starting with the first picture, S1 asks S2 *Are they (studying English?)* S2 answers *Yes* or *No* according to the picture. If correct, S2 asks the next question.

UNIT 8

Interview (page 188)

Use with the Let's Learn lesson.

Activity summary: Students ask and answer questions about after-school activities. The activity reinforces days of the week, verb phrases, and the question *What do you do on (Mondays)?*

Steps:

1. Distribute one page to each student. Review the verb phrases and question-and-answer pattern.

2. Model the activity as students watch.

a. Walk up to S1 and ask *What do you do on Mondays?* S1 answers *I (go to art class).* Write *Monday* next to the appropriate verb phrase, and then hand the page to S1 and say *Please write your name.* S1 writes his or her name on the paper and gives the paper back to the teacher.

b. Move to S2 and ask the next question.

3. Once students understand the activity, have them move around the classroom, asking questions about the objects on the page. Note that the form limits students to asking one question per student.

Variations:

1. When students finish, have them write out sentences about their classmates' activities.

2. If S1 answers *Yes* to the question, have S2 ask questions to extend the conversation such as *Do you like (soccer practice)?* etc.

3. Make a class survey of how many students do each activity. Make a chart on the board. Ask *Do you (go to art class on Mondays)?* Students who go to art class on Mondays raise their hands as they answer. Have the class count hands. Ask *How many students go to art class?* Students answer *(15) students.* (Note: Students have not learned this question form yet, but should be able to answer it in this context.) Write the number of students on the board.

Bingo: After-school Activities (page 189)

Use with the Let's Build lesson.

Activity summary: Students play **Bingo** using activities and days of the week. The activity reinforces activities and the structure *What do you do on Saturdays?*

Steps:

1. Make a set of cue cards by cutting out the cards and putting them in a bag.

2. Give each student a page and have them cut out the cards (without the text cues). Review the vocabulary.

3. Have students create their own Bingo grids by arranging their cards as they like on the grid. Students should cross out one square.

4. Choose a student volunteer. Begin by asking the student *What do you on Mondays?* Have the student draw a cue card from the bag and answer (e.g., *I do homework on Mondays.*). Have the class say *He/She does homework on Mondays.* Students who have the same answer indicated on their boards should turn that card over. The first student to get Bingo is the next helper.

5. Check the winning student's squares by asking the student to make sentences about the activities on the overturned squares (e.g., *I listen to music on Saturdays.*).

Variations:

1. Have students write sentences based on their boards.

2. Have groups of three work together. Students arrange their boards as they like. S1 asks S2 about S3's board: *Does he/she walk the dog on Tuesdays?* S2 answers. S2 then asks S3 a question about S1, etc.

Teaching Contractions

Begin by showing students the original words (e.g., *I am*). Say the words and have students repeat. Have students continue to say the words with you as you gradually move the two cards toward each other. As the cards get closer, you will be speaking faster and faster, with less of a pause between the two words. Once the cards are overlapping, you will naturally be forming the contraction. At this point, replace the two cards with the one contraction card (e.g., *I'm*). Alternate showing students the two separate word cards and the contraction card so that they can practice saying both forms. Be sure to explain, if necessary, that both forms have exactly the same meaning.

I	am	I'm
That	is	That's
What	is	What's
It	is	It's
is	not	isn't
They	are	They're
are	not	aren't
do	not	don't

does	not	doesn't
There	is	There's
Where	is	Where's
Who	is	Who's
She	is	She's
He	is	He's
We	are	We're
You	are	You're
can	not	can't
How	is	How's

Teacher and Student Card List   Level Two

1	erase the board	38	an umbrella	75	kitchen
2	speak English	39	a lunch box	76	bathroom
3	write my name	40	a wallet	77	next to
4	read books	41	20/twenty	78	in front of
5	a pencil sharpener	42	21/twenty-one	79	behind
6	a picture	43	22/twenty-two	80	spaghetti
7	a workbook	44	23/twenty-three	81	type
8	a paper clip	45	24/twenty-four	82	wink
9	a clock	46	25/twenty-five	83	do a cartwheel
10	a door	47	26/twenty-six	84	play Ping-Pong
11	a window	48	27/twenty-seven	85	an omelet
12	a calendar	49	28/twenty-eight	86	a peach
13	pencil sharpeners	50	29/twenty-nine	87	a pear
14	paper clips	51	30/thirty	88	a pancake
15	clocks	52	40/forty	89	yogurt
16	workbooks	53	50/fifty	90	cereal
17	calendars	54	60/sixty	91	tea
18	pictures	55	70/seventy	92	hot chocolate
19	windows	56	80/eighty	93	grapes
20	doors	57	90/ninety	94	pancakes
21	run	58	100/one hundred	95	peaches
22	swim	59	play baseball	96	hamburgers
23	sing	60	use chopsticks	97	stew
24	dance	61	ice-skate	98	cheese
25	a key	62	do a magic trick	99	pasta
26	a candy bar	63	bed	100	steak
27	a comic book	64	bathtub	101	January
28	a comb	65	sofa	102	February
29	a coin	66	stove	103	March
30	a brush	67	lamp	104	April
31	a tissue	68	sink	105	May
32	a watch	69	toilet	106	June
33	a camera	70	TV	107	July
34	a key chain	71	refrigerator	108	August
35	a music player	72	telephone	109	September
36	a calculator	73	living room	110	October
37	a train pass	74	bedroom	111	November

112 December	148 at the zoo	185 art class
113 wake up	149 at the movies	186 English class
114 get out of bed	150 at the store	187 math class
115 make breakfast	151 in the restaurant	188 dance class
116 get dressed	152 on the bus	189 karate class
117 morning	153 on the train	190 soccer practice
118 a shopkeeper	154 in the taxi	191 piano class
119 a cook	155 spring	192 swimming class
120 a nurse	156 summer	193 go to the bookstore
121 a farmer	157 fall	194 do homework
122 a taxi driver	158 winter	195 listen to music
123 a train conductor	159 cook dinner	196 talk on the telephone
124 an office worker	160 wash dishes	197 practice the piano
125 a police officer	161 read e-mail	198 ride a bicycle
126 a teacher	162 do homework	199 walk the dog
127 a student	163 evening	200 take a bath
128 teachers	164 dancing	201 three o'clock
129 police officers	165 fishing	202 six fifteen
130 doctors	166 sleeping	203 eight thirty
131 pilots	167 coloring a picture	204 ten forty-five
132 engineers	168 singing a song	
133 train conductors	169 running	
134 firefighters	170 walking	
135 taxi drivers	171 throwing a ball	
136 students	172 playing soccer	
137 dentists	173 studying English	
138 study English	174 talking on the telephone	
139 talk on the telephone	175 watching TV	
140 watch TV	176 reading comic books	
141 practice the piano	177 riding bicycles	
142 afternoon	178 flying kites	
143 at school	179 eating apples	
144 at home	180 take a walk	
145 at work	181 look at stars	
146 at the library	182 play outside	
147 at the park	183 take a bath	
	184 night	

Word List

Page numbers refer to pages in the Student Book.

A

a 4
a.m. 73
about 2
address 20
after 68
afternoon 47
alligator 3
am 2
an 14
apples 60
apple tree 47
April 37
are 2
aren't 7
art 66
at 3
August 37

B

bad 38
bag 10
ball 58
baseball 21
bath 65
bathroom 22
bathtub 22
bed 22
bedroom 22
behind 24
better 38
bicycle 56
big 8
board 3
books 3
bookstore 68
breakfast 39
brush 12
bus 47
busy 64

C

calculator 14
calendar 4
camera 14
can 11
can't 29
candy bar 12
cartwheel 29
cell phone 16
cereal 30
chair 27
cheese 32
chopsticks 21
class 66
clock 4
clocks 6
coin 12
cold 39
coloring 58
comb 12
come 46
comic book 12
cook 40
cooking 57

D

dance 11
dancing 58
December 37
dentists 42
dinner 57
dishes 57
do 12
doctors 42
does 14
doesn't 15
dog 68
doing 56
don't 10
door 4

E

eating 60
eighty 19
e-mail 57
engineers 42
English 3
erase 3
evening 57
every 39
everywhere 27

F

fall 55
farmer 40
February 37
fifty 19
firefighters 42
fishing 58
floor 27
flying 60
for 28
forty 19
free 64
Friday 72

G

get 38
get dressed 39
go 66
goes 68
good 2
good-bye 2
grapes 32
great 64
gym 47

S

sad 39
Saturday 64
school 3
seasons 55
see 2
September 37
seventy 19
she 11
she's 38
shopkeeper 40
sick 38
sing 11
singing 58
sink 22
sixty 19
sleeping 58
small 9
soccer 60
sofa 22
song 58
soon 38
sorry 64
spaghetti 28
speak 3
spring 55
square 9
stars 65
steak 32
stew 32
store 50
stove 22
student 40
study 47
studying 60
summer 55
Sunday 64
sure 46
swim 11
swimming 56

T

table 26
take 65
talk 47
talking 57
taxi 50
taxi driver 40
tea 30
teacher 40
telephone 22
thank you 28
thanks 2
that 4
that's 4
the 3
then 64
there 22
there's 22
these 6
they 7
they're 7
thirty 19
this 4
those 6
throwing 58
Thursday 72
time 73
tired 39
tissue 12
to 46
today 39
toilet 22
too 28
train 50
train conductor 40
train pass 14
Tuesday 65
TV 22
twenty 19
two 35
type 29

U

umbrella 14
under 26
use 21

V

very 65
video game 16

W

wake up 39
walk 65
walking 58
wallet 14
want 28
wash 57
watch 12
watch 47
watching 60
we're 56
Wednesday 72
welcome 38
what 5
what's 5
where 20
where's 22
who 38
who's 38
whose 10
window 4
wink 29
winter 55
work 48
workbook 4
write 3

Y

yellow 8
yes 5
yogurt 30
you 2
you're 38
your 17
yo-yo 16

Z

zoo 48

LET'S GO 2

Congratulations!

This certifies that _____

has successfully completed Let's Go 2 on _____

Date _____

Signature _____

Good Job Award

LET'S GO 2

Date

Signature